Business Group Management in Japan

Monden Institute of Management: Japanese Management and International Studies **(ISSN: 1793-2874)**

Editor-in-Chief: Yasuhiro Monden *(Mejiro University, Japan)*

Published

Vol. 1 Value-Based Management of the Rising Sun
edited by Yasuhiro Monden, Kanji Miyamoto, Kazuki Hamada, Gunyung Lee & Takayuki Asada

Vol. 2 Japanese Management Accounting Today
edited by Yasuhiro Monden, Masanobu Kosuga, Yoshiyuki Nagasaka, Shufuku Hiraoka & Noriko Hoshi

Vol. 3 Japanese Project Management:
KPM — Innovation, Development and Improvement
edited by Shigenobu Ohara & Takayuki Asada

Vol. 4 International Management Accounting in Japan:
Current Status of Electronics Companies
edited by Kanji Miyamoto

Vol. 5 Business Process Management of Japanese and Korean Companies
edited by Gunyung Lee, Masanobu Kosuga, Yoshiyuki Nagasaka & Byungkyu Sohn

Vol. 6 M&A for Value Creation in Japan
edited by Yasuyoshi Kurokawa

Vol. 7 Business Group Management in Japan
edited by Kazuki Hamada

Monden Institute of Management
Japanese Management and International Studies – Vol. 7

Business Group Management in Japan

editor

Kazuki Hamada
Kwansei Gakuin University, Japan

NEW JERSEY • LONDON • SINGAPORE • BEIJING • SHANGHAI • HONG KONG • TAIPEI • CHENNAI

Published by

World Scientific Publishing Co. Pte. Ltd.
5 Toh Tuck Link, Singapore 596224
USA office: 27 Warren Street, Suite 401-402, Hackensack, NJ 07601
UK office: 57 Shelton Street, Covent Garden, London WC2H 9HE

British Library Cataloguing-in-Publication Data
A catalogue record for this book is available from the British Library.

BUSINESS GROUP MANAGEMENT IN JAPAN
Monden Institute of Management: Japanese Management and International Studies — Vol. 7

ISBN-13 978-981-4289-50-4

Printed in Singapore.

Japan Society of Organization and Accounting

Mission of JSOA and Editorial Information

For the purpose of making a contribution to the business and academic communities, the Japan Society of Organization and Accounting (JSOA), a reformed and expanded organization from the Monden Institute of Management, is committed to publishing the book series, entitled *Japanese Management and International Studies*, with a refereed system.

Focusing on Japan and Japan-related issues, the series is designed to inform the world about research outcomes of the new "Japanese style management system" developed in Japan. It includes the Japanese version of management systems developed abroad. In addition, it publishes research by foreign scholars and concerning foreign systems that constitute significant points of comparison with the Japanese system.

Research topics included in this series are management of organizations in a broad sense (including the business group) and the accounting that supports the organization. More specifically, topics include business strategy, organizational restructuring, corporate finance, M&A, environmental management, business models, operations management, managerial accounting, financial accounting for organizational restructuring, manager performance evaluation, remuneration systems, and management of revenues and costs. The research approach is interdisciplinary, which includes case studies, theoretical studies, normative studies and empirical studies, but emphasizes real world business.

Each volume contains the series title and a book title which reflects the volume's special theme.

Our JSOA's board of directors has established an editorial board of international standing, which is served by the Monden Institute of Management. In each volume, guest editors who are experts on the volume's special theme serve as the volume editors.

Editorial Board

Contents

Preface

Currently, Japanese companies are positively promoting the "integration and/or separation of businesses" with the aim of gaining a competitive advantage. Although various individual and combined business models exist, the common goal is to enhance the value of the business.

Nowadays, the competition that exists among business groups is more important than that among individual firms. Therefore, the strategies for managing numerous individual firms have become important from the viewpoint of the business group as a whole.

In Japan, there are many core companies that engage in unique inter-firm relationships, called "Keiretsu", which confer substantial influence upon the members of the group through continuous transactions, even in the absence of capital-alliances. Therefore, our research also considers these uniquely Japanese attributes. The management methods employed in Japanese companies include the following: (1) application of evaluation systems; (2) execution of mergers and acquisitions (M&A); (3) utilization of segment information; (4) management of inter-firm relations; and (5) adoption of organizational learning.

In this book, we explore and elucidate business group management (BGM) and inter-firm management in Japanese companies, both theoretically and practically through case studies, survey research, and other methodologies. The analyses, hypotheses, and conclusions presented in this book will be useful for business practitioners and for academic researchers.

This book consists of the following five parts.

Part 1: Accounting Information for Group Management and Management Control Systems

The first paper by Hamada examines the managerial accounting methods used in business group management by analyzing the role played by the group headquarters. In particular, it is examined how the managerial accounting system and consolidated performance evaluation system are designed and utilized in Japanese companies.

The second paper by Tomo, Yori, and Asada investigates the current situation and problems associated with the application of management control systems in companies that are falling under the control of holding company. The meaning of business reformation, the extent of authority delegation, and the roles of the holding company are examined.

Part 2: M&A, Including MBO, and Outsourcing for Group Reformation

The first paper by Suzuki investigates the effects of M&A on financial performance. This paper regards M&A as a means to transfer business resources from one company to another, whereby a firm or business is itself a type of resource. From this standpoint, the effects of M&A on business sustainability performance are evaluated.

The second paper by Kaneda examines management buyouts (MBOs) of Japanese companies. In MBOs, corporations tend to retain the original management and employees, generally avoiding massive layoffs. Thus, some large corporations prefer to use MBOs to spin off subsidiaries. As an example, the spinning off of subsidiaries from Nissan Motor Company, during which the management changed its style of corporate management, is presented.

The third paper by Matsuoka discusses outsourcing. The purpose of outsourcing has evolved, and strategic outsourcing or value-creation outsourcing has emerged in recent years. This paper describes the historical transitions undergone by outsourcing and looks in particular at the current managerial meaning of strategic outsourcing.

The fourth paper by Monden explains the acquisition price of M&A as a practical example of the *incentive price*, using the case study of the merger between City group and Nikko. The estimated synergy of M&A will be allocated to both the acquiring firm and the acquired firm. The central problem in this allocation is how to determine the acquisition premium for the stockholders of the acquired firm considering the interest of stockholders of the acquiring firm.

Part 3: Analyses of Accounting Information for Consolidated Business Groups and Segmental Business Units

The first paper by Takano discusses how management accounting information is used for BGM through the analysis of consolidated accounting information. The associated analyses with case studies are provided in this paper.

The second chapter by Hiraoka investigates segment reporting for business evaluation using a case study. Starting in April 2010, Japanese companies will be obliged to introduce a "management approach" to segment reporting. However, Panasonic Electric Works is already applying this approach to arrangement. Through a case study of segment reporting at Panasonic Electric Works, this paper shows how an analysis of "business evaluation" can be made.

Part 4: Management of Inter-Firm Relations

The first paper by Minagawa discusses how management accounting can achieve the goal congruence among supply chain partners. Among the critical issues to be resolved for efficient supply chain management is how to reduce the risks that associate with opportunistic behaviors by partners.

The second paper by Ozawa demonstrates the hypothesis that for Toyota to maintain its strong negotiating position, it is necessary to have a system in place that rewards dealerships based on their sales performances, rather than one that increases sales by reducing invoice prices in the low-demand season.

The third paper by Hoshi discusses the royalties of franchise contracts and profit allocation. The basis for assessing royalties in a franchise contract in a convenience store business is usually the gross profit or the gross profit plus the "loss amount," which corresponds to the cost of purchased merchandise that was subsequently discarded because it was past its consumption-date. This paper examines the effect of loss inclusion in the royalty base, so that the profit allocation issues that arise in a convenience store business can be clarified.

The fourth paper by Kubota investigates the factors that influence the control mechanisms of joint ventures. The success of inter-company alliances or joint ventures is dependent upon the management control systems for inter-firm relations. In general, compared to the situation in Western companies, the managers of Japanese companies are inclined to get involved in on-site, shop-floor-level manufacturing, and to conduct informal controls. This paper clarifies the Japanese inter-firm control mechanism through the research survey of the top management of manufacturing companies in Japan.

The fifth paper by Sakaguchi explores the question as to whether or not inter-firm cooperation contributes to the performance level of Japanese firms, based on a survey of 97 Japanese manufacturing companies. Inter-firm cooperation, the relationship between cooperation and performance, and the emerging problems in Japanese inter-firm cooperation are examined.

The sixth paper by Monden discusses incentive price used as a transaction price for allocating the joint profits to the member firms of the network organization. The criterion to determine such an incentive price is the contribution grade of how each party has contributed to gain the joint profit, and it will be measured based on the tangible and/or intangible assets or the expenses paid to develop such assets.

Part 5: Inter-Organizational Learning and Autonomous Organizations

The first paper by Kondo discusses the management of population-level learning and inter-organizational relations in Japan. In this paper, the differences in the various learning patterns of various inter-firm relations are summarized. In addition, appropriate organizational learning strategies to be adopted by each organization to adapt flexibly to changes in the management environments, while controlling dysfunctional results, are discussed.

The second paper by Ito investigates management control systems for empowered organizations. The concepts and principles of empowered organizations contrast with those of centralized organizations, which are designed and managed using a "command-and-control" logic. The relationship between the organization principle and management accounting is analyzed in detail. Tentative conclusions are reached based on case studies of high-achieving Japanese companies, such as Toyota, Kyocera, Kao, and 7-Eleven.

I am very grateful to Ms. Juliet Lee Ley Chin, the Social Sciences commissioning editor of World Scientific Publishing Company, for her invaluable efforts in making this book a reality. Furthermore, Ms. Kim Tan, the book editor, is acknowledged for her handling of the manuscripts. Lastly, I would like to express my special thanks to Prof. Yasuhiro Monden, founder of the Monden Institute of Management, who made it possible for me to publish this book as a book series (Vol. 7) of the Institute.

Kazuki Hamada
25 April 2009

About the Volume Editor

Kazuki Hamada
Professor of Institute of Business and Accounting,
Kwansei Gakuin University
1-155 Uegahara-1bancho, Nishinomiya, Hyogo 662-8501, Japan
President, Japan Society of Organization and Accounting
Majoring in Management Accounting
BA and MBA from Kwansei Gakuin University,
Ph.D. from Tsukuba University
k-hamada@kwansei.ac.jp

Main publications

"Total Productivity Management and the Theory of Constraints: An Integrated Application of Supply Chain Management Methods," in Monden, Y. *et al.*, eds., *Japanese Management Accounting Today*, World Scientific, 2007.

"Managerial Roles of Financial and Non-Financial Measures in Supply Chain and Engineering Chain Management," in Monden, Y. *et al.*, eds., *Value-Based Management of the Rising Sun*, World Scientific, 2006, Chapter 23.

"A Method for Simultaneously Achieving Cost Reduction and Quality Improvement," "A Management System for the Simultaneous Attainment of Customer Satisfaction and Employee Satisfaction," in Monden, Y., ed., *Japanese Cost Management*, Imperial College Press, 2000, Chapter 7 and Chapter 19.

Evolution of Management Accounting Method, Chuoukeizai-sha, 1998 (in Japanese).

"Target Costing and Kaizen Costing in the Japanese Automobile Companies," *Journal of Management Accounting Research*, Vol. 3, 1992 (co-authored with Monden, Y.).

List of Contributors

Takayuki Asada
Professor, Graduate School of Economics, Osaka University
1-7 Machikaneyama, Toyonaka, Osaka 560-0043, Japan
Ph.D. from Kobe University
asada@econ.osaka-u.ac.jp

Shufuku Hiraoka
Professor, Faculty of Business Administration, Soka University
1-236 Tangi-cho, Hachioji, Tokyo 192-0087, Japan
Ph.D. from Meiji University
shiraoka@soka.ac.jp

Noriko Hoshi
Professor, Faculty of Business Adminstration, Hakuoh University
1117 Daigyoji, Oyama, Tochigi 323-8588, Japan
Ph.D. from Tsukuba University

Katsuhiro Ito
Professor, Faculty of Economics, Seikei University
3-3-1 Kichijyoji-kitamachi, Musashino, Tokyo 180-8633, Japan
MBA from Hitotsubashi University
kito@econ.seikei.ac.jp

Naoyuki Kaneda
Professor, Faculty of Economics, Gakushuin University
1-5-1 Mejiro, Toshima-ku, Tokyo 171-8588, Japan
Ph.D. from Carnegie Melon University

Hiroki Kondo
Lecturer, Faculty of Business Administration, Mejiro University
4-31-1 Nakaochiai, Shinjyuku-ku, Tokyo 161-8539, Japan
Ph.D. from Kyushu University
kondo@mejiro.ac.jp

Yuichi Kubota
Associate Professor, School of Economics, Osaka Prefecture University
1-1 Gakuen-cho, Naka-ku, Sakai, Osaka 599-8531, Japan
Ph.D. from Kobe University

Syunzo Matuoka
Professor, Faculty of Business, Hannan University
5-4-33 Amamihigashi, Matubara, Osaka 580-8502, Japan
MBA from Osaka Prefecture University

Yoshiteru Minagawa
Professor, Faculty of Commerce, Nagoya Gakuin University
1-25 Atsuta, Nishimachi, Atsuta, Nagoya, Aichi 456-8612, Japan
Ph.D. from Nagoya University

Yasuhiro Monden
Professor, Faculty of Business Administration, Mejiro University
4-31-1 Nakaochiai, Shinjyuku-ku, Tokyo 161-8539, Japan
Professor-Emeritus of Tsukuba University
Ph.D. from Tsukuba University
monden@mejiro.ac.jp

Hiroshi Ozawa
Associate Professor, Graduate School of Economics, Nagoya University
Furocho, Chikusa-ku, Nagoya, Aichi 464-8601, Japan
Ph.D. from Nagoya University

Junya Sakaguchi
Associate Professor, School of Accountancy, Kansai University
3-3-35 Yamate-cho, Suita, Osaka 564-8680, Japan
Ph.D. from Kobe University

Kozo Suzuki
Director of Management Section
Tama Waterworks Reform Promotion Center
Tokyo Metropolitan Government
6-7 Midorimati, Tachikawa, Tokyo 190-0014, Japan
Ph.D. from Tsukuba University

Manabu Takano
Associate Professor, Department of Commerce
Seinan Gakuin University
6-2-92 Nishijin, Sawara-ku, Fukuoka 814-8511, Japan
Ph.D. from Meiji University

Makoto Tomo
Associate Professor, Faculty of Economics, Seijo University
6-1-20 Seijo, Setagaya-ku, Tokyo 157-8511, Japan
Ph.D. from Osaka University
seijo@xtomo.com

Makoto Yori
Professor, Graduate School of Accountancy, University of Hyogo
8-2-1 Gakuennishi, Nishi-ku, Kobe, Hyogo 651-2197, Japan
Ph.D. from Kobe University
biwakoshiga@gmail.com

Part 1

Accounting Information for Group Management and Management Control System

1

Management Accounting Information for Consolidated Group Management

Kazuki Hamada
Institute of Business and Accounting, Kwansei Gakuin University

1. Introduction

Japanese companies can be roughly divided into two types: (1) corporate groups that were formed before World War II, such as Mitsui, Mitsubishi, Sumitomo; and (2) corporate groups that are affiliated with city banks, such as former Daiichi Kangyo Bank, Fuyo (former Fuji Bank, former Yasuda Bank) and the former Sanwa Bank. The business relationships among the large companies in these groups are only fair and not direct in many cases. However, for business groups that place large companies in the center, the business relationships between the large companies and their associated small/medium companies are close. The other type of corporate group is the vertical group, in which the parent company is at the top, as is the case at Toyota, Hitachi, Panasonic, Canon, and so forth. These groups are based on business operating relationships and close connections between the constituent companies.

In recent years, in both types of corporate groups, many companies have been split to delegate the authority for speedy decision making, to ensure complete responsibility for own profit/loss, and to reduce the fragmentation of effort required for the launching on new business ventures and the development of new products. When a company is broken, the bad assets are often retained at its headquarters. Therefore, the delegation of authority and company fragmentation may produce some good results but may also weaken the headquarters of the company. In addition, the company may encounter problems with the pursuit of local optimization at each company, synergy creation in subdivisions, waste of resources, and increase of adjustment costs.

The group headquarters has to optimize its functions and manage from the view of the whole group rather than that of the parent company. For some companies, the effects of decentralization can be detrimental, forcing revision of management methods and even reconsideration of the decision to decentralize. In this paper, the group headquarters is in charge of the management of the entire group.

The purpose of this paper is to examine the methods that can be used for group management from the standpoint of management accounting, with a consideration of the role of the group headquarters. In particular, the characteristics of management accounting information that facilitate group management and the design and use of consolidated performance evaluation system are discussed. In Japan, the ban on pure holding companies was lifted in principle in 1997, and some companies subsequently adopted this system. For a company that seeks to change to this type of company structure, it is usual to start as an operating and holding company that runs its own business and is managed like a pure holding company. In any case, many companies currently execute such group management now. Therefore, I consider this paper taking this type into consideration.

2. The Role of Group Headquarters and Three Types of Group Management

2.1. *The importance of "management of dispersion and unification"*

The group headquarters functions to

(1) Adjust and unify the component businesses from the view of the whole group, while promoting the self-management of group companies.
(2) Develop the new businesses and to abolish defunct businesses.
(3) Cooperate and conduct the joint development projects with companies outside the groups.
(4) Support the companies in the group.

The philosophy underlying these roles of the group headquarters relate to balanced "management of dispersion and unification."

For the management to promote self-management, management methods such as clarification of the individual missions of each company, delegation of authority, clarification of the ranges of responsibility and authority, introduction of market mechanism, and clarification of performance evaluation standards must be implemented. For reinforcement of group centripetal force, management methods such as the clarification of missions and the unification strategies across the entire group, information sharing, joint responsibility for ethics, personal exchange, common training programs, and consolidated performance evaluation are required.

For management of dispersion and unification, it is necessary to combine both management methods in a satisfactory manner. From the standpoint of management accounting, I think it is important to consider carefully the formulation of group missions and unification strategies, the establishment of individual missions and strategic goals in each company, the design of appropriate performance evaluation systems in which the ranges of authority and responsibility are considered, and the procedures for accounting information sharing and mutual communication.

2.2. *The three types of group management and the roles of the group headquarters*

Group management can be roughly divided into three types. The management of dispersion and unification is necessary for all the types listed below, and even within a single type of group management, the emphasis placed on dispersion and unification may be quite different.

The first type of group management is that led by a group headquarters (Type I), which not only formulates and transmits group missions and group strategies, but also decides on the missions and concrete targets for the headquarters business divisions and group companies. The concrete measures applied by the business divisions and group companies are decided by themselves. The group headquarters allocates a role to each company, to achieve synergy among the companies in the group, and to attain global optimum. Both periodic performance evaluations and intra-period controls are performed, and management is executed based on detailed information. From the evaluation results, essential businesses are established and superfluous businesses are abolished. Information sharing is promoted between the headquarters and group companies, and the group headquarters decides the necessary technology and support in terms of funding, tie-ups, and so forth.

The second form of group management is led by business divisions and related companies (Type II). In this organization, the group headquarters not only formulates and transmits group missions and group strategies, but also defines the individual missions for the business divisions and related companies. However, the group headquarters does not decide on concrete strategy targets, and the business divisions and related companies manage independently. In addition, the group headquarters introduces a market mechanism, manages the overall group, and executes performance evaluations regularly. The *de novo* establishment and abolition of businesses are performed based on the evaluation results. Information sharing and cross-sectional evaluations are carried out as much as possible to maintain the centripetal force of the group. When requested by a business division or a related company, the group headquarters may support a new technology, a fund scheme, or a plan to strengthen the business.

The third form of group management is financial management (Type III). The group headquarters transmits group missions and group strategies to maintain centripetal force. As the relationships between the individual business divisions and related companies may be poor and they may lack common strategies, there may be little synergy between them. The group headquarters executes only a periodical performance evaluation and decides on the direction of the business. Upon receipt of a request from a business division or a related company, the group headquarters may support a new technology, a fund scheme, or a plan to strengthen the business.

Hitachi is divided into the M (management) consolidated company, V (vision) consolidated company, and F (financial) consolidated company. The M consolidated company performs strategic management within Hitachi with regard to pursuit synergy. The V consolidated company leads businesses that share a management vision and brand and that are members of the Hitachi group. The F consolidated company executes only financial consolidation.

2.3. *Functions of the group headquarters*

The functions of headquarters can be divided into functions related to the management of the overall group and functions that support the group businesses and related companies. Moreover, the former can be divided into activities of strategic formulation and adjustment, resource allocation, and strategic control. The operational details of these three activities depend on the type of the group management used, as described below.

Strategic formulation and adjustment:

(1) Strategic formulation and communication of the vision, missions, and strategies of the whole group; for all types of group management.
(2) Formulation and communication of the business divisions and related companies; for Type I and Type II.
(3) Establishment and indication of the individual goals of the business divisions and related companies; for Type I.

Resource allocation:

Investigation of an optimal group management system and formulation of a resource allocation plan; these activities should always be executed for Type I group management, and should be performed as the circumstances demand in Type II and Type III.

Strategic control:

(1) Decisions as to performance evaluation indicators; for all types of group management, with detailed decisions for Type I.
(2) Monitoring accomplishment of overall goals and each divisional goal in the intra-period; for Type I.
(3) Interpretation of enforcement results and performance evaluation and decisions as to rewards; for all types, although the grasping detailed results and evaluation is needed for Type I.

Support functions, which are implemented to support the businesses in the group and the related companies, include personnel affairs, accounting, legal affairs, personnel training, technologic support, intellectual assets strategies, and research and development particularly basic research and high-risk, high-return studies. These operations are necessary for all the group management types.

3. Group Management and Management Accounting Information

3.1. *Group performance accounting*

The objectives of accounting for group decision making are outlined in points (1) and (2) of *Strategic formulation and adjustment* (Section 2.3), and in *Resource allocation* (Section 2.3), if group support functions are excluded. In contrast, the objectives of group performance accounting are covered by point (3) of *Strategic formulation and adjustment* (Section 2.3), and in *Strategic control* (Section 2.3). In this paper, I focus on group performance accounting.

In performance accounting, the establishment of goals, the performance evaluations, and performance control over a short period are the most important issues. Of course, the short-term goals must be consistent with the declared strategies, individual plans, and long-term goals. However, in recent years, the importance of an emergent strategy has been emphasized, and the domain of performance accounting is no longer considered to be narrow but is expected to expand in accordance with the business strategy. As indicated in Fig. 1, performance evaluation for a short period is designed to take into account the strategies, and the performance evaluation results are considered to influence strategy formulation. In other words, the group evaluation system has handled relations of (a) in Fig. 1 traditionally, but to consider the relations of (b) in Fig. 1 is important.

Fig. 1. The relationship between strategies and the periodical performance evaluation system.

3.2. *Characteristics of performance accounting information that are useful for group management*

In this section, I will comment on the usefulness and characteristics of management accounting information based on the characteristics of group performance accounting described in the previous section.

The group headquarters not only informs about the financial goals (group goals) in the short term. However, it is also important to clarify the relationships between the group missions and group strategies, so that the division managers and company managers understand their individual missions. Thus, they understand the roles of their own division and company by understanding the direction of the whole group and their own stand-point, which allows them to evaluate the current situation and results in an autonomous manner.

In the group headquarters-led model, the headquarters informs the business divisions and related companies of their goals and their performance evaluation indicators, and allows them to report in detail regularly (every month), while at the same time permitting them to report necessary information on a weekly, daily or real-time basis. In the business divisions/related companies-led model, the headquarters informs these units only regarding performance evaluation indicators, and allowing them to report results regularly (every month), while proving the opportunity to report weekly or daily if necessary. In the financial management model, the headquarters allows the companies to report results regularly (every month).

For group headquarters-led management and business divisions/related companies-led management, it is necessary to clarify the issues of authority and responsibility, since this dictates the positioning within the overall group and increased autonomy. Moreover, since various forms of businesses are carried out in the group, it is important to define unambiguously using a matrix the relationships between the functions of the headquarters/related companies and the various businesses, and to manage regarding a factor of the matrix as a business unit (responsibility center). In addition, authority and responsibility are decided by considering the relationships between the functions and businesses. When a bundle of business units is small, it is good to be able to consider plans and measures concretely, but it is not possible to consider from a general point of view and to consider synergy in a wide range. On the contrary, when a bundle of business unit is large, it is possible to consider goals and synergy from a general view, but it is difficult to consider concrete measures.

It is necessary to determine in advance transfer prices, internal interest rates for fund raising from headquarters, the calculation method for internal dividends on adopting an internal capital system, and the allocation methods for corporation expenses occurred in the business divisions and related companies, to compute the profit/loss for the headquarters, each functional division at the headquarters, and each related company, as well as the profit/loss for each business division and business. It appears that clear definition of these parameters make it easier for the constituent units to act autonomously. Of course, these performance calculation methods need to be consistent with not only the short-term goals, but also the strategies of the whole group.

Accounting procedures for performance evaluation should be conducted fairly. Cost burden rules often tend to be different. For example, internal business divisions bear the common costs of the headquarters, while related companies do not. Internal business divisions also often have courtesies which are mutually beneficial but unofficial arrangements, while related companies do not. It is important to standardize these accounting procedures.

It is necessary to expedite reporting by standardizing accounting procedures. For the purposes of managing, complete information is not essential, as estimated values or predicted values can be used.

4. Example of Using a Performance Evaluation System for Group Management

An appropriate performance evaluation system is essential for the procurement of useful performance accounting information. In recent years, the numbers of overseas subsidiaries in global companies, such as electric companies and office machine companies, which deal with many products, have increased, such that integral information on the businesses at home and abroad has become crucial. When the horizontal and vertical divisions of labor systems are taken, not only the evaluation of each company and each function, but also the evaluation of each business is necessary, as I mentioned in the previous section. One example of a matrix evaluation system is provided by Canon.

At Canon, most of the sales and production activities are carried out by subsidiaries. The business divisions do not have their own production and sales companies. Essentially, a single production company produces the products of some of the business divisions and all the sales companies sell the products of all the businesses. In light of this corporate structure, the matrix performance evaluation system was introduced for the following reasons.

(1) When the independent management system of each business division becomes too strong, some production companies and sales companies are built by business division in the same area, with the potential for increased wastage of resources.
(2) Business divisions need to run businesses not only from the view of their own business, but also from the overall view.

(3) As production companies are in charge of some businesses and sales companies execute management by channel, a unified management is necessary.

The profit/loss made by each company and each business division are computed in this evaluation system, and management aimed at maximizing both of these parameters is enabled. Since close communication is important in matrix management, the directors of the business divisions regularly visit the sales companies and production companies, to exchange information and to share group accounting information.

At Murata Manufacturing, the profit/loss levels of each department and each product (consolidated profit/loss for each product) are calculated, and two-dimensional matrix management based on these parameters is executed. The department profit/loss in the company is the starting point for profit/loss management and is a generic term for profit/loss by process, by place, and by corporation. Murata Manufacturing differs from Canon in that its matrix evaluation is enforced in detail within the company. Research and development, business planning, and general management are conducted intensively in the headquarters. If these activities are added, the management becomes three-dimensional.

During the calculation of department profit/loss, cases may arise in which a general administration/sales department and a research and development department at the parent company and some of the subsidiaries conduct their activities at a location other than their usual place of business. In such cases, the costs are assigned directly or allocated adequately among the divisions and corporations. In the calculation of consolidated profit/loss for each type of product, general administration/ sales costs and research and development costs are assigned directly or allocated by received benefit beyond the position. The budgets and actual profit/loss results are controlled monthly.

The main rules for profit/loss management are established unambiguously. These rules include transfer prices, which are decided using an addition method. However, a special price is set when a product cannot be sold at the transfer price. This method has been adopted because it guarantees the gross margin for the headquarters, and limits losses for the subsidiaries. In addition, transfer prices are determined in yen, to make overseas companies susceptible to exchange rate fluctuation. Moreover, an interest rate system is introduced, which means that funds for equipments/ inventories and all the working capital are supposedly borrowed from the headquarters, so that interest can be charged. However, the internal capital system is not adopted. This system is peculiar to Japan and its purpose is to assign intra-divisional capital and to allow the divisions to act autonomously as independent companies. When the internal capital system is adopted, it will let you misjudge because the past profit is reserved as surplus funds. Furthermore, standard costs are calculated and used to set the sales prices and intra-transfer prices, as well as for cost management, budgeting, and inventory evaluations.

The knowledge gains and the points to be considered from these examples are as follows:

(1) The consolidated performance evaluation system is useful in generating a unified consciousness across the group, and it should be devised as strategic executive means, as well as evaluation of the achievements in the short term.
(2) For the matrix organization to be the premise underlying matrix performance evaluation, the issues of authority and responsibility need to be clarified, to facilitate autonomous management.
(3) For autonomous management, transfer prices to evaluate performance and allocation rules for common costs and corporate costs must be established.
(4) Consolidated monthly closing procedures must be adopted, and an information system should be devised to disseminate important information as soon as possible, weekly and daily.
(5) Information sharing is necessary for matrix management. Therefore, it is important to establish a location for communication.

5. Using Management Accounting Information to Generate Synergies

It is necessary for the group headquarters to generate value that is greater than the sum of the values of the parts, so that group management is effective. Therefore, it is important to generate synergies. Group missions and visions give definitive guidelines for the value to be created by synergy. In addition, it is important to monitor continuously the situation of each business, so that synergy is created. Group synergy comprises planned synergy and emergent synergy. Planned synergy is expected at the time of planning, whereas emergent synergy emerges during the enforcement process and cannot be anticipated at the time of planning. Synergy arises from joint ownership of know-how, strategic adjustment, joint ownership of tangible assets, and concentration of negotiating power.

When synergy effects are estimated, the effects and feasibilities tend to be overestimated and the costs tend to be underestimated. Therefore, managers need to analyze more carefully the synergy effects and the associated financial costs, and to evaluate these items using a consolidated performance evaluation system, as mentioned above. The evaluation does not have to be strictly accurate. The effects of synergy are linked to increased profit and reduced costs.

In this section, I will consider the relationships between emergent synergy and performance accounting information. The places in which creativity is stimulated and promoted are indispensable for the generation of emergent synergy. It is extremely important that information and knowledge are allowed to flow within the group and are used diversely, and that devices and places are established in which information and knowledge are considered and linked freely. Therefore, it is important to build networks of human information and knowledge and to use personnel system.

Professor Yoshiya Teramoto mentions that the following items are necessary for the organization of learning, presupposing autonomous diversity of the organization members.

(1) Knowledge sharing, which is the sharing of explicit knowledge, tacit knowledge and sense of value;
(2) Holistic viewing;
(3) Flexible networking, which the flexible linkage and combination of people and organization; and
(4) Hypothetical experimenting, which involves the proposing of hypotheses regarding countermeasures and verification through experimentation.

Considering the generation of synergy from the stand-point of performance accounting using this way of thinking, it is necessary to establish the places that are used to accumulate performance accounting information and that facilitate knowledge sharing. To produce emergent synergy, reporting and communication only in the top and bottom directions, but also in the right-and-left directions are important. In addition, it is important to collect management accounting information in all locations at all times, and to educate users. Moreover, it is necessary to generate not only management accounting information, but also qualitative information.

From a holistic view, it is necessary that the goals of the overall group, those of each division, and the personal goals are consistent, and that achievements can be evaluated as needed. It is important that management accounting information is provided in a timely fashion. For flexible networking, the measurement of effects through the connection of persons and the organization is needed. For hypothetical experimentation, it is necessary that the influences of the measures that correspond to the various situations regarding profits and costs can be measured using simulations.

6. Summary and Conclusions

Group headquarters plays various roles. I believe that it is essential for group companies to be integrated while acting autonomously, and it is essential that they are managed from the overall view. I have discussed how valuable balanced "management of dispersion and unification" is for the field of management accounting, as well as the features and effective uses of useful management accounting information. In addition, I have considered how best to design and use a group consolidated performance evaluation system, so as to promote the management from the overall view.

I have emphasized the importance of defining clearly the group visions and the visions of each business division/related company, so as to encourage these units to act autonomously while maintaining a sense of unity. The authority and responsibility within each business unit, as defined by two axes, i.e., company (function of the company) and business, as well as the evaluation standard of the unit, should be clarified. In addition, it is indispensable to clarify the transfer prices and allocation rules for common costs and corporate costs.

I consider the matrix evaluation system to be effective, since various forms of business are executed in group companies and not only the performance of each company, but also that of each business beyond the company is needed. Establishing an appropriate performance evaluation system facilitates the maintenance of the centripetal force and autonomous management. As examples, I have mentioned Canon and Murata Manufacturing.

The evaluation system should be used not only to evaluate consolidated performance, but also to generate group synergies, i.e., planned synergy and emergent synergy.

Regarding further group management, conflicts, such as those related to transfer prices, will occur if an individual business division and each related company is overemphasized in performance evaluation, since subsidiaries and related companies are linked by the flow of trade. Therefore, relative importance attached to consolidated performance evaluation or performance evaluation of each business division/related company is crucial. Although I also considered the focusing of intra-group companies, consideration of the relationships with the companies outside the group is also necessary.

References

Asada, T. (2005). Characteristics of the holding company in the Japanese company, in *Organization Design for Increase of Corporate Value and Management Accounting*, edited by Monden, Y., published by Zeimu Keiri Kyokai, Chapter 14 (in Japanese).

Hamada, K. (2006). Performance Accounting Information for Consolidated Group Management, Kaikei, 170(4) (in Japanese).

Ishigaki, H. and Nagasawa, I. (2004). From management accounting to management oriented accounting, *Chiteki Shisan Sozo*, September (in Japanese).

Izumitani, H. (2001). The company can be examined if its "profit" can be examined: all of Murata style "matrix management", *Nihon Keizai Shinbunsha* (in Japanese).

Onuma, Y. and Kawano, T. (2005). Construction of next generation group management model, *Chiteki Shisan Sozo*, January (in Japanese).

Sawai, R. (1998). A elaborate plan to realize global excellent company group and its promotion measures for consolidated management innovation, in *A Practical Casebook for Management of Group Innovation and Related Companies,* edited by Nihon Noritu Kyokai (in Japanese).

Tanahashi, K. (2006). Promotion and management system of global/group consolidate management in Canon, in *From "Choice/Concentration" to "Realization of Next Growth Strategy: A Practical Casebook for the Promotion of Management Innovation*, edited by Kigyo Kenkyukai (in Japanese).

Tani, T. (1990). Corporate strategy and performance accounting, *Kaikei*, 137(5) (in Japanese).

Teramoto, Y. (2005). Management of contexts conversion: study about "synthesizing fusion" and "co-evolution" by organizational networking, *Hakuto Shobo* (in Japanese).

Tuda, N. (2003). Group management and a holding company system, in *An Ideal Type of the Global & Group Management in 21st Century: Strategy of Group*

Corporate Value Maximization and Management System, edited by Kigyo Kenkyukai (in Japanese).

Yamamoto, N. (2006). Global group management by new governance, in *From "Choice/Concentration" to "Realization of Next Growth Strategy: A Practical Casebook for the Promotion of Management Innovation*, edited by Kigyo Kenkyukai (in Japanese).

Yokota, E. (2005). A consideration about management control for autonomous organization and its unification, *Kaikei*, 168(6) (in Japanese).

2

Management Control System of Japanese Pure Holding Companies

Makoto Tomo
Faculty of Economics, Seijo University

Makoto Yori
Graduate School of Accounting, University of Hyogo

Takayuki Asada
Graduate School of Economics, Osaka University

1. Introduction

It became possible for Japanese companies to establish a pure holding company (HD) through the revision of the Japanese Antitrust Law in 1997. After 1999, more than a hundred of listed companies have established pure HD. Those companies might have various motives to keep pace with changes of the equity market environment, the globalization of M&A, the revision of the Anti-monopoly Law, and so on. We studied the present conditions and the issue of a management control system (MCS) for pure HD through an interview and literature study. Especially, we focused on the business reorganization, empowerment, and role of the headquarters. In this paper, we will propose our hypothesis concerning the MCS for HD.

2. Significance and the Purpose of the Study

The earlier studies about the pure HD did not distinguish between Japanese HD systems and Western HD systems. They classified them by HD's functions. We found some different HD's cases from the prototype of earlier studies — Japanese holding companies manage the diversified subsidiaries under different circumstances. We will describe the robustness and innovativeness of Japanese HD's MCS, and the ways in which they are different from Western models of HD. In addition, this paper is based on the case method by interview, literature study, and financial data analysis. Thus, this study is at the stage of hypothesis formation (Tables 1 and 2).

3. The Meaning and the Purpose of a Pure HD System

A pure HD owns other companies and does no business itself. The HD delegates authority business functions to subsidiaries and controls them.

Table 1. The company for a hearing.

Corporate name	Establishment year of HD	Sales	Core business
JS Group	2001	1,124	Housing-related business, commercial-building-related business
Nippon Mining HD	2002	3,802	Petroleum, metals
JFE HD	2002	3,260	Steel, engineering, shipbuilding
Fuji Electric HD	2003	908	Power, control devices, semiconductor devices, vending machines
Sojitz	2003	5,218	Machinery & aerospace, energy & mineral resources, chemicals & plastics
Konica Minolta HD	2003	1,028	Multi-function peripherals, optics, medical and graphic imaging
Asahi Chemical	2003	1,624	Fibers, chemicals, electronics, health care
Mitsubishi Chemical HD	2005	2,623	Petrochemicals, synthetic plastic products, pharmaceuticals
Dowa HD	2006	459	Nonferrous metals, environmental management & recycling

Data: 2007.3 consolidated accounting, sales amount: 1 billion yen, HD: holdings.

Table 2. Main questionnaire entries.

- The purpose of establishing pure HD and organizational restructuring, and the current state of such restructuring.
- The basic policy to restructure the product department and sales department.
- The corporate governance system and the structure of organizational integration.
- The extent of involvement in subsidiary's management decision: subsidiary's strategy, goal setting, and so on. What kinds of support function for subsidiary do headquarters have?
- Where does HD obtain the income? Where does the HD reserve the enterprise group profit?
- What are the performance evaluation measures of the subsidiary?
- What kinds of demands do the subsidiaries have? Do headquarters have the official system to deal with them?
- What kinds of transfer price rule are in enterprise group? Can the subsidiaries purchase goods from outside vendor, even though another subsidiary in the group makes them?
- What kind of organizational structure do you have about the shared service: disperse to the subsidiaries or concentrate on HD? What is the purpose?

The purpose of the pure HD organization was as follows:

(1) The restructuring, which aimed at the profitability improvement.
(2) The delegation of business decision authority and encouraging the manager of subsidiary.
(3) The integration of the enterprises which have different corporate cultures.
(4) Placing the companies which have different business models under the same umbrella.
(5) The adaptation to the structural changes of the customer market.
(6) Protecting business rights from hostile takeover. (Modified by Asada, 2007, p. 4.)

It is difficult to determine what purpose each HD had. Most of the HD might have the purpose to achieve the economies of scale by M&A and diversification of risks by company split-up. However, in general, HD might have more purpose.

Moreover, the purposes after several years since HD was established might be different from those purposes when HD was originally established.

However, we thought the main purpose was aforementioned. The reason is the poor business performance company tends to adopt pure HD organization as follows.

4. Organizational Restructuring

4.1. *The pattern of organizational restructuring*

The organizational restructuring can be divided roughly into two patterns — mergers and corporate spin-offs. Of course, there might be the case that they adopt corporate spin-off and mergers at the same time. We typified the surveyed enterprises as follows:

(1) Integration type (substitute of mergers): To reduce the conflict by mergers by taking the form that two companies operate as subsidiary under headquarters instead of mergers.

   Case example: Konica Minolta Holdings, Inc. (Konica and Minolta), JFE Holdings, Inc. (Kawasaki Steel and NKK), JS Group Corporation (TOSTEM and INAX), Sojitz Corporation (Nichimen and Nissho Iwai): Headquarters and subsidiaries were merged a year later. The pure HD was used during a preparation period until they merged.

(2) Group restructuring type: The reorganization in a corporate group.

   (i) Spin-off type: Shifting from "company system: pseudo intra-corporation system, investment center system" to HD system.

   Case example: Asahi Kasei Corporation (To closure of the unrelated diversification with poor profitability), Fuji Electric Holdings Co., Ltd. (To increase the independency and profitability of investment centers), DOWA Holdings Co., Ltd. (To increase the unifying force by assembling the young human resources under 45 years to headquarters.)

   (ii) Shifting from operating HD to pure HD type: To equate with subsidiaries and department in the operating HD.

   Case example: Mitsubishi Chemical Holdings Corporation. (The chemistry department was spun off as subsidiary to equate with pharmaceutical subsidiary.)

   (iii) Corporate parallel type: Case example: Nippon Mining Holdings, Inc. (The mining corporation and the oil corporation were located under the newly established pure HD as subsidiaries.)

4.2. The purpose of organizational restructuring

According to Table 3, most of the surveyed companies' sales were less than No. 2, except for the sash business in JS Group Corporation. These companies might exploit organizational restructuring, selection and concentration, for competitive advantage.

Table 4 shows the degree of diversification of the surveyed corporations compared with their competitors in their industry by entropy

Table 3. Position in the industry of the surveyed corporations.

Company name	Field	Sales	Domestic competitor	Sales	Ratio
		(a)		(b)	(a)/(b)
JS Group	Sash	543	Nippon Light Metal	173	3.14
	Housing Equipment	270	TOTO	512	0.53
Nippon Mining HD	Oil	677	Nippon Oil Corporation	5,964	0.11
	Nonferrous Metal	279	Mitsubishi Materials	1,452	0.19
Mitsubishi Chemical HD	Chemistry	1,246	Sumitomo Chemical	1,790	0.70
	Pharmaceutical	305	Takeda Pharmaceutical	1,305	0.23
JFE HD	Steel	2,754	Nippon Steel	4,302	0.64
	Engineering	306	Chiyoda Kakoh Co. Ltd.	485	0.63
Fuji Electric HD	Electrical Machinery	908	Toshiba	7,116	0.13
Konica Minolta HD	Office Machine	1,028	Canon	4,156	0.25
Dowa HD	Nonferrous Metals	459	Mitsubishi Materials	1,452	0.32
Asahi Kasei	Chemistry	677	Sumitomo Chemical	1,790	0.38
	Housing	405	Sekisui House	1,596	0.25

Sales: The sales (a consolidated accounting classified by segment) of 2007.3 terms, unit: 1 billion yen.

Table 4. Domestic competitor comparison of the diversification degree.

Company name	Entropy index	Domestic competitor	Entropy index	Ratio
	(a)		(b)	(a)/(b)
JS Group	88	Nippon Light Metal	187	0.5
		TOTO	14	6.2
Nippon Mining HD	111	Nippon Oil Corporation	60	1.8
		Mitsubishi Materials	231	0.5
Mitsubishi Chemical HD	199	Sumitomo Chemical	262	0.8
		Takeda Pharmaceutical	40	5.0
JFE HD	60	Nippon Steel	115	0.5
		Chiyoda Kakoh Co. Ltd.	148	0.4
Fuji Electric HD	212	Toshiba	207	1.0
Konica Minolta HD	158	Canon	124	1.3
Dowa HD	198	Mitsubishi Materials	231	0.9
Asahi Kasei	220	Sumitomo Chemical	262	0.8
		Sekisui House	179	1.2

Entropy index $\sum_{i=1}^{n}\{P_i \times \log_2(1/P_i)\}$, Pi: composition ratio of business DI.

index. The entropy index was measured with the data in Kaisha shikiho, summer 2007 edition: quarterly corporate report (Toyo Keizai Shinpo-Sha). It shows that the larger an entropy index is, the higher a diversified level is.

The diversification degree of surveyed corporation was higher than the competitor. It is thought to be the cause that the scale of sales of surveyed operations are smaller than the competitor, in addition, they sell or withdraw the poor performance business when they adopt the pure holding company system.

For example, Nippon Mining Holdings, Inc. handed over a part of pharmaceutical business to Sumitomo pharmaceuticals. It also transferred shares of Convenience store chain, "AM/PM", to Reins International Inc.

Asahi Chemical also got out of business, such as acrylics, food, alcohol, and housing timber material, at the time it adopted a pure HD organization. It also handed over white-distilled-liquor business to Asahi Breweries, food business to JT, and so forth.

Thus, it is thought that pure HD's diversified level was low because the poor performance businesses was sold out.

5. The Result of Field Study of Pure HD System

By our survey of actual conditions, we made several findings contrary to common knowledge about pure HD systems. They are indicated below.

- The purpose is the succession of family business.
- There is a case which has utilized the company system simultaneously to utilizing a HD system.
- There is a case that the listed pure HD has listed subsidiaries.
- Establishing the pure HD does not always aim to maximize a shareholder value.
- There is weak pure HD, which cannot collect the funds from the subsidiaries and which cannot intervene in subsidiaries' business.
- There is pure HD, which does not have a strategic function.
- There is a case to encourage the loyalty by using the HD. This is an application of the "Ba" theory. Ba means a place for knowledge creation.

These might suggest the existence of singular pure HD system in Japan, where three types (financial strategy type, strategic planning type, a strategy management type) of HD do not suit. The three types are the classifications according to the headquarters' span of management to the subsidiaries. We call this a static classification in this paper.

(1) In the financial strategy type, the headquarters lay weight on the achievement of financial target, although it does not intervene in the

planning and the operation process of the subsidiary. It tends to have the small headquarters and the shared service subsidiaries.

(2) In the strategic planning type, the headquarters take part in the strategy formulation of subsidiaries. It does not lay weight on the achievement of financial targets.

(3) In the strategy management type, the headquarters formulate interactive systems, from strategic decision, monitoring, to performance evaluation, with headquarters and subsidiaries. A Balanced Score Card (BSC) and a project budget, and so forth were used in the interactive systems, for example (Asada, 2005a, p. 146).

We will set up some hypotheses mainly based on the following two questions.

The first question concerns the function of pure HD. The second question concerns the purpose, the manner, and the methods of establishing the pure HD organization.

We cannot describe the MCS of HD by the static classification, which is the relationship between headquarters and subsidiaries at some point.

Therefore, we show diagrammatically a "dynamic classification" in Fig. 1. The "dynamic" means that we described the restructuring process being used by pure HD. Thus, each company's position in this figure will change continually.

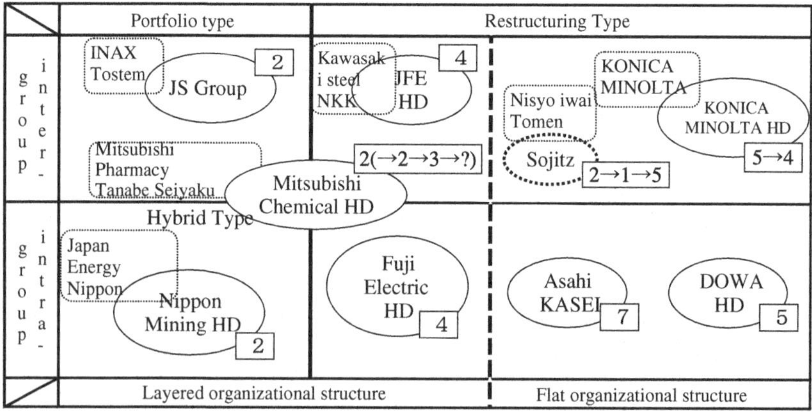

Fig. 1. A dynamic classification of surveyed companies.

The vertical axis shows the type of restructuring target — whether they are only group companies or not. The horizontal axis shows the subsidiaries' organization restructuring type — whether they are merged with other divisions or not. The portfolio type organization has the independent subsidiaries, which did not merge completely. The restructuring type organization has the restructured subsidiaries: spin off or merger.

There are two types of MCS such as flat and layered. The layered type has intermediate headquarters: such as regional headquarters or business domain headquarters. In addition, the intermediate headquarters practically formulate strategy and do decision making for its subsidiaries.

The surveyed companies were plotted on Fig. 1 by foregoing criterion. The ellipse of solid line show the present pure HD. The main companies before becoming a pure HD are shown in the box of dotted line box about on the ellipse. The box of solid line shows the number of the main subsidiaries along with the restructuring process.

Mitsubishi Chemical Holdings has been positioned on each four quadrants. This is because the restructured core business subsidiaries were both inner and outside group companies. Moreover, the purpose of reorganization by pure HD was portfolio type and a restructuring type.

5.1. *Portfolio type*

There were two portfolio type companies (JS Group and Nippon Mining Holdings Inc.). INAX and Tostem established JS GROUP as a joint HD. INAX and Tostem are keeping the prior organization and corporate name, though they are jointly conducting the development of some products. Before establishing Nippon Mining Holdings Inc., both Japan Energy Corporation (oil industry) and Nippon Mining & Metals Co., Ltd. (metal industry) were listed companies. After establishing the pure HD, it keeps the two corporations, though they were delisted.

Nippon Mining & Metals Co., Ltd. sold the 80% share of am/pm Japan Co., Ltd. to Rex Holdings Co., Ltd. in the process of establishing the pure holding company in August 2004.

The number of core business companies of the portfolio type is fewer than that of the restructuring type. Both JS Group and Nippon Mining Holdings Inc. only have two core business companies. Mitsubishi Chemical Holdings also has only three core business companies. On the other hand, the restructuring type holdings have from 4 to 7 core business companies.

In the portfolio type, it thought that the core business company has a high degree of autonomy. In addition, the headquarters are seldom involved in the management decision process of the core business companies. Therefore, the performance evaluation indicator for them tends to be the investment efficiency from the financial view. The earnings of the core business subsidiary are paid to HD as a dividend at a rate proportional to the external dividend. And the rest of the earnings are retained in the core business companies. In this case, the main function of the HD is to create the missions of the group, control by rule, and audit on operation.

5.2. *Restructuring type*

There are two patterns in the type of restructuring. First, there is the method of integrating the similar functions of the two enterprises, and doing the spin off. JFE Holdings, Inc. and Konica Minolta Holdings correspond to this type. JFE Holdings, Inc. was established by merging Kawasaki Steel and NKK. JFE Holdings did not place Kawasaki Steel and NKK under the HD, but integrated the steel manufacture business and the engineering business, and so forth, of the two companies, and placed each business under the HD as a subsidiary. Furthermore, in the restructuring process, JFE Holdings transferred the subsidiaries of resin business to GE plastics. Konica Minolta HD reorganized each business field into five business subsidiaries and put them under the HD. Konica Minolta HD closed the camera and photo business that were the initial business in March 2006 after about three years of the pure HD establishment. It was a part of the "selection and concentration" strategy.

The second pattern is to spin off divisions into separate companies. This is an advanced type of an in-house company system. Asahi Chemical, Fuji Electric HD, and DOWA HD correspond to this type. Asahi Chemical spun off divisions into seven subsidiaries, such as fiber, chemistry, and so forth, under the HD. Fuji Electric HD and DOWA HD are similar to Asahi Chemical.

5.3. *Hybrid type*

Mitsubishi Chemical HD consists of two-domain identity as shown in Fig. 2. In the chemistry DI, Mitsubishi Chemical merged the subsidiary (Mitsubishi Plastics Inc.) on October 2007. In the pharmaceutical DI, Mitsubishi Pharmacy merged with Tanabe Seiyaku Co., Ltd. on

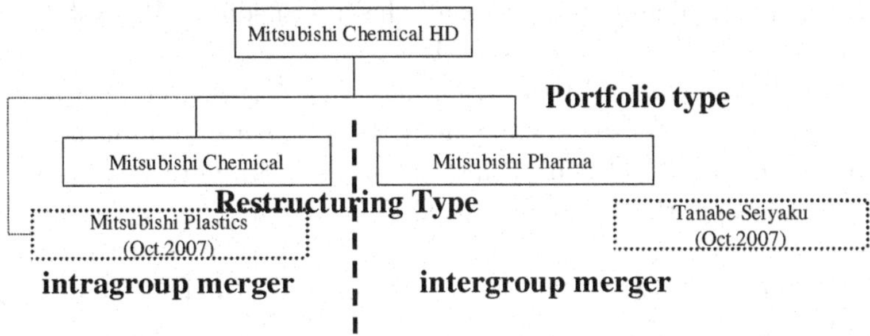

Fig. 2. Mergers and restructuring of Mitsubishi Chemical HD.

October 2007, and Tanabe Mitsubishi Pharmaceuticals was established. In this case, the reorganization took place with outside group and in-house corporation concurrently.

This case was the hybrid type. The HD is a portfolio type that has two core subsidiaries (chemical and pharmacy). The core subsidiary level is a restructuring type. The chemical subsidiary and pharmacy subsidiary have adopted different restructuring manner. The chemical subsidiary reorganized with in-house corporation, on the other hand, the pharmacy subsidiary reorganized with outside group.

6. Organizational Structure of Pure HD, and Relation of Authority

6.1. *The layered organizational structure*

The pure HD system is compared with the in-house company system. There is the view that the pure HD system is the advanced type of the in-house company system. However, there was the case that was using both the pure HD system and the in-house company system by our research.

For example, the in-house company system was adopted in Nippon Mining & Metals Co., Ltd., which is the core business company of Nippon Mining Holdings, Inc., and in the JFE engineering, which is a core business company of JFE HD. Moreover, the segment system was adopted in each core business company of Mitsubishi Chemical and Fuji Electric. The segment system is a kind of advanced in-house company system.

Furthermore, some enterprises had the intermediate HD system that the core business subsidiary was a HD.

For example, Nippon Mining Holdings, Inc. corresponds to this case. It has only two core business companies, Japan Energy (oil business) and Nippon Mining & Metals Co., Ltd. (metal business). On the oil business, Japan Energy has the following subsidiaries: Japan Energy development Co. Ltd. (petroleum development), Kashima Oil Co., Ltd. (petroleum refining and chemistry), JOMO-NET Co., Ltd. (management of gas station).

On the metal business, Nippon Mining & Metals adopts the in-house company system. It has the following in-house companies: a resource and a metal company, an electronic materials company, a metal processing company, and so forth. Furthermore, each in-house company has a subsidiary. The metal business has layered headquarters' structure.

Thus, it cannot necessarily be said that the pure HD system is an advanced type of the in-house company system. When the independence between the core business companies is high, and those scales are large, the in-house company system and so forth is often used together.

The purpose of not dividing the core business company in detail is to maintain the independence of the business and the advantage of specialization. Besides, it is to exclude the possibility of the business repetition in the future, and to leave room for the organization restructuring. There is a possibility that the overlapping business is caused in the future by change of technology and market if the core business company is divided in detail. In addition, even when a layered headquarters structure is adopted, the pure holding company specializes in the strategic function.

It should be concluded that the combination of the company split-up by the pure HD system and the in-house company system in the core business company level is one of the features of the Japanese pure HD system.

6.2. *Going public of a core business subsidiary, and the conglomerate discount*

It is said that there is a possibility that the conglomerate discount is generated in stock prices of the pure HD. The conglomerate discounts are that valuation of the diversified company relatively lower than single business company in the stock market is.

Table 5. The PER comparison with a competitor.

Company name	PER	Competitor	PER	Ratio	Competitor	PER	Ratio
JS Group	21.4	Nippon Light Metal	14.2	1.5	TOTO	30.2	0.7
Nippon Mining HD	8.6	Nippon Oil Corporation	19.9	0.4	Mitsubishi Materials	9.3	0.9
Mitsubishi Chemical HD	13.6	Sumitomo Chemical	15.7	0.9	Takeda Pharma-ceutical	20	0.7
JFE HD	13.6	Nippon Steel	15.3	0.9	Chiyoda Kakoh	21.1	0.6
Konica Minolta HD	11.3	Canon	19.6	0.6			
Fuji Electric HD	16.9	Toshiba	18.4	0.9			
Dowa HD	13.6	Mitsubishi Materials	9.3	1.5			
Asahi KASEI	17.5	Sumitomo Chemical	15.7	1.1	Sekisui House	19	0.9

Table 5 shows the PER (per-share earning ratio) of the surveyed company and competitor. The ratio in the table was calculated as below: the numerator is the PER of the surveyed company and the denominator is the PER of the competitor.

Only the PER of DOWA HD was higher than the PER of competitor. As for JS Group and Asahi Chemical, the PER was higher than the competitor only in some business fields. The PER of other companies was lower than competitor.

The PER was relatively lower than competitor. This is the reason why most companies were not top-sales company in their fields. However, the possibility that the conglomerate discount had been generated cannot be denied. (The type-of-industry classification was based on the quarterly corporate report of Toyo Keizai, Inc.)

Going public of the core business company becomes one of the choices, when there is a possibility that the conglomerate discount is generated.

There is the case of Mitsubishi Tanabe Pharma Corporation that Mitsubishi Pharma Corporation (pharmaceutical subsidiary of Mitsubishi Chemical HD) merged with Tanabe Seiyaku in October 2007. Tanabe

Seiyaku was a listed company; on the other hand, Mitsubishi Pharma Corporation was unlisted company (a 100% subsidiary of Mitsubishi Chemical HD). Mitsubishi Tanabe Pharma Corporation is subsidiary of Mitsubishi Chemical HD, though the share holding ratio of Mitsubishi Chemical HD fell to 56.34% by the merger. The subsidiary (Mitsubishi Tanabe Pharma Corporation), and the parent company (Mitsubishi Chemical HD) keep listed company. In October 2005, Mitsubishi Pharma Corporation, that had become an unlisted company, continued IR by itself as if it was a listed company. The briefing of settlement of accounts had been held alone. Moreover, the Annual Report, the business report, the environmental report, and the brief announcement of the most recent financial statement following the end of the fiscal year, and so forth were published by itself. It seems that this intended the re-listing in the future.

This is a special case, in general, in the process of establishing pure HD, the listed subsidiary tends to be converted into a totally held subsidiary. For instance, Nippon Mining Holdings, Inc. delisted Nippon Mining & Metals Co., Ltd. (subsidiary of Japan Energy Corporation). In the pure HD system, it seems that the higher independence of the subsidiary company is, the harder allocation of strategic resources is.

In such a case, listing of the subsidiary is one of the options. This is because each subsidiary can get the discipline by the market valuation for the appropriately funding. Listing of the subsidiary existed before the pure HD system adoption. It is the characteristic of Japanese pure HD, which might have the listed subsidiary.

6.3. *Dividend policies to holding company and subsidiary's earning retention place*

The power relationship between the pure HD and the core business company is reflected on the dividend policy to the headquarters by the core business subsidiary and earning retention place. The HD normally has the authority to decide the dividend policy of core business subsidiary.

If so, it must be indifferent wherever the HD reserves the earnings in the group. However, many companies think that the autonomy of a core business company is influenced by the dividend policy of a subsidiary and the place of the retention of earnings.

Therefore, in the enterprise that values independence of the core business company, the dividend payout ratio of the core business subsidiary to the headquarters tends to be the same as the dividend payout ratio for

Table 6. The dividend policy of core business subsidiary and earning retention place.

Type	Company	Retained profit place	Policy of dividend to HQ
P	JS Group	Subsidiary	Under an external dividend ratio
P	Nippon Mining HD	Subsidiary	Equal to external dividend
H	Mitsubishi Chemical HD	HQ + subsidiary	50% of profits (2007.3)
R	Fuji Electric HD	Subsidiary	Equal to external dividend
R	JFE HD	HQ + subsidiary	97% of profits (2007.3)
R	Konica Minolta HD	HQ + subsidiary	20% of profits (2007.3)
R	Asahi Kasei	HQ + subsidiary	50% of profits

P: portfolio type, H: hybrid type, R: restructuring type.
Source: Compute by the term financial report ended March 2007 of each company.

external stockholder. In this case, it can be said that the core business company keep the earning retention. On the other hand, when the headquarters reallocate the capital strategically, all the profits of the core business subsidiary might be collected by dividend.

Table 6 shows the dividend rate of the core business subsidiary in the surveyed company. In JS Group, Nippon Mining Holdings, and Fuji Electric, the distribution ratio to headquarters by the core business subsidiary was lower than the external distribution ratio. These kept the earning retention in themselves. In Konica Minolta HD, the subsidiary was dividing 20% into the headquarters. In Mitsubishi Chemical HD and Asahi Chemical Industrial Co., Ltd., the subsidiary was dividing 50% into the headquarters.

In JFE HD, the subsidiary was dividing 97% into the headquarters for the period on March 2007. JFE have been investing strategically such as M&A by the headquarters lead against the worldwide reorganization of the iron and steel industry.

Thus, the dividend policy of core business subsidiary and the earning retention place depend on the business environment and the financial autonomy of core business subsidiary.

6.4. *Division of profits into stakeholders*

One of the functions of the pure HD is to balance the conflicting interests of stakeholders and to manage the distribution of profit to them.

Table 7 shows the reward system for stockholders, managers, and employees. Three companies (JSG, JFE HD, and Konica Minolta HD) committed the target of dividend payout ratio. Four companies had the stock option program for the manager. In JS Group, the stock option was applied even to the employees besides managers. In addition, the performance linkage remuneration was applied to the manager.

It is one of the purposes of the pure HD system to introduce a different personnel system and a reward system of each subsidiary characteristic. Six companies had the personnel system of each subsidiary characteristic. The performance-based evaluation reward to the employee had been introduced into seven companies.

It seems that the fewer adoption of personnel system of each subsidiary characteristic shows the independency of the core business subsidiary is not so high.

7. Summary and Future Tasks

It should be concluded, from what has been mentioned above, that several Japanese pure HDs have some purposes different from those of Western holdings. The pure HD has a wide variety of backgrounds and actual conditions.

We showed diagrammatically a "dynamic classification" regarding the restructuring process and the MCS in pure HD. In addition, we tried to describe the variety of purposes and MCS which Japanese enterprise adopt with respect to the pure holding company.

The following hypotheses we are able to propose at the present stage, although we will describe the detail in another paper.

1. The pure HD is not an advanced type of the in-house company system.
2. The in-house company system might be used together under the core business subsidiary.
3. There is the issue concerning the evasion of the conglomerate discount in the pure HD system. Listing of the core business subsidiary is one of the options.

Table 7. Division of profits for stakeholders.

	Stockholder	Manager		Employee		
Company name	Commitment of dividend payout ratio	Stock option	Performance-based system	Different type of personnel system	Pay-per-performance system	Stock option
JS Group	30% or more	○	○	○	○	○
Nippon Mining HD	×	○	×	○	○	×
Mitsubishi Chemical HD	×	○	×	○	○	×
JFE HD	About 25%	×	×	○	○	×
Konica Minolta HD	15% or more	○	×	×	○	×
Fuji Electric HD	×	×	×	○	○	×
Dowa HD	×	×	×	×	×	×
Asahi Kasei	×	×	×	○	○	×

4. The power relationship of the pure HD and the core business company is reflected in the dividend policy to the headquarters by the core business subsidiary and earning retention place. The dividend policy of core business subsidiary and the earning retention place depend on the financial autonomy of core business subsidiary. The less autonomy of core business subsidiary has, the more authority headquarters appropriation of subsidiaries' earnings has.
5. One of the functions of the pure HD is to balance the conflicting interests of stakeholders and how to distribute the profit to them.

In this paper, we addressed a part of question mentioned at the beginning. The remaining questions are left as a future task.

References

Asada, T. (2005a). The strategy and management of a holding company, in *The Organization Design and Management Accounting in Order to Improve Corporate Value*, edited by Monden, Y., Zeimukeiri Kyokai (in Japanese).

Asada, T. (2005b). The feature of the holding company system in Japanese companies, in *The Organization Design and Management Accounting in Order to Improve Corporate Value*, edited by Monden, Y., Zeimukeiri Kyokai (in Japanese).

Asada, T. (2007). Management accounting subject of a pure holding company, *Kigyou Kaikei*, 59(8) (in Japanese).

Business Research Institute, The Construction of a group management organization and management innovation towards the consolidated management age, *Business Research Institute* (in Japanese).

Diamond Harvard Business Editorial Department (1996). *The Principle and Management Strategy of a Holding Company*, Diamond Co. (in Japanese).

Hamada, K. (2006). Performance management accounting information for consolidated group management, *Kaikei*, 170(4) (in Japanese).

Hattori, N. (2005). *The Strongest Selection About M&A*, Nikkei BP (in Japanese).

Hiki, F. (2000). Group management and management accounting: On the cases of Western companies, *The Journal of Management Accounting*, Japan, 8(1,2) (in Japanese).

Makoto, Y. (1997). The significance and subjects of a in-house company system, *Research Annual Report*, Vol. 4, Department of Economics, Shiga University (in Japanese).

Makoto, Y. (2001). 'Doppo' management and strategy of Mycom, *Group Management Strategy; Theory and Practice*, The Tokyo Keizai Jyouho Shuppan, edited by Hayashi, S. and Asada, T. (in Japanese).

Makoto, Y. (2006). The present condition and subject of a holding company: The case study of a trading company, *The Hikone Ronso*, Shiga University, Vol. 362 (in Japanese).

Mutoh, Y. (1996). The merits and subjects of a holding company, *DHB*, April–May (in Japanese).

Mutoh, Y. (2003). *An Actual Condition of Holding Company Organization*, Nihon Keizai Shinbunsha (in Japanese).

Sakurai, M. (2004). The significance of corporate restructuring and decentralization in management accounting, *Kigyou Kaikei*, 56(5) (in Japanese).

Sonoda, T. (2006). Performance management of a pure holding company, *An Innovation and Enterprise Reconstruction*, Keio University Press (in Japanese).

Tamamura, H. (2006). *A Holding Company and a Modern Enterprise*, Koyoshobo (in Japanese).

Tanaka, T. (1999). Management and accounting of a holding company, *Kigyo Kaikei*, 51(9) (in Japanese).

Tsuda, N. (2003). Mitsubishi Chemical: Group management and a holding company system, *The Strategy and Management System in Order to Maximize the Value of a Group Company*, Kigyo Kenkyukai, Kenkyu Sousyo, No. 119 (in Japanese).

Part 2

M&A Including MBO and Outsourcing for Group Reformation

3

Influence of M&A on Financial Performance: Measuring the Performance of M&A from Sustainability of Utility

Kozo Suzuki

Tama Waterworks Reform Promotion Center, Tokyo Metropolitan Government

1. Introduction

In recent years, the potential resale profitability of corporations has been considered important in the purposes of "merger and acquisition" (henceforth, M&A). There have been many cases of the acquisition, restructure and resale of companies that were under-performing or undervalued in stock-price. Furthermore, very often sales occurred to save the time and effort of restructuring. And, of course, it can be an end in itself to gain huge profit through resale. The latter, though, has been less successful or attractive since autumn 2008.

On the other hand, it is argued that the reconstruction and restructuring of companies or enterprises contribute to human society and sustainable development. If the society or markets need the goods or the services supplied by a mismanaged business, it may encourage successful companies to try through M&A. In this context, M&A is useful since the necessity of continuing the activities of production has not changed. Therefore, M&A as the transfer of external management resources is an essential requirement in a capitalist society.

In this paper (based on Suzuki and Ogura (2007, pp. 77–91)), the important elements of M&A will be examined. Especially, it will stress cost reduction and "research and development" (henceforth, R&D) as a part of M&A, since they are processes to attract external resources, and in many cases, they are required for the continuation of business.

The Japanese manufacturing industry in 1990s will be used as a focus because business viability and the contribution to society of business enterprises, such as drug companies for example, had been thought of as important in M&A activities in that period. The acquisition of external management resources was also another main purpose. Looking back upon M&A at that time may yield useful suggestions toward future sustainable development.

2. The Effects of M&A

In this paper, M&A is positioned as an introductory means of attracting external management resources (Das and Teng, 2000, p. 31). And the effectiveness of that is shown by positive analysis. The conditions in which M&A for cost reduction realizes the purpose are also shown. Furthermore, the performance of financial or other effects and relations with M&A are examined.

The first reason for considering cost reduction as being important is that M&A for cost reduction actually exists (Suzuki, 1999, pp. 75–78). The second reason is for the evaluation of M&A.

The following positive outcomes will be realized if M&A for cost reduction is set as the object of the research. This is because the effects of the introduction of external resources through M&A can be easily grasped numerically. So, as a result, M&A can be evaluated economically.

Generally, M&A has many goals, with R&D, expansion of the market share, reduction of risks, and cost reduction being some. But when reflecting on the pattern of accounting income, M&A for cost reduction differs from the other purposes.

For R&D, expansion and risk reduction, there is a high possibility of them being connected with a reduction in earning statements. In other words, they may, initially, cost money. But in the case of cost reduction, complicated processes are followed. That is, the accounting income is improved after the additional injection of management resources brings about an increase of cost, i.e., there will be a reduction of profits. In other words, the aim is to, eventually, save money.

There is a likelihood of an improvement in the accounting income by the introduction of external management resources. However, there is also a high possibility of accounting income being diluted by the result of the administrative behavior of others, both inside the company and outside the company, such as outsourcing companies. This is more and more likely over time. As stated previously, cost reduction is one of the various purposes of M&A; however, there is a question over the effect of M&A on corporate management.

To further illustrate these points, M&A for R&D is contrasted with the cost reduction by M&A in this paper. The relation between the evaluation of M&A by business administrators and the financial effects of that M&A is analyzed through this comparison. The financial effect means the improvement effect on financial statements. This is an improvement phenomenon of many indices that appear on financial statements after carrying out M&A. The method of this research does not merely evaluate the effect of M&A from numerical changes in financial indicators. It acknowledges the evaluation of business administrators involved in the process and also the differences appearing in financial indicators that relate to the effects on the nonfinancial sides of management.

3. The Outline of the Verification Method and Questionnaire

From the above viewpoint, a model based on the following rough hypothesis is made.

H_0: Many activities involved in the M&A process influence the performance of management and bring about and improvement in financial achievements.

In this hypothetical verification, two kinds of data are analyzed through a covariance structure analysis. One is the data collected by questionnaire (Appendix 1). This is a subjective self-evaluation undertaken by the business administrators, who carried out M&A. The other objective data are the financial statistics in the financial report of the company that participated in the questionnaire. This analysis is adjustable based on the consideration of whether the objective performance (e.g., financial statements) is in reasonable agreement with or largely incompatible with the subjective performance (e.g., administrative questionnaires).

The characteristic feature this method of analysis is having added the subjective evaluation of the managers via questionnaire to the more traditional method of evaluating the effectiveness of M&A based on financial indicators.

With the aim to survey the general conditions of M&A in Japanese manufacturing industry, this questionnaire was distributed to the management-planning departments of 1,714 listed companies belonging to the manufacturing industry in Japan in the Year 2000. Effective responses were received from 102 companies and, of these, 95 responses were used in this paper.

In this investigation, respondents were asked to focus on a single M&A case that they judged to be the most important among any M&A carried out in the past 10 years by the company. In the questionnaire, the observed variables of cost reduction (Question 9) and R&D (Question 10) were selected as focus elements of M&A.

Furthermore, the effects of the participant's M&A was measured from six main viewpoints (Question 12):

1. General economic well-being
2. Cost reduction
3. Profit
4. Speed of management
5. Market share
6. R&D

Cost reduction was further classified into eight cost-related activities that follow the value chain based on the cost for reduction that the M&A manager regarded as important (Question 9):

1. Control of plant-and-equipment investment
2. R&D costs
3. Raw material & parts costs
4. Physical distribution costs for supplying
5. Manufacturing costs
6. Sales costs
7. General & administrative costs
8. Physical distribution and delivery costs

R&D activities were also classified into six items based on the contents of the R&D that the managers thought of as important (Question 10):

1. Gathering information
2. Contribution of technology

3. Synergistic effect
4. Reduction of R&D cost
5. Shortening of period for R&D
6. Introduction of patent.

Question 12 asked respondents to indicate the existence and degree of certain possible effects. Question items 9 and 10 were measured on a scale of 1–5 in order of the perceived importance of each item, 5 being of most importance and 1 being of least importance.

4. Creation of Analytic Models

Next, the models for covariance structure analysis are constructed. In these models, the following three qualitatively different constructs or latent variables are specified.

1. The activities (divided into cost reduction and R&D) carried out by the M&A.
2. The performance of management.
3. The improvement effects on financial indicators.

The causal relationship between the three constructs is also verified and examples of many management activities that affect those relationships are also investigated. In addition, before conducting the covariance structure analysis, the measurement models of three latent variables were prepared. Based on the above procedure, latent variables are defined as follows:

m_1: *Cost reduction* (activity via M&A)
m_2: R&D (activity via M&A)
} (Latent variable 1).
P: Performance of management (Latent variable 2).
X: The improvement effect on financial indicators (Latent variable 3).

Latent variables m_1, m_2, and P have been explained above. The financial statistics used to make the measurement model of the latent variable X represent the difference between three annual averages of accounting data from before M&A and three annual averages of accounting data from after the company undertook it's M&A. Twenty-five kinds of statistical data on financial indicators were drawn from the 95 companies that responded to the questionnaire.

Table 1. Latent variables and observed variables.

Latent variables		Observed variables
1	m_1	md: physical distribution cost of supplying
		mg: general & administrative cost
		mh: physical distribution cost of delivery
	m_2	ra: reduction of R&D cost
		rb: shortening for period of R&D
		rc: synergistic effect
2	P	pa: general economic well-being
		pb: cost reduction
		pc: R&D
3	X	xa: current profit ratio
		xb: turnover-of-total-capital-employed operating income to sale
		xc: margin of profit

In regards to latent variable X (in Table 1), a principal component analysis by correlation-matrix method is applied to this data. This analysis highlighted factors showing the change in the financial conditions of the sample companies.

Furthermore, for each latent variable, the three top items from the various data possible were determined as representative. In the case of X, this was three out of 25 possible items. As a result, the observed variables of m_1, m_2, P, and X are as above-mentioned (Table 1).

5. Characteristics of the Relationship Between Cost Reduction, Performance, and Financial Indicators in M&A

First, the relationship between the latent variables of m_1, P, and X are examined. Therefore, the Model 1 (Fig. 1) is made and the Hypothesis 1 is verified.

H_1: In M&A, cost reduction promotes the improvement of financial indicators.

As a result of testing Model 1 for goodness of fit (the number of samples: 95), the significant probability of the suitability of the model is set to 0.124, exceeding 0.05. The comparative fit index (CFI), that is a measurement

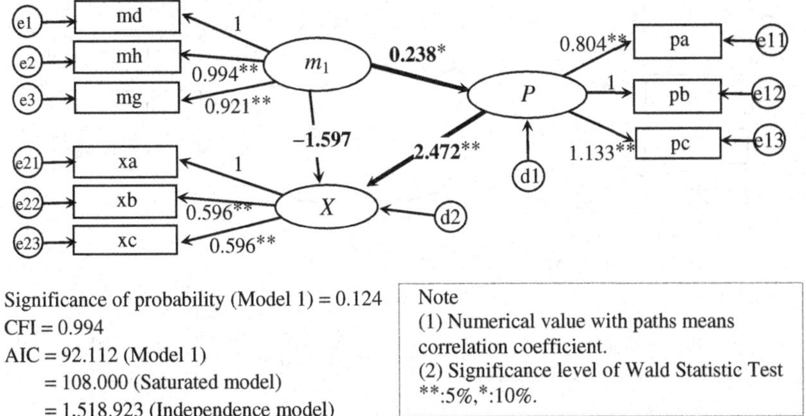

Fig. 1. Model 1.

of the goodness of fit, is 0.994. And since Akaike information criterion (AIC) of this model is within the minimum standard, so Model 1 can be said to be acceptable.

The Wald Statistic Test, which, based on the "null measurement" of hypotheses, assesses the levels whereby, "There is no influence from m_1 to P.", and "There is no influence from P to X.", measures 1.819 and 2.474, respectively. Therefore, the former hypothesis is rejected by a significance level of roughly 10%. The latter is also rejected by roughly 5%. But since the Wald Statistic Test on the direct causal relationship from m_1 to X is −1.549, the null hypothesis, "There is no influence from m_1 to X.", is not rejected.

6. Amended Model

In Model 1, the direct influence on X from m_1 becomes negative (−1.597), though this is not significant. Therefore, this path (from m_1 to X) is deleted from the Model 1 based on the Simon and Blalock method. Thus an amended model (Model 2) and the Hypothesis 2 are verified (Fig. 2).

H_2: In *M&A*, the *cost reduction* that raises the performance of management promotes the improvement of financial indicators.

On the significant probability and the goodness of fit, this Model 2 has no problems. On the Wald Statistic Test, the null hypothesis of "There is

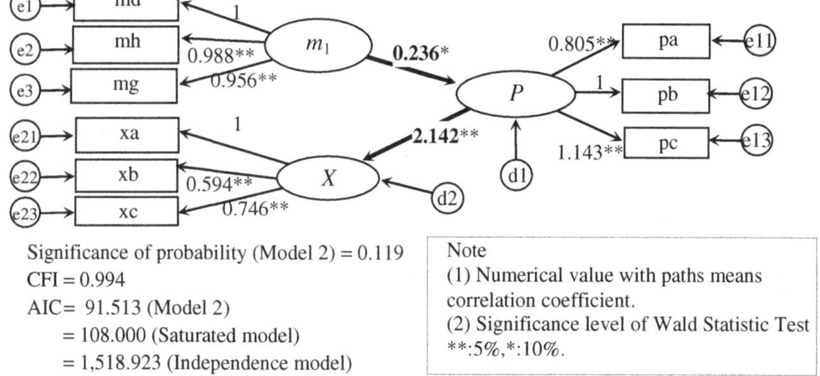

Fig. 2. Model 2.

Standardized total effect

	m_1	P	X
P	0.283	0.000	0.000
X	0.072	0.253	0.000

Standardized direct effect

	m_1	P	X
P	0.283	0.000	0.000
X	0.000	0.252	0.000

Standardized indirect effect

	m_1	P	X
P	0.000	0.000	0.000
X	0.072	0.000	0.000

Fig. 3. Effects between latent variables in Model 2.

no influence from m_1 to P." is 1.765, and the null hypothesis of "There is no influence from P to X." is 2.102. Therefore, the former is rejected by a significance level of 10% and the latter is also rejected with the level 5% (Fig. 3).

Next, the direct influences from m_1 to P and P to X are positive. The comprehensive influence from m_1 to X is similarly positive.

Therefore, in M&A, cost reduction and the improvement effective on financial indicators have positive correlations (Fig. 3). Thus, it is observed that the cost reduction that raises the performance of management acts on the improvement of financial indicators.

Therefore, Hypothesis 2 is accepted and it is suggested that cost reduction influences the improvement effective on financial indicators indirectly.

Next, to make a comparison with R&D to cost reduction, Model 3, which transposes m_1 to m_2, is created (Fig. 4). The influence from m_2 to P is rejected as a result of the same calculation method. Similarly, the influence from m_2 to X is also rejected.

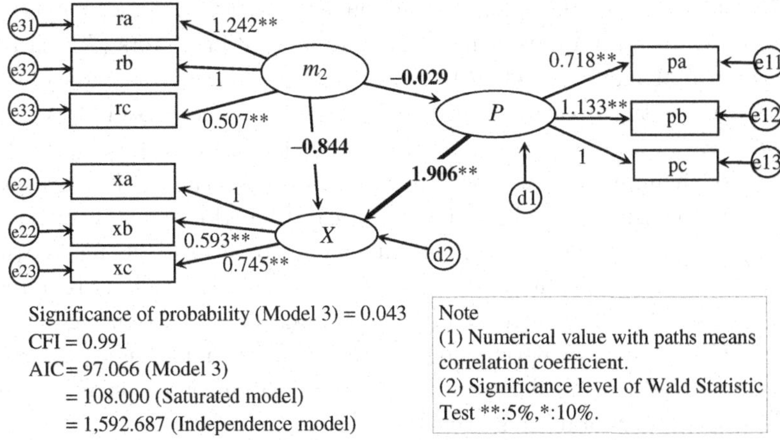

Fig. 4. Model 3.

7. The Result of Verification

The latent variable, m_1, has the highest goodness of fit when the following three costs, physical distribution cost of supply, general and administrative costs, and the physical distribution costs for delivery, are applied as observed variables. That is, such costs have the tendency to act favorably as activities of cost reduction in M&A.

General and administrative costs contain the portion equivalent to a fixed cost, such as personnel expenses and administrative expenses. In those cost reductions, the single, top-down integration of the value chain or cost structure is needed. Since M&A integrates all partner companies, strong centralized control is realized. That is, that reduction of general and administrative costs in the observed variables indicates that a strong controlling power is important to influence the cost structure of any partner company.

On the other hand, costs for incoming physical distribution cost of supply or outgoing deliveries are costs in peripheral parts of production. With the integration of those as items of expenditure, there is a high possibility to directly affect cost reduction.

Next, P is explained from three observed variables of general economic well-being, cost reduction, and R&D. They are evaluation indices related to profit-and-loss account. Moreover, X is close to profitability as mentioned above. So, the tendency is observed that the performance of M&A is recognized on the profit-and-loss basis.

About latent variables, cost reduction (m_1) carried by *M&A* may be connected with the improvement effects on financial indicators (X) via the performance of management (P). Thus, in M&A, there is a tendency for cost reduction to be clearly reflected in financial indicators. However, it is restrictive to only measure improvement in the performance of management and an improvement effective on financial indicators. Even if cost reduction is considered as important, neither the performance of management nor the upward trend of financial conditions is necessarily automatically or unconditionally realized. Consideration of it is required. Characteristically, the financial numerical value of an accounting report measures the surface achievements of a company. If that is right, the cost reduction in M&A will clearly appear as an improvement result of the surface portion of corporate management.

8. Conclusion

Considering all of the above, the following four problems with the decision-making on M&A can be highlighted.

1. In M&A, cost reduction produces the improvement of financial indicators. But R&D influences neither performance of management nor the improvement of financial indicators.
2. A tendency is found that managers of companies attach importance to financial indicators by M&A.
3. A tendency is found that the motive to M&A and financial motivation are coincident because cost reduction is evaluated as a performance of management and financial effectives can be considered as measurable.
4. The M&A that is recognized as effective on management and that brings an improvement of financial indicators in profit-and-loss account corresponds to following conditions.

   (1) It realizes the integration of the value chain and the decision-making processes of both companies.
   (2) It integrates overlapping activities in both companies, such as physical distribution and delivery costs.

That is, when introducing the management resources of other companies via M&A with the aim to improve the management effectiveness or financial indicators, M&A must be considered according to management purposes rather than purely those of finance, i.e., profit. M&A involves the introduction of external management resources to a new environment, resulting in new viewpoints for practical use of M&A toward continuation of business or sustainable development.

References

Das, T. K. and Teng, B. T. (2000). A resource-based theory of strategic alliances, *Journal of Management*, 26–31, 31–61.

Suzuki, K. (1999). Strategic cost reduction by making relationships between companies in Japanese manufacturing industries, *The Journal of Management Accounting*, 7–1(2), 65–89 (in Japanese).

Suzuki, K. and Ogura, N. (2007). The influence of M&A and alliance on the financial performance: Measuring the performance of M&A and alliance from cost reduction, *The Journal of Management Accounting*, 15–2, 77–91 (in Japanese).

Appendix 1

Questions 1–8 concerned general backgrounds and other information not immediately relevant to this paper.

(Question 9) M&A and cost reduction

Activities of cost reduction	Degree of importance					1: No importance
1. Control of plant-and-equipment investment	1	2	3	4	5	2: Little importance
2. R&D costs	1	2	3	4	5	
3. Raw material & parts costs	1	2	3	4	5	
4. Physical distribution costs of supply	1	2	3	4	5	3: Average importance
5. Manufacturing costs	1	2	3	4	5	
6. Sales costs	1	2	3	4	5	4: Important
7. General & administrative costs	1	2	3	4	5	
8. Physical distribution and delivery costs	1	2	3	4	5	5: Great importance

(Question 10) M&A and R&D

Activities of R&A	Degree of importance					1: No importance 2: Little importance 3: Average importance 4: Important 5: Great importance
1. Gathering information	1	2	3	4	5	
2. Contributing of technology	1	2	3	4	5	
3. Synergistic effect	1	2	3	4	5	
4. Reduction of R&D cost	1	2	3	4	5	
5. Shortening of period for R&D	1	2	3	4	5	
6. Introduction of patent	1	2	3	4	5	

(Question 12) Effects of M&A

Effects of M&A	Degree of effect					1: Not effective 2: Not so effective 3: Average effective 4: Effective 5: Very effective
1. General economic well-being	1	2	3	4	5	
2. Cost reduction	1	2	3	4	5	
3. Profit	1	2	3	4	5	
4. Speed of management	1	2	3	4	5	
5. Market share	1	2	3	4	5	
6. R&D	1	2	3	4	5	

Note: Question 11 was not used in this analysis.

4

Management Buyout of a Japanese Business Group

Naoyuki Kaneda

Faculty of Economics, Gakushuin University

1. Introduction

During the late 1980s, high prices for stocks and real estate were features of the asset price bubble in Japan. In this booming economy, large corporations, engaged in equity financing, increased their debt obligations to increase production capacity, and made investments in financial securities and real estate, to generate profits for their portfolio. With the collapse of the asset bubble, many Japanese corporations suffered from high fixed costs, together with overcapacity and the burden of unrealized losses for their financial assets and real estate investments.

Furthermore, some large corporations engaged in expanding their businesses into diverse areas in the late 1980s. After the collapse of the "bubble economy," these corporations restructured their business groups to concentrate their business resources in the areas of their core competencies.

With the introduction of the financial "Big Bang" in Japan, new accounting rules were introduced that emphasized consolidated financial statements rather than nonconsolidated ones. Traditionally, investors scrutinized the financial statements of the parent company to evaluate the corporations and the investment opportunities. As a result, the performance of subsidiaries was not highly regarded among the management tiers of many Japanese corporations. Thus, after the introduction of the new accounting rules, listed companies had to improve the performance of their subsidiaries, to survive in the deflationary economic environment. Poorly performing subsidiaries needed to be closed or sold to other business groups.

Management buyout (MBO) involves the buying out of firms by their management and a private equity fund. As mentioned above, during the late 1990s, many Japanese corporations created spin-off companies and acquired subsidiaries to strengthen their strategic position. In an ordinary merger and acquisition, subsidiaries are acquired by strategic buyers and ex-subsidiaries are under the complete control of the acquirer. In this type of situation, the existing management and employees may be dismissed or laid off. In a management buyout, subsidiaries are acquired by financial buyers, such as private equity funds. In many cases, the existing management teams of the ex-subsidiaries continue to manage the companies post-MBO. Many companies retain their employees rather than laying them off after the buyout. These characteristics of MBOs are considered to be more acceptable to the Japanese business community, in which it has been the common practice, at least since World War II, not to lay off employees.

Financial buyers are usually private equity funds that aim to earn significant returns from their leveraged investment. Their targets are mature companies, which bring stable cash-flows from their business, rather than new ventures. The managers of these funds usually plan to exit from the investments in an initial public offering or in a subsequent MBO several years later.

In current Japanese business practice, there are three types of MBO. In the first type, the management teams of listed firms buy out the company's shares to privatize the company. In the second type of MBO, the management teams of the subsidiaries of one business group acquire the shares of the subsidiary and become independent after the buyout. In the third category of MBO, managers acquire the shares of the spin-out division and become independent after the buyout (Kaneda and Sonoda, 2009).

In the following sections, we present examples of MBOs that appeared during the restructuring of Nissan Motor Company. The companies in question are Zero and Vantec, which became independent after the buyouts that occurred as part of the Nissan Revival Plan. These MBOs are in the second category, in which the management of the subsidiary acquires the corporate shares.

In this paper, we deal with two issues in relation to each MBO. First, we examine the changes in management and operations. In the case of the two Nissan MBOs, their shares were sold in a time of financial difficulties. The performance of the subsidiaries was poor and was expected to improve under the new scheme. It is very important to recognize the impact of the change in management style and the reason for improvements in management and operations, if any (Kaneda and Sonoda, 2009).

Second, we examine the change in corporate governance as a result of each buyout. Traditionally, the cornerstone of corporate governance in large Japanese corporations has been the main bank. Main banks are typically those banks that provide a large proportion of the capital loaned to the corporation. These banks closely monitor the financial status of the corporation and provide liquidity to support the corporation during periods of financial difficulty.

In the late 1980s, many large corporations gained access to direct financing and relied to a lesser extent on financial intermediaries, such as banks and various credit companies. In the late 1990s, the Japanese banking system suffered its worst financial crisis ever. Corporate governance through the main banks had been significantly weakened and was not functioning very well. It is significant to examine how private equity funds monitor acquired companies and strengthen their corporate governance to improve the value of the corporation.

2. Financial Difficulties and Restructuring at Nissan Motor Company

Nissan Motor Company is one of the automobile manufacturers of Japan. The company was established in 1933 and used to be the second largest automobile manufacturer. After the collapse of the asset bubble in the early 1990s, sales of automobiles stagnated. The financial crisis in the late 1990s resulted in a further decline in automobile sales in Japan. In 1999, Nissan Motor Company found itself in severe financial difficulties with stagnant revenues and a debt of two trillion yen.

In March 1999, Renault acquired 36.8% of Nissan Motor Company's shares and entered an alliance with Nissan. This alliance gave Nissan precious time in which to restructure. Carlos Ghosn, then Executive Vice President of Renault, was appointed as Chief Operating Officer of Nissan Motor in June 1999.

Under Ghosn's leadership, the Nissan Revival Plan (NRP) was introduced in October 1999. NRP basically consisted of (1) cost reductions in marketing and production; (2) cost reductions in financial management; and (3) making investment from improved cash flow streams to increase corporate value (Okuno, 2004). Cost reductions in marketing and production were achieved by closing factories and reducing the number of suppliers. Cost reductions in financial management were achieved by reducing inventory and selling noncore assets. A large Japanese corporation traditionally holds group companies' shares to maintain strong business relationships. NRP terminated this practice for the Nissan Group and most of the shares in noncore group companies were sold. NRP considered only four group firms to be core assets among its existing shareholdings in group companies. Aside those four subsidiaries, stockholdings in most of the subsidiaries were planned to be sold off during the restructuring.

With respect to the spinning off of noncore companies in the NRP, Nissan Motor would be reluctant to sell these shares to competing automobile manufacturers and financial buyers as part of ordinary acquisition deals, since these subsidiaries would still have close ties to the major business of Nissan Motor. If these deals went through, the long-term effects on Nissan's business operations might be detrimental. In this sense, an MBO might be a convenient tool for the stakeholders in these subsidiaries.

3. Corporate Governance and MBOs

The existing literature provides useful insights into the issue of corporate governance with respect to MBOs.

Jensen (1986) proposed the "control hypothesis" for debt creation. Managers of the corporations are the agents of corporate shareholders. In this scenario, managers and shareholders have conflicting interests with regard to the management of the corporation. Managers have incentives to grow their corporations beyond the optimal size for shareholders, as corporate growth increases the resources that are under the control of the management. Conflicts of interest between shareholders and managers are severe when the firms generate a substantial free cash flow.

Managers with substantial free cash flow may promise to increase dividends or to repurchase stocks, to avoid low-return projects or "empire-building." However, these promises are dubious, since they are not binding contracts. In contrast, debt creation forces managers to pay out future cash flows as part of a binding contract. Consistent with this theory, the stock price rises with unexpected increases in payouts to shareholders, unless firms have ample profitable projects in their business plan. Conversely, the stock price falls with reduction in payments or seasonal equity issuance.

In the case of MBOs, the "control hypothesis" for debt creation provides useful perspectives on the issue of monitoring. The major targets of MBOs are firms that operate in an established business and generate substantial free cash flow. In this situation, conflicts of interest over payout policies can be serious. Managers may undertake low-return projects to create a corporate empire. However, in the process of a typical MBO, firms usually have large debts in addition to the equity investments of management and private equity funds. Management has strong incentives to service the debt after the leveraged buyout. Otherwise, they may face dismissal from the corporate seat.

Kester (1991) pointed out the importance of corporate governance for corporate diversification. In the late 1980s, some large Japanese corporations diversified their business in the absence of synergies. Managers in mature industries have sufficient cash that can be used for corporate growth rather than value creation. When management invests the free cash flow in a low-return project, there is little monitoring by the banks, whereas in the cases of bond issuance and bank loans, management has to adhere to strict monitoring by the markets and banks. Thus, diversification into mature industries is more likely to result in less successful value creation.

Jensen (1993) indicated that firms may improve efficiency and increase value with higher leverage and smaller boards, even with low-growth firms in which agency costs to free cash flow are high.

Based on case studies of leveraged buyouts and venture capital funds, Jensen (1993) listed the principles underlying a well-performing company board. First, successful associations are organized as limited partnerships, which prohibit the cross-subsidization of one division with cash from another division. From the viewpoint of management control, this implies that each division should be evaluated based on its own performance. Second, successful boards tend to have high levels of equity ownership by the managers and board members. This strengthens the commitment of management and board members to the company's management. Third, board members represent the larger shareholders of each company. If board members represent numerous small shareholders, their monitoring becomes ineffective. Fourth, successful boards are small boards, consisting of no more than eight persons. In the early 1990s, many Japanese corporations had large boards and were criticized for the ineffectiveness. Fifth, in successful boards, CEOs are the only insiders on the board. Sixth, the CEO is not the chairman of a well-performing board.

If private equity funds acquire the shares of subsidiaries, the management makes business decisions in the new corporate governance structure. It is very important for the management to interact with the private equity funds in terms of the daily business decisions and to understand the strategy of the funds.

In the following sections, we examine how each subsidiary was spun off from the Nissan Group and review the changes in operations and corporate governance that occurred post-buyout.

4. Vantec, a Logistics Company

Yokohama Yuso, latterly Vantec Corporation, was established as a wholly-owned subsidiary of Nissan Motors in 1954. It was the first division to be split off from Nissan Motors. Their major business was originally automotive logistics. They renamed as Vantec Corporation in 1997, merged with Overseas Air Cargo, and became independent through MBO in the process of the Nissan Revival Plan in 2001. They expanded their business operations further into global logistics, merged with Tokyu Air Cargo. They continuously endeavor to upgrade the corporate values through M&A from different industries.

We interviewed one of the board members who was responsible for the first MBO.[1] In the first buyout, the shares were acquired by its board members and 3i-Kogin Buyouts, which was a joint venture launched by 3i Group Plc, one of the Europe's leading venture capitals and private equity firms, and Industrial Bank of Japan, which subsequently merged with two other city-center banks and became Mizuho Financial Group, Inc.

After the buyout, some more Japanese directors and a couple of British directors were appointed as the board of directors. The company's management had the full confidence of the equity fund. 3i-Kogin joined the process of making Vantec's business plan, which helped strengthen the partnership between them. According to the original business plan, the management had some flexibility in terms of their decision making. However, the decisions by Vantec with respect to mergers and acquisitions were delayed, as they had to ask for official approval from the headquarters in Europe (Okuno, 2004). In addition, it took time to explain Japanese business customs and details of the business plan in English.

After the first MBO, the company divided the roles between directors and executive officers, since directors were also regarded as executive officers, followed by the traditional governance system. A Compensation Committee and a Nomination Committee were also established without corresponding to the Japanese Corporation Law. The management understood that the fund did not require the binding committee system, since they trusted the management style of Mr. Okuno, the President.

In the first buyout, all executive officers were requested to hold company shares (Okuno, 2004). It encouraged them to strengthen their commitment. Directors and executive officers used to recognize themselves simply as employees of the parent company, whereas after the buyout they became shareholders as well as executive officers, who could lose their investment if the company did not perform well. This is an example of the second principle of Jensen (1993). Vantec Group Holdings has 7 members of board of directors, which is within the range proposed in the fourth principle of Jensen (1993).

Vantec closed a deal with 3i-Kogin for their second MBO in 2003, and Mizuho Capital Partners became their major shareholder. We will explain Vantec's operations after MBO, referring to Kaneda and Sonoda (2009).

After the MBO, more executive officers and managers from outside the company were hired. They developed an internal management system, including a personnel system that would be a model for other companies. This new personnel system enables employees to be evaluated by their immediate bosses. Their evaluation had to be fair and accurate, or they could be demoted. Under the previous system, individual performance never effected their position and salary in a negative way. On the contrary, the new system allows employees to get incentives, depending on their performance to the company. Vantec's management reformation seems to be undertaken by simple principles that are leading to improve employees' mind-set.

At the time of the MBO, cost reduction was the top priority for them to survive in response to Nissan's requests of cut-back, followed by the Nissan Revival Plan. Wage cut was the answer for that since it was higher than the industry average. As salary cut might not be the good solution to motivate employees, they introduced a results-based remuneration system to encourage well-performers. They set individual target for managers and executive officers for their contributions to annual profit of the company. Their salaries were set based on achievement upon their targets.

They endeavored to reduce costs by finding suppliers offering cheaper products. They also enhanced to improve turnover of trucks and loading efficiency. In addition, they returned the loaned personnel to Nissan Motors. These measures improved the morale of the nonloaned personnel in the company and revitalized the firm.

They endeavored to increase their sales through non-Nissan or nonauto industries to expand their customer base. Logistics services for convenience stores and restaurants were increased and office relocation services and international freight services were developed as their new businesses. This is how they enlarged their business and developed business strategies for their future growth. Their objectives also include offering services to corporate clients that would like to outsource their logistics operations to them.

They also expanded their business through mergers and acquisitions to increase the corporate values. Merger with Overseas Air Cargo and Tokyu Air Cargo, acquisition of Ikeda Unyu were typical example of their strategic M&A. Tokyu Air Cargo is currently known as Vantec World Transport and it is a key company in the Vantec group, providing air cargo services. The acquisition shows the fact that a company post-MBO would be a leading company in consolidating industries under support of private equity funds. Unifying all systems of the companies involved is also a key to increase corporate values. Enterprise Resource Planning system is currently under the preparation to launch, as it merges Vantec and Vantec World Transport in April, 2009.

5. Zero, An Automobile Carrier[2]

The predecessor of Zero is Nissan Rikusou, which was established as a hundred-percent subsidiary of Nissan Motor in 1961 and transports new cars from the Nissan factory to domestic car dealers. Overall, seventy-five percent of its sales are from automobile transportation and automobile-related activities, such as automobile body maintenance. Although the business of Nissan Rikusou was listed as noncore in the NRP, their operations are invaluable for the automobile manufacturer. Some of the directors of Nissan Motor opposed the sale of Nissan Rikusou shares based on the indispensible nature of the subsidiary's business. Other automobile manufacturers have their own carrier subsidiaries within their business groups. Car carriers require large motor pools and expensive specialized equipment for their activities. It is difficult for a new entrant to penetrate this segment of the industry.

In certain instances, management and employees might prefer not to be acquired by competitors, as the takeover might entail drastic restructuring and redundancies. In the case of Nissan Motor, the MBO has proven to be beneficial, both for the Nissan Rikusou management and employees. The buyout was carried out in May 2001, and the company was renamed Zero, which symbolizes the starting from zero as a new company.

Nissan Rikusou management sought a private equity fund for the buyout of their company. In the end, most of the investment came from Tokio Marine Capital, with AIG Japan Capital Investment assuming a smaller share of the investment. The two funds acquired eighty-five percent of the shares of Nissan Rikusou and the management and business partners acquired fifteen percent of the shares.

Zero went public in August, 2005. Before pursuing an initial public offering (IPO), Zero asked their large shareholders to sell their shares, to mitigate the selling pressure at the time of the IPO. The shareholders agreed to sell their shares exceptionally as private equity funds. Even after the company went public, Zero's shares have been held by Zenith Logistics, SBS Holdings, and Mitsuike Corporation as stable stockholders. The President of the company, Mr. Iwashita, has made significant advances in terms of investor relations through his personal network. In the following few paragraphs, we describe the changes in the operations of Zero, referring to Kaneda and Sonoda (2009).

As mentioned above, the shares of Nissan Rikusou were sold off according to the NRP. The management started to plan the buyouts even before the official company decision. They took advantage of this head start in preparation for the MBO. They achieved the MBO in six months, whereas this process usually takes one year. This was basically a "management" buyout, with the management assuming the leadership of the process. The - employees had concerns about the buyout itself because they felt that they were losing the economic protection afforded by the once-mighty Nissan Motor. In the NRP, Nissan Rikusou was asked to cut price by thirty percent, and it was emphasized that the company could not survive without this drastic cost reduction.

After the buyout, the management established an in-house management system. As a first step, the management changed the remuneration system, to enhance the employees' business mindset. The salaries were set higher than the industry average and had to be cut to meet the NRP-required cost reductions. The company did not reduce the number of employees to lower the fixed costs. As a subsidiary of Nissan Motor,

Nissan Rikusou relied on the parent company for most of its business. The employees did not promote their services to their customers and they are not proactive in improving their operations.

A pay structure system was not really established before the buyout. The previous system for paying drivers was not incentive-based. If they worked overtime, their wages were higher even if they worked inefficiently. In the new system, the company started to evaluate and pay drivers through a partially result-oriented remuneration system. Thus, the new system provides incentives to work effectively with adequate safety precautions. Before the MBO, the work force included persons who were originally hired by Nissan Rikusou immediately after graduation from college, as well as staff loaned from Nissan Motor. Since the buyout, the company also hires experienced workers from other companies and industries. The IPO provided a tremendous opportunity to increase the value of the company name, and the company has taken advantage of its status as a listed company to incorporate highly skilled labor into its workforce.

The second issue related to management reform is promotion of sales to take advantage of the independent status of the firm. As a Nissan subsidiary, the business connection between Zero with Nissan Motor presented some obstacles to extending the business relationship to competing automobile manufacturers. As mentioned above, most car carriers are subsidiaries of car makers. Zero exploits its unique position as an independent operator in the industry to promote sales with non-Nissan manufacturers. Thus, the company has increased sales to both Nissan and non-Nissan automakers. Before the buyout, the drivers were not very enthusiastic to pick up loads to fill the vacant spaces in returning trucks. Once the management emphasized the importance for sales of maximizing carrying capacity, the drivers' mentality changed. The next task is to change the remuneration system to create "sales drivers," who will sell more eagerly their carrying capacity. Similar to the case of Vantec, Zero may acquire firms in other sectors, since the market for car carriers is stagnant and it is difficult to grow in this business sector. After an acquisition, it may be advantageous to slash indirect costs by sharing services.

The third issue in management reform is the emphasis that must be placed on the cost of a service. Before the buyouts, the managers and employees were not very cost-conscious. The sales representatives would offer a price that was not based on cost accounting. As part of the management reform post-MBO, the management monitors and improves operational efficiency using performance measures. With respect to human resources, the company has returned loaned personnel to Nissan Motor, as did Vantec, to improve management flexibility. Zero and Vantec are exceptional in stopping the loaning of personnel from the previous parent company. In these aspects, Zero has become an independent transportation operator that is not under the direct control of the automaker.

Nevertheless, Zero continues to cooperate with Nissan Motor in some operations, e.g., in the sharing of trucks to deliver different products to the same destinations, thereby reducing waste and environmental impact. Zero also has extended overseas operations in China as a partner of Nissan Motor.

As mentioned above, an MBO generates a firm that is severed from the parent company. It also enables the firm to penetrate new markets as an independent operator. The MBO provides opportunities to reform the management, operations, and employee mindset, leading to dramatic changes in the way the business of the company is conducted.

Endnotes

1. We interviewed Mr. Yasuaki Suzuki, Director and Senior Executive Officer of Vantec Group Holdings Corporation, and Mr. Yoshio Sato, Public Relations Manager of Vantec Group Holdings Corporation, in February 2007.
2. We interviewed Mr. Yasuhiro Ogawa, Manager of Corporate Planning Department of Zero Co., Ltd. in April 2006.

References

Jensen, M. C. (1986). The agency costs of free cash flow: Corporate finance and free cash flow, *American Economic Review*, 76(2), May.

Jensen, M. (1993). The modern industrial revolution, exit, and the failure of internal control systems, *Journal of Finance*, 48(2), July.

Kaneda, N. and Sonoda, T. (2009). Spin-off through MBO and management issues, *Kigyou-kaikei*, 61(7), July (in Japanese).

Kester, W. (1991). The hidden costs of Japanese success, in Chew, D. H. (1997), *Studies in International Corporate Finance and Governance Systems: A Comparison of the US, Japan and Europe*, Oxford Univ. Press.

Okuno, S. (2004). *Survival Plan*, Kindai Shuppansha (in Japanese).

5

Managerial Significance of Strategic Outsourcing

Shunzo Matsuoka
Faculty of Business, Hannan University

1. Introduction

In times of continued economic growth, a product was sold if produced. However, the cessation of economic growth is accompanied by a sharp downturn in the sales growth, and companies seek to reduce the more obvious costs such as personnel expenses and enlarged assets. Interest determines how efficiently a company performs its administrative and stockholder duties. Outsourcing has traditionally been utilized as a measure of reduction in cost and to enhance efficiency by management; however, it has become the strategic means of companies to maintain competition predominance.

It is important in outsourcing and group management that a company shares information with an associated company and other companies through management; therefore, a business process is administered smoothly through the information sharing within the company as well as with the outside company. When the competition intensifies, it is natural to use external resources such as outsourcing, or sharing a service. The promotion of group management and the outsourcing between different organizations can be a necessity. Following the collapse of the bubble boom, companies suffered from a rise in the fixed cost ratio due to surplus staff — an overinvestment. Group management is natural under these conditions. A company increases its efficiency through the indirect performance of duties by outsourcing — a measure utilized to reduce the costs. With the resulting surplus resources these measures can produce, management has clearly realized its importance.

Independent, plural companies become the group for group management, and this group management system is in place to plan business expansions and value-added improvements. Outsourcing is more attractive to companies without major capital assets. In group management, problems owing to the management of the individual company occur but can be reconciled. In group management and outsourcing, the optimization of the whole is provided by the optimization of the individual.

In the following text, outsourcer means a consignment company while outsourcee means a trustee company.

2. A Change in the Purpose of Outsourcing

2.1. *Outsourcing for speed and value added*

An outsourcee increases the value added of the business process re-engineering (BPR) process and performance, improving cost, service, and speed. The success of outsourcing lies in its ability to improve upon a company's existing duties. Currently, long-term outsourcing contracts of more than five years are common. The contracted outsourcee, in turn, improves the ability of the company to reduce the annual costs and enhance the service quality as well as the business and duties processes; in addition, the outsourcee must provide the technological improvements required of their specialization. The outsourcer utilizes the original know-how of the outsourcee and plans the reinforcement of the non-core aspects of the business after which the outsourcer reviews the operations of the company and advances the business development area that is more dominant than a competitor's.

2.2. *Introduction of new services through outsourcing*

Traditionally, companies have entrusted their work to outsourcing, which improved and added value to these duties. However, an outsourcee can provide new services to the outsourcer and absorb the latter's consignment of internal work. Indeed, it appears that new services are being introduced by the outsourcees to the outsourcers simultaneously with the transfer of services from the outsourcers to the outsourcees.

The built-operation-transfer (BOT) model is one example of an outsourcing activity that is introduced by the external company to the outsourcer. The outsourcee replaces the model with the new activity and when the activity becomes familiar to the company, the outsourcee moves it to the outsourcer. A BOT model is a transformation model of the third type of so-called outsourcing.

In light of the spread of business process outsourcing (BPO) in Japan, the BOT scheme may acquire an increasingly subtle importance. The BOT process involves the following: A private enterprise establishes an institution and administers it for a certain period. The outsourcee then transfers it to the outsourcer, a self-governing body, and the country afterwards. Security operations occur in the user company of the business model such as the BOT.

The third passenger terminal at Ninoy Aquino International Airport of the Manila metropolitan area in the Philippines employs this scheme. This investment was made by the private operators of the Philippine International Air Terminals Corporation (PIATCO). The terminal is administered for a certain period by PIATCO and the investment is collected in the process. This BOT method was transferred to the country that subsequently managed the international airport.

3. The Organization and Risk Reduction

3.1. *Source of the competition's predominance turns from tangible assets to knowledge assets*

Tangible assets were the growth factors of a company in the industrialization era. However, these came to be associated with the risks involved in large assets. In fact, as with real estate in good condition, the rise in price can become remarkable. However, it is always accompanied by the risk of price depreciation. Movable property, unlike real estate, always involves the risk of reduction in price. These risks are curbed when a company maximizes outsourcing and a lease.

Outsourcing can prevent the risks associated with idle assets. It is important to eliminate the risk of price depreciation and increase the price expectations of a company's fixed assets. The ability to achieve the latter has been an increasingly serious demand. As for holding fixed assets, it should be recognized that the expectations and risks are real.

The intangible assets of a company include high quality products and services; motivated, expert employees; and speed and an operating process that adequately supports customer satisfaction. In the age of information technology, intangible assets became more important than tangible assets to management. Value creation shifted from the management of tangible assets to the strategic management of the knowledge base for the practical use of the intangible assets. Intangible assets also include customer relations, innovative products and services, high quality, a business process that is responsive, IT and database processes, employee skill, motivation, and organizational ability. The strategy of value creation is required to positively utilize not only tangible assets, but also intangible assets, especially since intangible assets became the main source of the competition's predominance.

3.2. *Reduction in capital investments*

Outsourcing contributes to a reduction of the investment or holding of assets. When a company is founded, it controls the means to investment in outsourcing a part of its duties. Instead of creating a section if a new function is needed in a company, as with the development of a new product, the outsourcing of the function controls investments such as those required to build new facilities. The assets and financial risks of the company are, therefore, reduced.

In addition, a technical job can be performed by an outsourcee for the outsourcer. By utilizing the support of an outsourcee, the outsourcer was able to find the means of supplying the continuous production of their product without incurring significant investment costs. The outsourcer can provide the outsourcee the inside resources newly added into the development and innovation process of a new product, advanced technical production intensively here. These actions are more strategic.

3.3. *Streamlining the administrative body*

The assembly and the subassembly line of many outsourcers have begun to be transferred from outsourcer to the subsystem maker, an associated company and outsourcee. This occurred in the 1960s. Japanese companies have since begun to outsource the assembling of the parts and the finished product itself. These are the characteristic strategies of this type of outsourcing. During the periods of sharp increases in product types and the reduction of the product life cycle, outsourcers concentrated on a few primary outsourcees to fulfill their production needs. The outsourcee, as the system component maker, was in charge of organizing the scope of jurisdiction. The outsourcee was, therefore, relegated the task of cluster management.

This administrative task became complicated with rapid economic growth and significant increases in product types. The outsourcer was freed to a considerable extent from this necessary activity of its operational management by the process of outsourcing. The organizational structure, which became complicated, was streamlined by this flexible outsourcing of various types of production activities and some development duties. In general, the lead time and the life cycle of the product were shortened. The product type was extended beyond that which was previously merely maintained.

4. Essentials of Strategic Outsourcing

4.1. *Construction of the core competence*

It became extremely important that the modern company built a core competence that it could develop. Everything but the core competence is outsourced thereby increasing the tendency to streamline production. The core competence is the by-product of the integrated powers of the companies. It can be superior in comparison with that of other companies, which has become a unique competitive power; however, in the future, entry into the new product market will become simpler to sustain competition predominance. For example, the finished product maker uses the part manufactured by the maker and can demand a profit that is higher than other manufacturers when the part maker produces a superior part, which is the element of superiority in that it is not possible for the other part makers to replicate the item.

Sony owns the synthetic technology to miniaturize a product and produces new products such as the world's smallest Walkman and the digital video camera with passport size technology. Fuji film acquired the painting technology of the multilayer film and developed film production technology from cameras to audio tape systems to the production of videotapes.

4.2. *Value creation outsourcing*

Outsourcing is a process utilized by an organization to reduce costs by relegating duties to outsourcees. As of late, companies outsource a significant amount of work involving a wide range of functions to specialized agencies. The objectives of outsourcing lay primarily in production, personnel affairs, accounting, distribution, research and development, and sales. This strategic judgment produces high value added that can be enjoyed by the outsourcing company and plays a cost reduction role.

The essence of strategic outsourcing is different from the outsourcing used solely to reduce costs. The outside specialty organization's skill, knowledge, and know-how are utilized; therefore, strategic outsourcing can be defined as specific duties being maximized through a series of processes to add new value to the company. Strategic outsourcing is distinguishable from the conventional subcontracting method that aims to reduce costs, insofar as it is a value creation type of outsourcing. The outsourcer allocates financial resources in the field of its strength. The outsourcer thereby relegates the duties associated with its fringe areas to the outsourcee, and manages the know-how of the outside organization. The value creation business model in which a user company cannot act alone is further developed when technology development is consigned to the outsourcee who then controls the fate of the business. The source of the competition predominance of a company is shifting from facilities or a fund to knowledge and wisdom.

Outsourcing that leads to value creation collects all knowledge from the concept stage to the design stage. If there is a design idea that promotes a product as more compact, easy to assemble and repair, then it is respected by the designer, the production and manufacturing staff, and all those participating from the concept stage.

4.3. *Source of the competition's predominance: from a thing to a person*

Outsourcees are analyzed in the same manner as a company's materials, costs, and property. Management methods differ in their view. With outsourcing methods, a person is compared to and must be able to provide a service at a low variable cost. On the other hand, that person is also compared to property and must provide a high fixed cost value. In the end, however, the decision to outsource or not depends on the talent of the individual to raise the quality of the software, even with an excellent management performance and process. The outsourcer must occasionally provide personnel training to the outsourcee — as in the cases of Eastman Kodak and Seven-Eleven — namely in the absence of a crucial employee.

The ratio of knowledge to labor rises and the value of the means of production declines when the knowledge of the outsourcee becomes more significant in the promotion of efficiency of resources in management than the practical abilities of the external source. In other words, managing those who can bring about knowledge and wisdom becomes increasingly important to building and maintaining competition predominance. It is necessary to nurture talented individuals for the growth of the BPO industry and that this future BPO industry growth is publicized. BPO involves the sale of specialized work, and, thereby, it should be regarded as a specialized service.

Outsourcing a function of a particular section of a company cannot ignore the talented person supporting this section and function. Though a company is an organic body of its sections, it integrates a section into an external organization to achieve lower costs and high quality. Therefore, the company's conventional ability, knowledge, and the resources such as skill are invalidated.

5. Issues of Quality in Outsourcing

5.1. *Quality becomes the black box*

With the division of labor in a company, each sphere of business becomes too narrow and it is difficult to understand what a neighboring section does and the influence of one's work on an end product. This may negatively effect the associated sense of accomplishment and royalties. As for the division of labor and specialized progress, the level of efficiency may rise. However, technical engineers do not understand others or experience failure in the same manner either. Outsourcing is identical in this respect. The aggravation of the division of labor is still only beneficial in one's own company. Furthermore, if the division of labor of the company is outsourced, the know-how is not left with the outsourcee. If outsourcing progresses, a certain part becomes the so-called black box. It becomes difficult to discern how a product is made and how its quality is guaranteed. It becomes key to ascertain and manage the quality of the outsourcing. In the field of software, the establishment of a quality brand made in Japan is a rushed process. As for the future of manufacturing, a guarantee of quality in the outsourcing will become important.

5.2. *Customer satisfaction shifts from cost to quality*

Many companies must determine how they will quickly manufacture a product and provide the end-consumer needs of its associated services in a precise and quick Manner. These are the most important problems; for example, the part maker must satisfy the consumer of the finished product, which a division of the outsourcing company is used for. Cooperation between business partners is important in resolving this problem. In the future, this will intensify the competition among the supply chain providers. In the case of Dell, competition superiority for a reduction in costs was fulfilled by the promotion of efficiency of the supply chain; for example, the price of a Dell computer was around 60% of the competing model — thus overwhelming cost competitive in the Japanese PC market in 2000. However, in 2005, Dell was not a price leader in their market entry of E machines. At the time, the purchasing action of the consumer shifted to a focus on design — a serious break from price consideration. The American computer manufacturers Dell and HP are very good at outsourcing. They do not manufacture parts but relegate this task to outsourcing — a business model in which a company entirely purchases what it needs. Quality is guaranteed through a very severe set of standards whereby several hundred items are examined for this purpose. A product that does not meet the required standards is not received. Currently, Japanese quality standards are vaguely observed. The United States differs from this. Specifications contracts and a standard of 100% are made clear to the outsourcee from the beginning.

6. Outsourcing Is Not a Panacea

Outsourcing has its merits and demerits. For companies without production factories, outsourcing can provide speed in correspondence and a possible reduction in cost. However, in terms of technical maintenance, the technical succession and the progress of the technology may decline. If a reduction in the appointed date of delivery and costs are achieved by insourcing rather than outsourcing, the decision to insource should be made. Insourcing is different from the world of outsourcing. The decision to outsource the production of a product should be made while the future of the product is considered. Insourcing is new speech, but, there reflection for the excessive outsourcing is read. Insourcing prevents an outflow of the know-how that is found in excessive outsourcing, and these companies prefer to accumulate this internally.

7. Total Optimization Rather than Partial Optimization Is Important

The decision making to insourcing or outsource is required in cost arguments. Although there are factories that are self-owned and related production subsidiaries, some operations must still be outsourced to reduce the cost. If all factories and subsidiaries have a rate of operation of 100%, it is still optimal. However, it may be profitable to outsource a business unit even if there is an idle part in the operation. However, this may provide a deficit for the whole group. Hence, the reason for outsourcing is argued.

At the planning stage, the head of the unit and the planners only have information. However, at the design and quality stages, the production engineer and a design engineer participate jointly. At this stage, there may be concerns that technological outsourcing might result in leaks. Therefore, insourcing will be forced.

In addition, due to the lack of coordination between sections and the opposition from higher-ranking officials, it is possible that interest adjustments for these companies will be difficult; for example, the production section might insist on insourcing to maintain the rate of operation of the plant. Moreover, outsource might have an advantage in that correspondence regarding design changes will lead to the rapid development of new development parts.

In such situations, the decision making at the presidential level is required. One argument states that businesses must be conducted in a group to reduce the fixed cost ratio overall. Total optimization must be maintained in the place of individual optimization.

8. Summaries

Corporate management was brought into the fore to bring attention to the importance of utilizing internal resources as well as outsourcing; however, both group management and outsourcing have similar backgrounds. There are two approaches: dealing with the entire company or only sections. Outsourcing now demands investing important resources in the core of the company to secure competition predominance. Strategic outsourcing demands value added and cost reduction. Group management can easily lead to high value added as compared to individual management. Knowledge increased through group management, and the source of the profit changed. However, the management of talented individuals to secure competition predominance cannot be ignored. Outsourcing leads to the quality "black box" issue of quality. Customer satisfaction has shifted from cost to quality. Outsourcing is not a panacea for ensuring the appointed date of delivery, cost reduction, and speed for competition predominance. Some believe that insourcing enhances management efficiency.

Further Readings

Greaver, M. F. (1999). *Strategic Outsourcing*, AMACOM.

Hanada, M. (2008). Credit by the human resources development is the source of the guarantee of quality, *Quality Management*, 59(8), 10–17 (in Japanese).

Japan Association of Management Accounting (ed.) (2000). *Dictionary of Management Accounting*, Chyuou-keizaisya (in Japanese).

Kato, T. (1996). A risk and cost-effectiveness analysis in the strategic outsourcing, *Kigyou-kaikei*, 48(7), 40–44 (in Japanese).

Kawamoto, S. (2008). Outsource which can embody thought of Bandai, *Quality Management,* 59(8), 26–30 (in Japanese).

Kurata, K. (2008). It is a key to ascertain a quality control point during outsourcing. To the establishment of a brand made in Japan of the software quality, *Quality Management,* 59(8), 18–25 (in Japanese).

Minagawa, Y. (2008). *Management Accounting of the Supply Chain*, Koyoshobou (in Japanese).

Monden, Y. *et al.* (2005). *Management Accounting Text.* 3rd edn., Zeimukeiri-Kyoukai (in Japanese).

Okamoto, K. *et al.* (2008). *Management Accounting*, Tyuou Keizaisya (in Japanese).

Sakurai, M. (2000). *Management Accounting Dictionary.* Doubunkan publication (in Japanese).

Takeishi, A. (2003). *Divisions of Labor and Competition.* Yuhikaku (in Japanese).

6

Acquisition Price as an Incentive Price of M&A

Yasuhiro Monden
Professor-Emeritus, Tsukuba University

1. Research Purpose: How Can the Purchase Price of M&A Function as Incentive to Merger?

Decision making on mergers and acquisitions is dependent on consensual agreement between the firms concerned. Where managers of both firms, as representatives of their shareholders, are satisfied with the incentive return for their shareholders, mutual agreement is obtained; in other words, they will decide to merge the two firms.

Economically, the most important incentive is the expected "shared profit", which is distributed to both firms from a joint profit that is the incremental profit the firms would gain after merger by the synergy effect. Only where both firms are satisfied with that shared profit, will they decide to merge.

Therefore, the decision to merge is based on a "satisfying principle" of "Total amount of shared profit for each firm", which is the incentive for the merger. The "satisfaction" in of M&A means "mutual satisfaction" of both parties concerned with fair allocation" of joint profits.

The reason why the M&A decision is dependent on a "satisfying solution", not on an "optimal solution" is that all M&A-related firms need to "decide whether they should participate" in one coalition or not, and this is different from the other case of expanding the scale of the firm when one firm makes a decision on capital investment to expand its own production capacity. The decision to merge is made on mutual-agreement on final negotiations between both firms, and their decision criteria are mutually satisfactory for the benefit of each firm.

However, the leader firm of the coalition has influence when each of several firms decides autonomously whether they will participate in the new coalition or not. The leader of the "core firm" of the coalition or business group will decide, in advance, which company can be a candidate of a new participating firm who can maximize their "joint profit" and the leader also presents the incentive distribution plan to member firms to attract them in participating in the coalition.[1]

As above, M&A is based on decision making supported by mutual-agreement over the incentive of an incremental distribution amount generated by the synergy effect between several people, not on decision making of one single person. Therefore, M&A is substantially decided upon mutual satisfaction of several people, who are affected by the agreement. This can be expressed in the model of a corporative game.

The purpose of this paper is to demonstrate that the decision of purchase price under M&A, and the decision of the control-premium included in it, will follow the profit-sharing mechanism among the participating firms concerned, and will clarify its mechanism. The author named such price as "Incentive Price" that is the price that motivates and induces firms to participate in a network organization based on incentive by sharing profit. The purchase price or acquisition price for merger is functioning as Incentive Price.

2. Sources and Result of Synergy Effect: Innovation for Supply and Demand Balancing by M&A

For the synergy effect mentioned above to become a reality, it is necessary that participating firms improve and reform the balance of supply and demand after the merger, as shown below. The synergy effect will present as increased sales and reduced costs to equilibrate sales revenues and production costs as an intra-corporate total sum in the after-merger company. Therefore, integrating corporations by M&A has a function of balancing revenue and expenses in a microfinancial aspect. (Refer to Fig. 1).[2]

3. Control-Premium

Under M&A, the top management of the acquirer firm or the new top management dispatched by the acquirer to the acquired firm reforms a system of the acquired business by introducing some new business projects after M&A to add new value to the existing enterprise value realized under

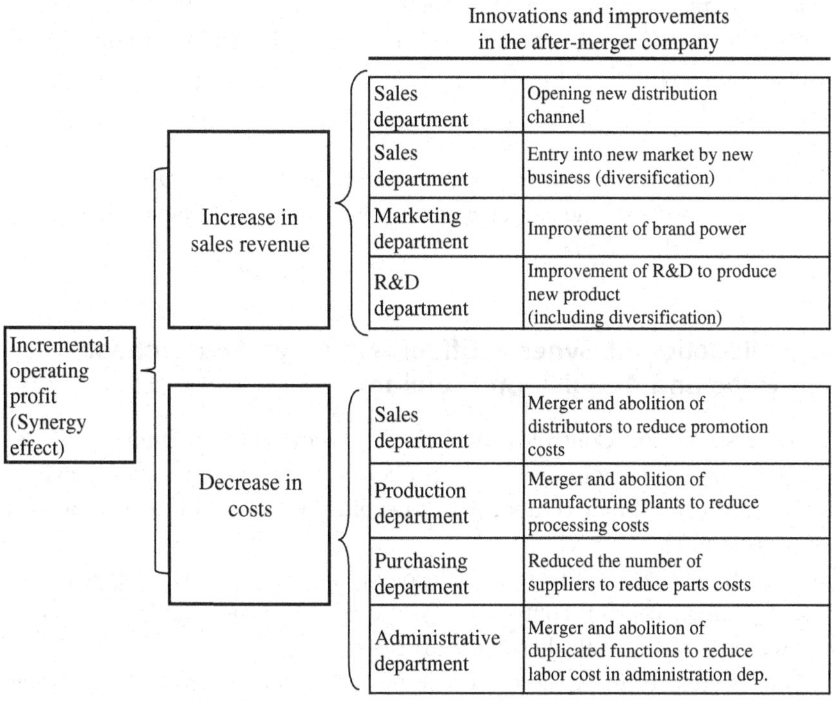

Fig. 1. Supply and demand equilibrium from M&A synergy effect. (Adapted from Maekawa *et al.* (2005) with modification.)

the previous top management. Such a new business project has an potential to increase the sales through new products developed by combined technologies of both firms, and the merger of marketing channels. This is called the "Synergy Effect" (merger effect) and the benefit of "Economies of Scale" provided by increase in the scale of the enterprise will enable the reduction of costs, and various restructuring may be carried out.

What is called the "Income Approach" is the method used to measure the synergy effect (accretion), which will be provided by new business projects after M&A, in assessing the target company. However, to actualize the synergy effect, it is necessary for (shareholders of) the acquiring firm or merging firm to hold enough share capital to have "Corporate Control Rights", which is a majority of voting rights. Because, having Corporate Control Rights over the after-merger company in M&A enables (shareholders of) the acquirer firm to make a decision of implementing new business practices and projects, at the General Meeting of

Shareholders. According to MacKinsey & Co. *et al.*, (2000), the value of that is called the "Control Premium" or "Acquisition Premium" is expressed as: (Refer to Fig. 2).

Control Premium
= [The value of the target company after control by M&A]
– [The value of the target company under the top management before the merger] (1)

4. Allocation of Synergy Effect Based on the Purchase Price and Acquisition Premium

The substance of Control Premium (or "acquisition premium") is, as clarified in the foregoing section, an allocation of synergy effect provided by M&A to the target company. In foregoing paragraph, it was expressed as equation (1).

The first term of the right side of above equation [the value of the target company after control by M&A] is "Purchase *Value* of Target Company", which could become Purchase *Price.*

The second term of the right side of above equation [The value of the target company under the top management before the merger] is "the stand-alone value of the target company as an independent firm" before acquisition. This stand-alone value is the value of the firm of the independent target company before the merger, and measured by the *book value of Net Asset* plus the "*sum of the present values of future income flows*" of the target company before merger. (Apply "DCF formula for residual profits" of Income Approach.) Therefore,

Control Premium = [Purchase value of target company]
– [Stand-alone value of target company] (2)

Further the relationship between the Control Premium and the Synergy Effect which both companies would gain after M&A can be shown as Fig. 2.

In Fig. 2, the synergy effect is divided into the "gain of the acquirer company" and the "control premium of the target company". This is the expected synergy effect allocated to both firms. Speaking precisely, the gain of the acquiring firm means the *expected* profit for shareholders of

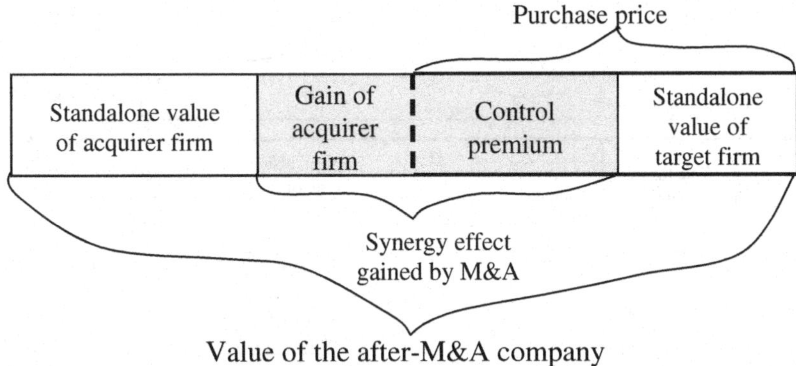

Fig. 2. The relationship between synergy effect and control premium.

acquiring firm, and the control premium means the *realized* profit for shareholders of target company though the latter actually realizes when the shareholders sell the rendered stocks to the stock market immediately. The agreement on M&A will be concluded upon whether or not managers of both firms, as representatives of shareholders of each firm, are satisfied with their benefits, through negotiation.

The problem here is that the gain for acquiring firm is only the expected value as contrary to the premium for target company that can be realized immediately because the premium for target company is included in the purchase price offered at the time of merger. Because of this problem, sometimes it is regretted after merger that synergy effect did not work as expected, and the premium amount was considered an "Overpaid" premium.

Since the purchase price is the price which induces shareholders of the acquired firm to merger with the acquiring firm or to participate in a network organization of acquiring firm, this is nothing but a kind of the "Incentive Price" that motivates parties to participate in a coalition.

5. Calculation Method of Merger Ratio

5.1. *Process of acquisition*

Firstly, refer to Fig. 3 for time-flow diagram of "Acquisition Process". In the Acquisition Process, the acquiring firm and the target firm will first

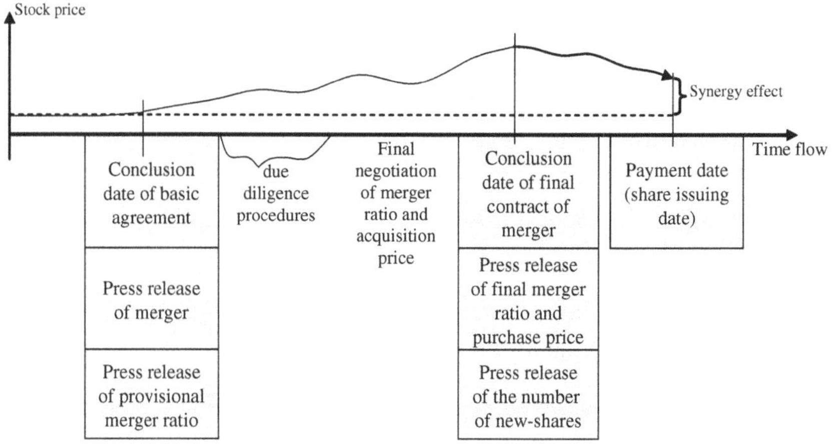

Fig. 3. Share price change during the acquisition process.

(1) conclude the "Basic Agreement" and carry out acquisition research of due-diligences procedures, (2) decide the final "Merger Ratio" and "Purchase Price", and (3) hand over the business (assets and liabilities of target firm) and pay the price in a form of acquirer's stocks for it. This process takes several months.

In this figure, both of the companies will announce their intention of merger to the public on the conclusion date of *Basic Agreement*. Thus, from this date, the share prices of both companies will usually begin to rise in anticipation of synergy effect gained by merger. On the conclusion date of the *final contract* of merger, they publish the *final* merger ratio payment and the number of new issued shares. Often, the share price falls in anticipation of decrease of the dividend amount per share because of increase of share supply in the market (i.e., dilution effect). Finally, the difference between the stock price average (dotted line) before the press release of merger on the conclusion date of Basic Agreement and the share price on the last date which is the new-share issuing date (merger date) becomes the total synergy effect reflected on the share price of acquiring firm.

5.2. *Calculation method of merger ratio*

As shown in Fig. 3, strictly speaking, the final determination date of Merger ratio is just prior to the actual merger date. Therefore, there could be a difference in share prices between Merger Ratio determination date and merger date (i.e., new-share issuing date or final conclusion date of contract of Merger). However, it is simplified here to call both days as "merger date" considering them as the same day.

Also, strictly speaking, the share price immediately after the merger could be different from the share price on the very merger date. However, in the following, we simplify to call the share price immediately after the merger, the "share price on the merger date". Furthermore, we assume that the share price on either date is adjusted to the fluctuations in the general market price such as TOPICS.

Now the "Merger Ratio" in a merger stands for how many stocks of the surviving firm per share of the nonsurviving firm shall be offered to the shareholders of the latter.

For example, in the *triangular merger* among the Citigroup in America and the Nikko Cordial Group in Japan, they decided the Merger Ratio based on the share price on the merger date (actually a day before merger) by the following calculation formula:

$$\begin{aligned}\text{Merger ratio} &= (\text{Nikko share price}) \div (\text{Citigroup share price})\\ &= 1{,}700\ \text{JPY} \div (27\ \text{dollars} \times 110\ \text{JPY per dollar}) \fallingdotseq 0.6.\end{aligned}$$

It followed that 0.6 Citigroup shares were allotted per one Nikko share. (However, Nikko share was set 1,700 JPY, which is equivalent to the price of TOB offered by Citigroup before the press release of merger.) This application of TOB price is according to the "principle of equal treatment of all shareholders". Therefore, in the above case of the merger ratio, the Nokko shareholder who held say 5,000 Nikko shares would receive 3,000 Citigroup shares (being 5,000 shares × merger ratio 0.6).

To calculate merger ratio, it is necessary to calculate the "*Stockholders' Value*" of each of nonsurviving firm and surviving firm. Stockholders' Value is calculated using the valuation methods of the firm value stated as follows:

(1) *Income Approach* (DCF method on Free Cash Flow, DCF method on Residual Profits).
(2) *Market Approach* (Published Market Price method, Similar Listed Company method).
(3) *Cost Approach* (Book-value Net Asset method, Replacement Value Net Asset method).

The following formulas are used to calculate merger ratio:

$$\text{Merger ratio} = \frac{\begin{array}{c}\text{[Shareholders' value of nonsurviving firm at merger date}\\ \div \text{ the number of issued shares of nonsurviving firm]}\end{array}}{\begin{array}{c}\text{[Shareholders' value of surviving firm at merger date}\\ \div \text{ the number of issued share of surviving firm]}\end{array}} \quad (3)$$

$$= \text{[Shareholders' value per share of nonsurviving firm]} \div \text{[Shareholders' value per share of surviving firm]} \quad (4)$$

Using this merger ratio, the number of newly offered shares of the surviving firm will be calculated applied by the following formula:

The total number of *offered* shares
= [Total number of issued shares of nonsurviving firm]
× [merger ratio]. (5)

6. Role of Stock Price in Calculating the Merger Ratio

Merger Ratio is calculated based on Shareholder Value of each firm as stated above. However, shareholder value is sometimes calculated by Published Market Price method of "Market Approach". On the assumption that the stock market is *efficient*, the share price must actually reflect various factors that have impacts on the fundamental earning capability of the firm, and the following should be correct:

Shareholders' value per share
= [Market price of the stock of the firm in question] (6)

Therefore, from equation (4), the following formula can be derived:

Merger ratio
= [The stock price of nonsurviving firm on merger date]
÷ [the stock price of surviving firm on merger date] (7)

From equation (7), the following will be derived:

The stock price of the nonsurviving firm on merger date
= Merger ratio
× [the stock price of the surviving firm on merger date] (8)

Therefore, from the equations (5) through (8), the following formula can be derived[3]:

Total market value of the number of newly *offered* shares
of the surviving firm on merger date
= Total market value of the nonsurviving firm on merger date. (9)

Therefore, the total market value of the nonsurviving firm on merger date is completely compensated by the number of new offered stocks of the surviving firm. And such total market value includes synergy effect allotment, which the shareholder of nonsurviving firm will obtain. Therefore, the allotment of the synergy effect is calculated by merger ratio as well. This will be explained in the next paragraph.

However, the actual share market is not always *efficient* in a short period; therefore, the investment bankers are reluctant to determine Merger Ratio only by comparing the share prices of both companies. For that reason, Merger Ratio is often determined by applying the three approaches (mentioned in the Section 2) to calculate the Shareholder Value. Notwithstanding that, the share price has in fact the biggest weight on determination of the Merger Ratio.

7. Formula for Synergy Effect Allocation and Determination of Acquisition Price

Synergy effects which could be obtained by the newly formed firm of merger are described below as mentioned in the Section 2:

(1) Incremental sales revenue after merger.
(2) Cost-reduction by reorganizing system after merger.

The various plans of (1) and (2) above will be realized since the surviving firm has control over the nonsurviving firm from the capital ownership viewpoint.

How much of those synergy effects the shareholders of *each* merger-related company will get must reflect on the *Shareholder Value of each company on merger date.* Therefore, if the stock market is efficient, the following relationship would hold.[4] (The equation (10) is corresponding to Fig. 2.)

Total market value of firm the newly formed firm on merger date
= {(Synergy effect allotment for shareholders of surviving firm)
+ (Stand-alone market value of surviving firm before the press release of Merger)}
+ (Synergy effect allotment for shareholders of nonsurviving firm)
+ (Stand-alone market value of nonsurviving firm before the press release of merger)} (10)

In the following, total annual synergy effect for both shareholders will be calculated as potential annual incremental operating profits by a detailed survey of incremental cost-reduction and incremental sales revenues, which the newly formed firm will gain. That is

Annual incremental operating profits of the newly formed firm after merger
= [Annual incremental sales profits]
+ [annual incremental cost-reduction] (11)

Thus,

Total market value of newly formed firm after the merger on merger date
= [Total *present value* of annual incremental operating profits of the combined firm after merger]
+ (Stand-alone total market value of the surviving firm before the press release of merger)
+ (Stand-alone total market value of the non-surviving firm before the press release of merger) (12)

It can be said that the equation (12) is equivalent to the formula of the "DCF method on Residual Profits"[5] of the Income Approach that calculates Enterprise Value.[6]

Total present value of synergy effect should be allocated to the shareholders of surviving firm and nonsurviving firm, respectively, based on their degree of contribution, with which each ex-firm will contribute to generating the synergy effect in the newly formed firm.

To my opinion, such degree of contribution should be determined on the basis of the amount of the comprehensive investment contained in their tangible and intangible assets, because the tangible and intangible assets of each firm would generate the synergy effect when they are merged. So the amount of the comprehensive investment should be used as an allocation base. The stand-alone market value of each firm before press release of merger can be used as such comprehensive investment amount before merger, because it is the market value of the fund that the shareholders of each firm have invested before the merger.

However, people cannot know before merger what the share price of both firms will be at the merger date. Then how could we determine the merger ratio before merger? And also how should the synergy effect be allocated?

Again, "the amount of the comprehensive investment contained in their tangible and intangible assets," that is, "stand-alone market value of each firm before press release of merger" can be used as the degree of contribution to the synergy effect or the synergy allocation criterion, and thus the synergy effect can be allotted in advance before knowing the share price on merger date. This is how they can determine the *provisional* merger ratio and the acquisition price on the date of initial press release. Let us see the formula of this logic.

Denote:

Shareholder value of the nonsurviving firm on merger date = X
Shareholder value of the surviving firm on merger date = Y
Stand-alone market value of nonsurviving firm before the press release of Merger = A
Stand-alone market value of surviving firm before the press release of Merger = B
Present value of synergy effect[7] = C.

Then,
the formula for allocating the synergy effect is as follows:

$$X = \{A/(A + B)\}\ C + A \tag{13}$$

= Synergy effect allotment to shareholders of non-surviving firm
+ Stand-alone market value of nonsurviving firm before press release of merger.

$$Y = \{A/(A + B)\}\ C + B \tag{14}$$

= Synergy effect allotment to shareholders of surviving firm
+ Stand-alone market value of surviving firm before press release of merger.

Summing up both equations (13) and (14),

Theoretical shareholders value (or theoretical market value) of the newly formed firm after merger = $X + Y = C + (A + B)$.

Therefore, from the equation (3), the following formula will be derived:

$$\text{Merger ratio} = \frac{(X \div \text{number of issued shares of nonsurviving firm})}{(Y \div \text{number of issued share of surviving firm before merger})}$$[8]

8. Market Transaction and Intra-Organizational Transaction for M&A

8.1. *M&A through market transaction*

As the cases of M&A are processed, there are Market Transaction cases or Intra-Organizational Transaction cases. However, generally, M&A is processed through market transaction in most cases.

In the case of "market transaction", a buyer and a seller trade the business itself as a kind of merchandise in the capital market. (Even though a seller firm is nonlisted firm, they still negotiate face to face.) Because of market transaction, the merchandise (a business in this case) has a "purchase price" as an asset transfer price. However, even in the case of market transaction, the purchase price still has the feature of an "Incentive Price" that has been described above.

Where lots of bidders are after one seller firm, a seller business is put up for bidding. Even if a seller were not put up for auction, they would go through negotiation for purchase price under price adjustment mechanism, and then the trade would be finally completed. Such a process is just a market transaction. In this case, shareholders of seller firm make comparative examination to find out which bidder they shall merge with to get the largest potential profits.

On the contrary, where there are lots of sellers and one bidder firm, the market will be a "buyer's market".

In the case of Separation of business where a firm is selling a certain section of the business, the process of transferring that business will be through market transaction.

8.2. *M&A through intra-organizational transaction*

This is merger or acquisition between member firms within the network organization. For example, there is a situation where the operational-allied firms become capital-allied firms within the network, and another situation where the capital-allied firms become parent and subsidiary companies.

As another angle, for example, the consolidated company group of Panasonic (ex-Matsushita Electric Industrial Co. Ltd.) carried out reorganization within group as follows in recent past years.

(1) Merger between subsidiaries within group, and between subsidiary and parent companies.
(2) Converting the subsidiary company into wholly-owned subsidiary through stock exchange.
(3) Converting the equity method affiliate into the subsidiary company through TOB.
(4) "Re-shuffle" that combines businesses by "business split-off" between subsidiaries or between subsidiary company and internal division of the parent firm.

Those transactions are essentially Intra-Organizational Transactions, but not Market Transactions. Such reorganization within a consolidated company group is also a sort of reformation within network organization.

9. Condition for Realizing M&A Agreement Under the Theory of Cooperative Game

Applying the principle of participation decision in M&A to the theory of cooperative game, it can be expressed in simple formula as follows. However, only gains of shareholders are mainly considered here, although all the interested parties will get gains (benefits) from merger.

Combined company's profits after M&A
$>$ sum of individual company's profits before M&A (15)

Above equation is prerequisite for M&A, and

Allocated profit for each company i after M&A
$>$ individual profit of each company i before M&A (16)

must hold for all participating companies as a required condition. The formula (16) is called the "*individual rationality*" in the theory of cooperative game.

Furthermore, where there are more than 2 firms participating in M&A, if the "Partial Coalition" could happen between certain firms, and the following equation come into effect, then, the member firm will withdraw from the Partial Coalition, so that a Merger of the "grand coalition" will occur (the grand coalition means the biggest coalition that all member firms will merge in M&A).

Combined Profits from "Partial Coalition"
$<$ [Sum of the allocated profit from "Grand Coalition"
to each member firm of "Partial Coalition"]. (17)

The Formula (17) is called "Rationality of partial coalition" or "Core condition" in the Theory of cooperative game.

In the above equation (15), "the left side figure minus the right side figure" leaves the "Synergy Effect" (also called the "operational synergy") of M&A, and it is also the source of the above "Rationality of partial coalition" and "Core condition".

Therefore, at least, it is a *necessary* condition of a Merger decision that the Synergy effect of equation (15) is realized. (However, strictly speaking, if the conditions of equations (16) and (17) do not hold, it cannot be said that *necessary and efficient conditions* for M&A have been fulfilled, and thus the allocation of synergy will not be stable.)

Further, the existing member firms within the consolidated business group cannot freely make a "partial coalition" with other companies, because of control power of the parent company through their capital ownership and on sending the directors, etc. As a result the rationality of partial condition (17) can be neglected. Therefore the consolidated business group can only consider the "individual rationality" (16), which will be satisfied by equations (13) and (14). In other words, for the consolidated business group if the condition (16) is satisfied the synergy allocation will be stable.

10. Conclusion: Other Factors in the Real World

In this paper, thc author asserted that the determination of the acquisition price under M&A or the control-premium included in it will follow the profit allocation mechanism among the combining firms concerned.

On the other hand, M&A practitioners may be influenced by the various following factors in determination of purchase price in reality (Okumura, 2007a, b).

(1) Bargaining Power for M&A: Acquisition price will depend on bargaining power of each seller and bidder during negotiation. For example, in case of the rescue of the company, the seller's bargaining power would become weaker, and in case where target shares are mainly held by specific institutional investors or Funds, the seller's bargaining power will become stronger. Furthermore, there are also many price-settings, which appear to have resulted from "bargaining tactics". Many practitioners also point out that because of the seller's strong bargaining power, the shareholders of the seller firm will often get *most* of the synergy value in advance, which should be generated by both of the merger-related companies after merger. This is also called "Winner's curse".

(2) Time Passage: If it passes too long time after the M&A press release, until final decisions of merger ratio, purchase price and the business plans to be taken after merger, some speculative price movement may happen, and the "excessively higher valuation" of the target may be carried out and result in the "over-paid" phenomenon.

(3) Personal Satisfaction of CEO: There is a tendency that the bigger the scale of the enterprise gets, the more compensation President gets. Many cases of M&A failed because M&A was carried out for apparent psychological (behavioral finance) factors such as "prestige for the President", rather than for the purpose of truly creating value. Or else, M&A are often just the results of personal motivation such as "Empire Building".

(4) Recent Trend of M&A Popularity: When a premium begins to rise under the tendency of a recent popularity of M&A market, such as

the popular cases of TOB price offered with 30% premium, the purchase price may be affected.

(5) Lack in Ability of Valuation of the Firm: Because the synergy effect only appears after merger, it is very difficult to forecast that before merger. Its value is only "God knows" or "anyone's guess" before the merger. This applies to investment bankers who support this forecast, or for the acquirer concerned.

Certainly, the purchase price and the control premium could be affected to some extent or largely by the above factors. However, as I see it, these factors are not substantial for the agreement of purchase price. The author is of strong opinion that a substantial underlying factor behind M&A decision lies in the mutual satisfaction with the incentive of allocated synergy effect. Based on this idea, a mechanism of deciding the control premium was explained in Section 5.

Finally, referring to the valuation of synergy effect which the author described as "God knows" in (5) above, it is of course impossible to forecast exactly how much annual incremental profit a target firm will bring in the after-merger company. However, to my opinion, if the "Principle of Conservatism" conventionally used in financial accounting is applied, it is fairly easy to forecast the restructuring effect which will be definitely generated in the next few years, and only that can be practically measured as synergy effect.

Endnotes

1. Incentive Price issue can be viewed in the framework of Agency Theory, where a Core Company in the network organization is considered as *principal* and a Member Company in network as *agency*. This can be considered as the issue that the principal gives an incentive to the multiple agents. (It is also explained by the *expectancy theory* as well.) However, for example, two allied firms within the network organization could be merged without instruction of any core company. In that case, it cannot be analyzed by the framework of agency theory.
2. Merger generates not only sales revenue increase and cost-reduction, but also temporary integration costs. For example, the information system department will suffer from additional costs of system-integration. Sales department and production department also suffer from additional costs for merger and abolition of shops.

3. [The number of new *offered* stocks] × [the stock price of surviving firm on merger date]
   = [(Total number of issued stocks of the nonsurviving firm on merger date) × (merger ratio)]
   × [the stock price of the surviving firm on merger date]
   (due to the equation (5))
   = [The number of issued stocks of the nonsurviving firm on merger date]
   × [the stock price of the nonsurviving firm on merger date]
   (due to the equation (8))
   = [Total market value of the nonsurviving firm on merger date] (9)
4. Total market value of the newly formed firm after the merger
   = [(Number of issued shares of surviving firm just prior to merger date) + number of new offering shares] × [the share price of newly formed firm after merger]
   = [(Number of issued shares of surviving firm just prior to merger date) × the share price of newly formed firm after merger]
   + [Number of new offering share × the share price of newly formed firm after merger]
   = [Shareholder value that shareholders of the surviving firm have on merger date]
   + [Shareholder value that shareholders of the nonsurviving firm have on merger date]
   = {(Synergy effect allotment for shareholders of surviving firm)
   + (Stand-alone market value of surviving firm before the press release of Merger)}
   + {(Synergy effect allotment for shareholders of nonsurviving firm)
   + (Stand-alone market value of nonsurviving firm before the press release of Merger)}
5. Basic equation of accounting profit method (JICPA (2007); this method is equivalent to the Ohlson Model.)

$$VE_1 = NA_1 + \frac{RI_1}{(1+k_e)} + \frac{RI_2}{(1+k_e)^2} + \frac{RI_3}{(1+k_e)^3} + \cdots + \frac{RI_\infty}{(1+k_e)^\infty}$$

$$VE_1 = NA_1 + \frac{RI_1}{(1+k_e)} + \frac{RI_2}{(1+k_e)^2} + \frac{RI_3}{(1+k_e)^3} + \cdots + \frac{RI_n}{(1+k_e)^n} + \frac{RCV_n}{(1+k_e)^n}$$

where

VE_1 = stock value at appraisal (at the beginning of the first period)
NE_1 = net asset book value at the beginning of the first period

RI_t = expected value of "residual profit", which belongs to the ordinary shareholders at period t

RI_t = $NP_t - NA_{t+1} \times k_e$

NP_t = expected value of net profit after tax at period t. (This is the net profit of current period under financial accounting)

RCV_n = the value of the accounting profit after period $n + 1$, which was discounted at the end of period n

k_e = owner's capital cost

NA_{t+1} = net asset book value at the end of period t

The reason why k_e is *owner's capital cost* is that the borrowed capital cost has been deducted from the operating profit already because NP_t is the net profit of current period under financial accounting.

6. The reason is that the following will hold where "DCF method on Residual Profits" is applied to each firm before merger.

Stand-alone stock value of *each* firm before press release of merger
= [Net asset book value of each firm at that time]
+ [Total present value of potential annual residual profits of the same firm]

Likewise, when the "DCF method on residual profits" is applied to newly formed firm after merger,

The following will hold:

The shareholders value of the newly formed firm after merger date
= The total of [the stand-alone shareholders value of *each* firm before press release of merger]
+ [Total present value of annual residual profits for the newly formed firm after merger].

7. The present value of synergy effect (= C) is the sum of the present values of RI_t that is the expected value of "Residual Profit" at period t, denoted in the end note (6) above.

8. The following is a supplementary explanation.
From the first equation in the end note (4), the following can be derived:

Since

Total market value of newly formed firm after the merger = $X + Y$,

Merger ratio
= {X/number of issued shares of nonsurviving firm}
÷ {($X + Y$)/(number of issued shares of surviving firm prior to Merger + number of new offering shares on merger date)}.

So Merger Ratio can be calculated as above, too. However, since "$X + Y$ = Total market value of newly formed firm after Merger", the denominator on the right side = the share price of newly formed firm after Merger.

And this can be rearranged as:

"Merger ratio = the stock price of nonsurviving firm on merger date
÷ the stock price of surviving firm on merger date"

This equation is the exactly same as the formula (7).

References

Japan Institute of Certified Public Accountants, Professional Group of Corporation Valuation (2007). Valuation approaches and methods of corporation value, as the material 1 of *Guideline for Corporation Value*, Research material (in Japanese).

MacKinsey & Co., Inc. Copeland, T., Koller, T., and Murrain, J. (2000). *Valuation: Measuring and Managing The Value of Companies*, 3rd edn. John Wiley & Sons.

Maekawa, N., Nodera, D. and Matsushita, M. (2005). *Basics of M&A*, Nikkei Inc. (in Japanese).

Miller, M. and Modigliani, F. (1961). Dividend policy, growth, and the valuation of shares, *Journal of Business*, XXXIV(4) (October 1961), 411–433.

Monden, Y. (1989). *Foundation of Transfer Price and Profit Sharing*, Dobunkan Pub. Co. (in Japanese).

Monden, Y. (1991). *Development of Transfer Price and Profit Sharing*, Dobunkan Pub. Co. (in Japanese).

Okumura, M. (2007a). Analysis and investigation of acquisition premium, in *Proceedings of Conference 2007 of Japan Association of Management Accounting* (in Japanese).

Okumura, M. (2007b). Analysis and investigation of acquisition premium, in *Handout Resume* in the Conference of Japan Association of Management Accounting, September 8th (in Japanese).

Part 3

Analysis of Accounting Information for Consolidated and Business Group and Segmental Business Units

7

Consolidated Accounting Information for Business Group Management

Manabu Takano
Department of Commerce, Seinan Gakuin University

1. Introduction

Although in business group management the final consolidated results are reflected in the consolidated financial statements, the institutional consolidated accounting information is not always useful for bringing about improvements in the performance of business group management. The overall financial situation and the strengths and weaknesses of the respective business groups can be deduced from the consolidated financial statements. Nevertheless, it is difficult to introduce business management practices that would improve the consolidated results using only the collated financial information for the entire business group. To improve business group management, in addition to the institutional consolidated accounting information, it is necessary to have the consolidated accounts of the divisions of a parent company, the divisions' affiliated companies, and associated companies.

This paper deals with consolidated accounting information for business group management, and examines the consolidated financial statements prepared by businesses and the nature of performance evaluation. In particular, we look at Canon, which manages its business group using business consolidation. Since only 10% of the listed companies in Japan have shifted to the holding company system (December 10, 2008; Nihon Keizai Shimbun), this paper concentrates on the "operating holding company" system.

2. Differences between Institutional Consolidated Accounting Information and Consolidated Accounting Information for Business Group Management

We propose that the institutional consolidated accounting information and consolidated accounting information necessary for business group management differ in the following two respects.

2.1. *Scope of consolidation*

The scope of consolidation is different between institutional consolidated accounting and consolidated accounting for business group management. In the institutional accounting system, the criteria by a rate of equity stake apply to the disclosure of consolidated financial statements. In contrast, in business group management, the scopes of the affiliated companies and associated companies in the consolidated accounts do not correspond to the overall scope of the business group management. As shown in Fig. 1, the scope of consolidation in consolidated accounting consists of Part A and Part B, whereas the scope of consolidation required for business group management consists of Part A and Part C. Part B represents the affiliated companies and associated companies that are not part of the strategy for improving the consolidated business results, although as a matter of form Part B is included in the scope of consolidation as an institutional object of consolidation. Part C represents the companies that constitute a supply chain and execute business processes, such as manufacturing and sales, although they are not included in the scope of institutional consolidation. That is, in business group management, those companies that are linked to

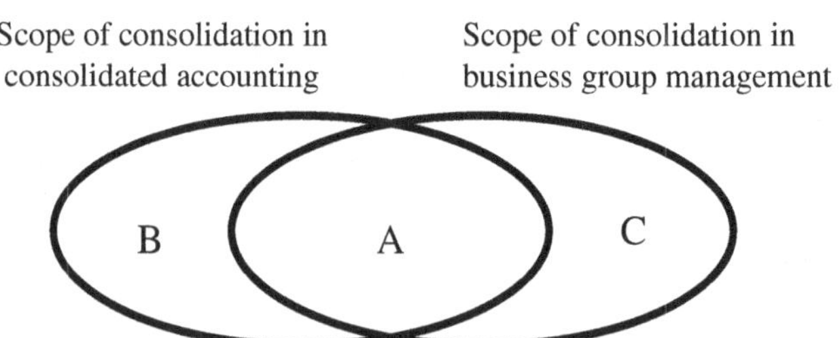

Fig. 1. Differences in the scope of consolidation between consolidated accounting and business group management. Adapted from Muto (2002, p. 14).

the business executive functions of the business groups and assume the strategies of business group management are included in the scope of consolidation, even though these companies are not the objects of institutional consolidation (Kimura, 1999).

2.2. *Types of consolidated accounting information*

The management of the business group analyzes the business group using the consolidated financial statements as part of the evaluation of the performance of the entire group. However, certain limitations and caveats are attached to the analysis of consolidated financial statements.

It is necessary to be careful about return on equity (ROE), which in recent years has been referred to as the index for the management target of Japanese companies, since ROE is high when the debt is large and equity capital is very low. The ROE increases if the equity capital is low and financial leverage is strong, even if the ratio of profit to net sales is low.

Although the analysis of consolidated financial statements has the aforementioned limitations, it provides outside interested parties with financial information on the entire business group, and it provides the management of the business group with valuable information on the financial situation of the entire business group, particularly with respect to the strengths and weaknesses of the business group and potential strategies for improving performance. However, the management of the business group cannot obtain concrete information that can be used to improve the consolidated results, even if it grasps the overall financial situation of the business group from analyzing the consolidated financial statements. Since the consolidated financial statements represent financial information on the entire group as a unit, they are insufficient for the needs of business management (Kimura, 2005). To obtain information that is useful for the management of a business group, it is necessary to break down the consolidated accounting information for the entire business group.

3. Information on Consolidated Accounting that is Indispensable for Business Group Management

3.1. *Consolidated financial statements by business*

There are various forms of business group management. If the business group is assumed to be an operating holding company, the parent company comprises more than one division, and under the control of the parent company the affiliated and associated companies assume the processes of manufacturing and sales. The formulation and implementation of strategy for each consolidated business are essential to improving the performance of the business group management, and the accounting information for each consolidated business becomes useful for the business group management.

Since the self-contained activities of consolidated businesses are carried out by affiliated and associated companies, which assume responsibility for development, production, and sales under the control of individual divisions of the parent company, each consolidated business has independent management responsibility for both income and expenses, i.e., profit responsibility. Accordingly, each consolidated business prepares a consolidated profit-and-loss statement, which makes it possible to grasp the level of profitability and to analyze growth potential in terms of the rate of increase in sales and the rate of new products that account for of the sales amount.

Furthermore, in consolidated businesses, consolidated balance sheets and consolidated profit-and-loss statement are prepared. These documents are helpful for decision making, as each division of the parent company can extract information on the accumulated profit or loss of the consolidated business, the debts payable, and the consolidated ROE (Hiki, 1998). Indeed, from 1997 through 2001. Mitsubishi Corporation adopted the consolidated in-house capital stock system, and consolidated balance sheet for each sales department was prepared (May 25, 1997 and March 23, 2001; Nihon Keizai Shimbun). At Mitsubishi, the consolidated in-house capital stock was determined by aggregating the balances of the surpluses of the group companies and adding the in-house capital stock, which was based on the results of the sales divisions and took into account foreign exchange losses. At Mitsubishi, the person in charge of each sales division took into consideration the balance sheet of the entire group by preparing a consolidated balance sheet for the sales division, and the business group was managed by setting a target value for the consolidated ROE (May 25, 1997; Nihon Keizai Shimbun).

Furthermore, in a consolidated business, a consolidated cash-flow statement is prepared. The consolidated cash-flow statement prepared by the business reveals various indices that can be used in analyses of the cash flow and cash-flow cycle of each consolidated business, thereby providing information that is helpful implementing improvements in the cash flow for each consolidated business. In addition, decision-making information for fund raising and information useful for developing the business strategy can be obtained by determining the free cash flow after subtracting the investment cash flow from the operating cash flow for each consolidated business (Fushimi, 1998).

3.2. *Performance evaluation index*

In business group management, as mentioned above, the consolidated financial statements are prepared by the business. Previously, the budget was drafted by the consolidated business, and performance was evaluated by comparing the budget against the results.

The indices for performance evaluation are roughly classified into financial and nonfinancial. For the financial indices, return-on-capital indices, such as ROI and ROE, are used in addition to income determination indices, such as sales amount and profits, which have been used traditionally. Since achievements related to cash flow and the parent company's dividend are required of each consolidated business (Asada, 1999), the cash flow and free cash flow are also used as indices for performance evaluation. Thus, for performance evaluation using financial indices, a well-balanced management uses various indices, such as income determination, return-on-capital, and cash-flow indices, instead of a single index (Asada, 1999).

With regard to nonfinancial indices, to evaluate qualitative factors, indices associated with the future growth potential of each business and indices associated with the degree of attainment of business plans are used. Future growth potential encompasses quality, productivity, market share, customer satisfaction, the results of new product development, and safety factors (Hoshino, 1999). The degree of attainment of a business plan means the extent to which a business strategy is executed (Moriyama, 2003).

These performance evaluation indices should be created based on the objectives, vision, and strategy of the entire group rather than on those of the individual divisions of the parent company. Each company in the business group must match its own performance evaluation criteria to those of the divisions of the parent company, to ensure consistency across the consolidated businesses (Terasawa, 2000). In addition, the establishment of performance evaluation indices motivates each employee within the group to attain the goals of the entire group (Hamada, 2007).

The above-mentioned performance evaluation is used in decision making by business group executives, who evaluate the performance of each consolidated business and make decisions as to resource allocation, such as the types of business investment that should be made or whether or not investment should be withdrawn. In general, the management of each consolidated business uses the performance evaluation index for the subsequent formulation and implementation of business strategies.

4. Case Study: Canon Inc.

4.1. *Adoption of the consolidated divisional organization*

Canon Inc. (hereinafter referred to as 'Canon') was founded in 1937 as a company that was engaged in the manufacturing and sales of cameras. Today, Canon is a global business group based in Japan and overseas that is engaged in development, production, marketing, and customer service in the areas of business machines, cameras, and optical equipment. The consolidated sales of Canon group in 2007 were 39.3 billion dollars, and the consolidated current net profit is about 4.3 billion dollars (U.S. accounting standards). The group consists of 239 consolidated subsidiaries and 131,352 employees.

In 1996, Canon worked out the "concept of global quality company group." This concept was incorporated into a matrix management system, and the consolidated divisional organization was adopted as the core mechanism to support this system. The matrix management adopted by the Canon group is a group-management technique (Fig. 2), in which the main bodies of Canon, the manufacturing company and sales company, are deployed longitudinally. In addition, the six operational headquarters, which include the imaging business machine headquarters, peripheral equipment headquarters, and ink-jet printer headquarters, are deployed transversely. This matrix management requires the maximization of individual company profits by creating a physical relationship between the individual companies (vertical axis) and operational headquarters (horizontal axis), and requires the maximization of the consolidated operational headquarter profits (Sawago, 1998). Through matrix management, Canon has come to place greater emphasis on the performance management of the operational headquarters and the company.

4.2. *Performance determination system for each consolidated operational headquarters*

Canon started to implement the performance determination system for each consolidated operational headquarters to put the consolidated

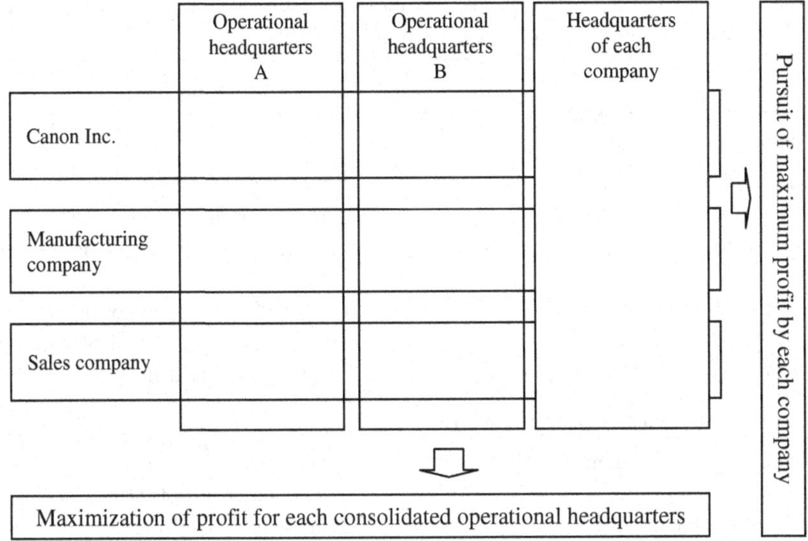

Fig. 2. Conceptual drawing of the matrix management at Canon. From Sawago (1998, p. 113, partly modified).

operational headquarters system into practice. This is a system of monthly performance management in which the budget by company and by operational headquarters is prepared and compared with past results.

A comprehensive and multifaceted performance evaluation of each operating headquarters, manufacturing company, and sales company is made semiannually based on a long-term perspective, in terms of management indices such as profitability, growth potential and safety, as well as indices other than management indices such as the technology, development capability, proprietary technology, and market share. Table 1 shows an example of the items and indices for the performance evaluation. At Canon, these evaluation items are rated and each business performance is ranked with overall points. However, such rankings are not directly associated with personnel evaluation or remuneration by the heads of the operational headquarters. Instead, the purpose of such rankings is to grasp the strong and weak points of one's own department or company with the aim of future improvement.

As just described, Canon aims at utilizing its management resources to the utmost extent on a global basis through matrix management by adopting the consolidated operational headquarters system and through the performance determination system for each consolidated operational

Table 1. An example of the items and indices for the consolidated performance evaluation at Canon. Adapted from Yanagihashi (2002, p. 8).

Evaluation item	Evaluation index
Management indices	
Profitability	Return on total assets (ROA), pretax profit ratio on sales
Growth potential	Sales growth ratio, profit growth ratio
Safety	Degree of dependence on loan, ratio of investment in plant, and equipment/cash flow
Indices other than management indices	
Technology development capability	Qualitative evaluation of technological potential
Proprietary technology	Number proposed per employee, income from license
Market share	Market shares of main products

headquarters to support matrix management in terms of accounting. At Canon, it has become easier to build up close communication between the operational headquarters and the manufacturing/sales companies through performance management and performance evaluation on a consolidated basis (Sawago, 1998).

5. Conclusion

In this paper, the consolidated accounting information by business is examined, as the consolidated accounting information is indispensable to business group management. Although the results of business group management will eventually be reflected in the consolidated financial statements, the institutional consolidated accounting information alone, in which the entire business group is treated as a unit, cannot provide information useful to the performance improvement of business group management. In business group management, it becomes necessary to break down the consolidated accounting information for the entire business group and extract the accounting information therefrom. Accordingly, the author feels that, in business group management, it becomes necessary to conduct business management through a consolidated business consisting of each division of the parent company as a core, and affiliated companies and associated companies under the control thereof. In a consolidated business, the consolidated financial statements by business are prepared, and performance is evaluated using multifaceted evaluation items. In fact, at Canon, the consolidated operational headquarters system that grasps the divisions of the parent company on a consolidated basis is adopted, and performance is managed monthly and evaluated semiannually by preparing the consolidated financial statements for each operational headquarters for the purpose of the business management of the business group.

In this paper, the consolidated accounting information for business group management is examined based on the structure of the operating holding company, but what kind of accounting information should be used in the case of business group management that adopts the structure of the holding company? Is there any essential difference from the structure of the operating holding company? Also, in the performance evaluation of a consolidated business, when the items requiring evaluation are too diversified, the target of the entire business group may be inconsistent with that of the consolidated business. In that case, would the management of the consolidated business, which is the object of the performance evaluation, not have difficulty in finding what should be targeted and what should be improved? These questions are left as future tasks to be resolved.

References

Asada, T. (1999). Issues of diversification and globalization in performance measurement, *Kigyou-kaikei*, 51(4), 18–23 (in Japanese).

Fushimi, T. (1998). Cash flow information to support management strategy, *Kigyou-kaikei*, 50(8), 42–53 (in Japanese).

Hamada, K. (2007). The role of group headquarters, and evaluation system of group performance: Matrix evaluation system, *The Commercial Review of Seinan Gakuin University*, 53(3–4), 1–24 (in Japanese).

Hiki, F. (1998). Consolidated information as management accounting information, *Sangyou-keiri*, 58(1), 88–97 (in Japanese).

Hoshino, Y. (1999). Incentives and diversity in the performance evaluation of Japanese companies, *Kigyou-kaikei*, 51(4), 24–31 (in Japanese).

Kimura, I. (1999). Management accounting information of group company organizations: From divisional companies to group companies, *The Journal of Management Accounting, Japan*, 7(1–2), 137–157 (in Japanese).

Kimura, I. (2005). *Management Accounting for Business Groups*, Zeimukeiri-kyokai (in Japanese).

Moriyama, C. (ed.) (2003). *Strategy for the Maximization of Company Values in a Business Group, and Management System,* Business Research Institute (in Japanese).

Mutou, Y. (2002). *Seven New Common Senses for the Business Group Management — From Investors' Viewpoint to Companies' Viewpoint*, Chuokeizaisha (in Japanese).

Sawago, R. (1998). *Canon — The Concept of Global Quality Company Group and Measures for Facilitating Consolidated Management Innovation,* in The Research Project for Consolidated Management Innovation (ed.). *Information Packet for Business Group Innovation and the Management of Associated Companies*, Japan Management Association, pp. 101–119 (in Japanese).

Terasawa, N. (2000). *True Picture of Business Group Management*, Nihon Keizai Shimbunsha (in Japanese).

Yanagihashi, K. (2002). Business group management and business group performance management at Canon, *Keiei Jitsumu*, 06, 4–9 (in Japanese).

8

Business Evaluation of a Company Group in Japan: A Case Study of Segment Reporting by Panasonic Electric Works

Shufuku Hiraoka
Faculty of Business Administration, Soka University

1. Introduction

The so-called "management approach" in segment reporting is based on the organization of segments internally for the purpose of making operating decisions and assessing performance (Epstein *et al.*, 2007; Huefner *et al.*, 2007). Japanese companies will be obligated to introduce this approach from March 2011 (Hiraoka, 2007); however, Panasonic Electric Works has been applying this approach in advance (Hiraoka, 2007). Using a case study of segment reporting by Panasonic Electric Works, this paper will show an analysis of business evaluation based on economic profit.

2. Organizational Innovation and the Management Approach

The Panasonic Electric Works Group introduced the intra-company system in November 1998. An intra-company is not a corporation but a kind of imitative company. In Japan, it is an investment center which has more authority than an operating division. Panasonic Electric Works organized five intra-companies, Electrical Construction Materials, Home Appliances, Building Products, Electronic and Plastic Materials, and Automation Control. However, each intra-company consolidated functional overseas subsidiaries, and each became a subgroup in accordance with the purpose of management. At the same time, economic profit was adopted as the basis for business evaluation. When Panasonic Electric Works became a subsidiary of Panasonic Electric Industrial in April 2004, the Panasonic group's brands were unified (Hiraoka, 2006).

Thereafter, Panasonic Electric Works introduced the marketing headquarter system to develop marketing strategies for every area and category. Therefore, Panasonic Electric Works took over some parts of the business belonging to Electrical Construction Materials, Home Appliances and Building Products from Panasonic Electric Industrial. On the other hand, it transferred some parts of Home Appliances to Panasonic Electric Industrial. In this way, business restructuring was performed between the parent company and its subsidiaries.

Having introduced the intra-company system, Panasonic Electric Works has been disclosing the segment reporting based on the management approach since November 1999. The originality of Panasonic Electric Works in segment reporting has been maintained even after becoming the subsidiary of Panasonic Electric Industrial. This remarkable tendency continues to manifest in the annual report. The segment's income statements, balance sheets, and cash flow statements have been disclosed since 2000. Such detailed contents cannot be seen in the other companies' reports. Of course, segment reporting must be derived from the management accounting information. The chief operating decision makers are able to not only arrive at better decisions, but also more accurately evaluate performance for the given business segment when using these reports together with other internal information; these data are collectively more detailed and more helpful than they would otherwise be for measuring and improving the corporate value.

3. Measuring the Entire WACC

In the case of Panasonic Electric Works, the economic profit of every segment can be measured using the information obtained based on the management approach. But before we can measure the economic profit of the business segment, we must calculate the cost of capital.

First, the entire cost rate of equity capital must be calculated. We can use the capital asset pricing model (CAPM) to perform the calculation. The β-value can be estimated as the regression coefficient between the variance rate of TOPIX (Tokyo Stock Exchange 1st Section Price Index) and that of the stock price of Panasonic Electric Works from April 2002 to March 2008 using the least squares method. The risk-free rate (R_f) is estimated as the average of rate of government bonds from April 2002 to March 2008. R_m is the expected return on the stock market. We assume it to be 8% here. The entire cost rate of equity capital (R_e) can then be calculated as follows:

The entire cost rate of equity capital on March 31, 2007:

$$R_e = R_f + \beta * (R_m - R_f) = 1.39\% + 0.91 * (8\% - 1.39\%) = 7.4\%.$$

The entire cost rate of equity capital on March 31, 2008:

$$R_e = R_f + \beta * (R_m - R_f) = 1.49\% + 0.85 * (8\% - 1.49\%) = 7.0\%.$$

Next, we must calculate the average of the ending and beginning liabilities with interest:

The average of the liabilities with interest as of March 31, 2007
= (51,049 + 51,678 + 36,552 + 51,889)/2 = 95,584 Yen (millions).

The average of the liabilities with interest as of March 31, 2008
= (36,552 + 51,889 + 54,998 + 21,726)/2 = 82,582.5 Yen (millions).

The tax rates are calculated in the same way as the segment's taxes rate, as follows:

The tax rate
= income taxes/income before income taxes and minority interests.

The tax rate as of March 31, 2007
= 30,935/79,945 = 0.387.

The tax rate as of March 31, 2008
= 32,226/82,665 = 0.390.

We must also calculate the average of the market capitalization:

Market capitalization
= stock price * the number of issued and outstanding.

Market capitalization on March 31, 2006
= 1,413 Yen * 733.21 millions = 1,036,026 Yen (millions).

Market capitalization on March 31, 2007
= 1,351 Yen * 733.21 millions = 990,567 Yen (millions).

Market capitalization on March 31, 2008
 = 1,025 Yen * 751.07 millions = 769,847 Yen (millions).

The average of the market capitalization as of March 31, 2007
 = (1,036,026 + 990,567)/2 = 1,013,296.5 Yen (millions).

The average of the market capitalization as of March 31, 2008
 = (990,567 + 769,847)/2 = 880,207 Yen (millions).

The interest as of March 31, 2007 is 3,647 Yen (millions), and that as of March 31, 2008 is 3,699 Yen (millions). Therefore, we can calculate the entire weighted-average cost of capital (WACC) as follows:

WACC as of March 31, 2007 (%)
 $= \{3{,}647 * (1 - 0.387) + 0.074 * 1{,}013{,}296.5\}/(95{,}584 + 1{,}013.296.5) * 100$
 $= 7\%$

WACC as of March 31, 2008 (%)
 $= \{3{,}699 * (1 - 0.390) + 0.070 * 880{,}207\}/(82{,}582.5 + 880{,}207) * 100 = 7\%$

In this connection, the entire rate of liabilities with interest before taxes is calculated as follows:

The interest rate as of March 31, 2007 (%)
 $= 3{,}647 * 100/95{,}584 = 3.8\ \%.$

The interest rate as of March 31, 2008 (%)
 $= 3{,}699 * 100/82.582.5 = 4.5\%.$

4. Measuring the WACC of Each Business Segment

We need to know the WACC of each business segment when we want to calculate the segment's economic profit. We apportion the market capitalization to the business segment on a distribution basis with the total equity (net assets) of the segment. In the annual reports of Panasonic Electric Works, the total equity of every segment on the consolidated balance sheets is listed by business segment. The total of the segment's total equities is as follows:

March 31, 2006: 439,675 Yen (millions)
March 31, 2007: 517,129 Yen (millions)
March 31, 2008: 538,461 Yen (millions)

The distribution amount of the market capitalization of each segment is calculated as follows:

As of March 31, 2007: Yen (millions)

Market capitalization distributed to Electrical Construction Materials
= 1,013,296.5 * (159,300 + 192,145)/(439,675 + 517,129) = 372,195.

Market capitalization distributed to Home Appliances
= 1,013,296.5 * (54,920 + 58,490)/(439,675 + 517,129) = 120,106.

Market capitalization distributed to Building Products
= 1,013,296.5 * (98,232 + 100,284)/(439,675 + 517,129) = 210,237.

Market capitalization distributed to Electronic and Plastic Materials
= 1,013,296.5 * (40,014 + 48,603)/(439,675 + 517,129) = 93,849.

Market capitalization distributed to Automation Control
= 1,013,296.5 * (58,161 + 78,215)/(439,675 + 517,129) = 144,428.

Market capitalization distributed to others
= 1,013,296.5 * (29,048 + 39,392)/(439,675 + 517,129) = 72,481.

As of March 31, 2008: Yen (millions)

Market capitalization distributed to Electrical Construction Materials
= 880,207 * (192,145 + 211,873)/(517,129 + 538,461) = 336,892.

Market capitalization distributed to Home Appliances
= 880,207 * (58,490 + 57,545)/(517,129 + 538,461) = 96,756.

Market capitalization distributed to Building Products
= 880,207 * (100,284 + 92,224)/(517,129 + 538,461) = 160,523.

Market capitalization distributed to Electronic and Plastic Materials
= 880,207 * (48,603 + 50,613)/(517,129 + 538,461) = 82,732.

Market capitalization distributed to Automation Control
= 880,207 * (78,215 + 81,367)/(517,129 + 538,461) = 133,068.

Market capitalization distributed to others
= 880,207 * (39,392 + 44,839)/(517,129 + 538,461) = 70,236.

Since the liabilities with interest of every segment are disclosed, the average of the beginning and ending is calculated for every segment as follows:

The average as of March 31, 2007: Yen (millions)

The liabilities with interest of Electrical Construction Materials (ECM)
= (61,419 + 1,610 + 51,129 + 1,788)/2 = 57,973.

The liabilities with interest of Home Appliances (HA)
= (620 + 25 + 1,151 + 25)/2 = 910.5.

The liabilities with interest of Building Products (BP)
= (23,941 + 2,030 + 17,789 + 3,264)/2 = 23,512.

The liabilities with interest of Electronic and Plastic Materials (EPM)
= (18,925 + 2,354 + 10,001 + 111)/2 = 15,695.5.

The liabilities with interest of Automation Control (AC)
= (13,136 + 14,194 + 14,062 + 16,484)/2 = 28,928.

The liabilities with interest of others
= (6,730 + 30,392 + 6,321 + 30,573)/2 = 37,008.

The average as of March 31, 2008: Yen (millions)

The liabilities with interest of ECM
= (51,129 + 1,788 + 47,143 + 45,229)/2 = 72,644.5.

The liabilities with interest of HA
= (1,151 + 25 + 555 + 0)/2 = 865.5.

The liabilities with interest of BP
= (17,789 + 3,264 + 26,104 + 3,588)/2 = 25,372.5.

The liabilities with interest of EPM
= (10,001 + 111 + 3,256 + 682)/2 = 7,025.

The liabilities with interest of AC
= (14,062 + 16,484 + 14,755 + 15,000)/2 = 30,150.5.

The liabilities with interest of others
= (6,321 + 30,573 + 8 + 27,422)/2 = 32,162.

Not only the income taxes, but also the income before taxes and minority interests are disclosed. Therefore, we can calculate the tax rate for each segment except Building Products, which has a deficit (Solomons, 1965, 1968). Let us suppose that Building Products' tax rate is equal to the total one.

As of March 31, 2007:

The taxes rate for ECM = 16,045/39,157 = 0.410
The taxes rate for HA = 1,976/7,169 = 0.2756
The taxes rate for BP = 0.387

The taxes rate for EPM = 1,907/7,479 = 0.255
The taxes rate for AC = 5,793/13,698 = 0.423
The taxes rate for others = 2,919/7,415 = 0.3937.

As of March 31, 2008:

The taxes rate for ECM = 18,391/43,541 = 0.422
The taxes rate for HA = 2,012/6,556 = 0.307
The taxes rate for BP = 0.390
The taxes rate for EPM = 2,145/7,729 = 0.2775
The taxes rate for AC = 5,633/14,693 = 0.383
The taxes rate for others = 5,363/13,157 = 0.4076.

Finally, the WACC of each business segment is calculated as follows:

As of March 31, 2007:

WACC of ECM
$= \{57{,}973 * (1-0.410) * 3.8\% + 372{,}195 * 7\%\}/(57{,}973 + 372{,}195) = 6.36\%$

WACC of HA
$= \{910.5 * (1-0.2756) * 3.8\% + 120{,}106 * 7\%\}/(910.5 + 120{,}106) = 6.96\%$

WACC of BP
$= \{23{,}512 * (1-0.387) * 3.8\% + 210{,}237 * 7\%\}/(23{,}512 + 210{,}237) = 6.53\%$

WACC of EPM
$= \{15{,}695.5 * (1-0.255) * 3.8\% + 93{,}849 * 7\%\}/(15{,}695.5+93{,}849) = 6.40\%$

WACC of AC
$= \{28{,}928 * (1-0.423) * 3.8\% + 144{,}428 * 7\%\}/(28{,}928 + 144{,}428) = 6.20\%$

WACC of others
$= \{37{,}008 * (1-0.3937) * 3.8\% + 72{,}481 * 7\%\}/(37{,}008 + 72{,}481) = 5.41\%$

As of March 31, 2008:

WACC of ECM
$= \{72{,}644.5 * (1-0.422) * 4.5\% + 336{,}892 * 7\%\}/(72{,}644.5 + 336{,}892)$
$= 6.22\%$

WACC of HA
$= \{865.5 * (1-0.307) * 4.5\% + 96{,}756 * 7\%\}/(865.5 + 96{,}756) = 6.97\%$

WACC of BP
$= \{25{,}372.5 * (1-0.390) * 4.5\% + 160{,}523 * 7\%\}/(25{,}372.5 + 160{,}523) = 6.42\%$

WACC of EPM
$= \{7{,}025 * (1-0.2775) * 4.5\% + 82{,}732 * 7\%\}/(7{,}025 + 82{,}732) = 6.71\%$

WACC of AC
$= \{30{,}150.5 * (1-0.383) * 4.5\% + 133{,}068 * 7\%\}/(30{,}150.5 + 133{,}068) = 6.22\%$

WACC of others
$= \{32{,}162 * (1-0.4076) * 4.5\% + 70{,}236 * 7\%\}/(32{,}162 + 70{,}236) = 5.64\%$

5. The First Method of Measuring Each Segment's Economic Profit

In addition to the above calculated results, we must measure the net operating profit after taxes (NOPAT) and the economic capital before we calculate the economic profit of each segment. We define NOPAT as follows:

$$\text{NOPAT} = \text{Operating income} * (1-\text{taxes rate}) - \text{amortization of the capitalized restructuring charge.}$$

We can recognize the impairment loss of the segment as one of the restructuring charges (Stewart, 1991). According to Young and O'Byrne (2001), a good case can be made for the subsequent amortization of the capitalized restructuring charge. We depreciate the capitalized impairment loss over five years equally. The impairment loss of the segment has been disclosed since 2007. Therefore, NOPAT as of March 31, 2008 (NOPAT_{08}) is defined as follows:

$$\text{NOPAT}_{08} = (\text{Operating income}_{08} - \text{impairment loss}_{08}/5) * (1-\text{taxes rate}_{08}) - \text{impairment loss}_{07} * (1-\text{taxes rate}_{07})/5$$

The NOPAT_{08} of each segment is calculated as follows:

$$\text{NOPAT}_{08} \text{ of ECM} = (44{,}706-46/5) * (1-0.422) - 446 * (1-0.410)/5 = 25{,}782 \text{ Yen (millions)}$$

$$\text{NOPAT}_{08} \text{ of HA} = (7{,}974-49/5) * (1-0.307) - 0 * (1-0.2756)/5 = 5{,}519 \text{ Yen (millions)}$$

$$\text{NOPAT}_{08} \text{ of BP} = (505-388/5)*(1-0.390)-5{,}429*(1-0.387)/5$$
$$= \Delta 405 \text{ Yen (millions)}$$

$$\text{NOPAT}_{08} \text{ of EPM} = (7{,}404-256/5)*(1-0.2775)-1{,}074*(1-0.255)/5$$
$$= 5{,}152 \text{ Yen (millions)}$$

$$\text{NOPAT}_{08} \text{ of AC} = (15{,}379-0)*(1-0.383)-1{,}191*(1-0.423)/5$$
$$= 9{,}351 \text{ Yen (millions)}$$

$$\text{NOPAT}_{08} \text{ of others} = (8{,}657-0)*(1-0.4076)-1{,}194*(1-0.3937)/5$$
$$= 4{,}984 \text{ Yen (millions)}.$$

Next, the beginning of the economic capital as of March 31, 2008 (EC) is defined as follows:

$$\text{EC} = \text{Liabilities with interest}_{07}$$
$$+ \text{ noncurrent liabilities without interest}_{07} + \text{Total equity}_{07}$$
$$+ \text{ impairment loss}_{07} * (1 - \text{taxes rate}_{07}) * 4/5$$

The EC of each segment is calculated as follows:

$$\text{EC of ECM} = 51{,}129 + 1{,}788 + 50{,}670 + 192{,}145 + 446*(1-0.410)*4/5$$
$$= 295{,}943 \text{ Yen (millions)}$$

$$\text{EC of HA} = 1{,}151 + 25 + 790 + 58{,}490 + 0*(1-0.2756)*4/5$$
$$= 60{,}456 \text{ Yen (millions)}$$

$$\text{EC of BP} = 17{,}789 + 3{,}264 + 28{,}274 + 100{,}284 + 5{,}429*(1-0.387)*4/5$$
$$= 152{,}273 \text{ Yen (millions)}$$

$$\text{EC of EPM} = 10{,}001 + 111 + 3{,}079 + 48{,}603 + 1{,}074*(1-0.255)*4/5$$
$$= 62{,}434 \text{ Yen (millions)}$$

$$\text{EC of AC} = 14{,}062 + 16{,}484 + 7{,}386 + 78{,}215 + 1{,}191*(1-0.423)*4/5$$
$$= 116{,}697 \text{ Yen (millions)}$$

$$\text{EC of others} = 6{,}321 + 30{,}573 + 2{,}480 + 39{,}392 + 1{,}194*(1-0.3937)*4/5$$
$$= 79{,}345 \text{ Yen (millions)}$$

The economic profit (EP) of each segment as of March 31, 2008 is calculated as follows:

$$\text{EP} = \text{NOPAT}-\text{EC} * \text{WACC}$$
$$\text{EP of ECM} = 25{,}782-295{,}943*6.22\% = 7{,}374 \text{ Yen (millions)}$$
$$\text{EP of HA} = 5{,}519-60{,}456*6.97\% = 1{,}305 \text{ Yen (millions)}$$
$$\text{EP of BP} = \Delta 405-152{,}273*6.42\% = \Delta 9{,}371 \text{ Yen (millions)}$$
$$\text{EP of EPM} = 5{,}152-62{,}434*6.71\% = 963 \text{ Yen (millions)}$$

EP of AC = 9,351–116,697 ∗ 6.22% = 2,092 Yen (millions)
EP of Others = 4,984–79,345 ∗ 5.64% = 509 Yen (millions).

From the calculations above, we can see that the economic profit of Building Products is only deficit. The total of the economic profits of all the segments is as follows:

Total of the economic profits
= 7,374 + 1,305 + Δ9,371 + 963 + 2,092 + 509
= 2,872 Yen (millions).

In the same way, the entire economic profit in the consolidated financial statement is as follows:

EP = (83,923–1,052/5)∗(1–0.390)
−(36,552 + 51,889 + 111,918 + 723,755
+ 9,387 ∗ [1–0.387] ∗ 4/5) ∗ 7.0%
= Δ13,945 Yen (millions).

Thus, the entire economic profit is not equal to the total profit of the segments because of the internal transactions between the segments and the head office.

6. The Second Method for Measuring Each Segment's Economic Profit

As calculated above, the entire cost of capital is larger than the total cost of the segments when we use the first method. The first reason for this is that the total of liabilities with interest for the segments is larger than the consolidated liabilities with interest due to the internal transactions within the Panasonic Electric Works Group. In other words, the cost rate of the liabilities with interest is smaller than the cost of equity capital. Therefore, the WACC calculated by the first method is smaller. The second reason is that the entire capital is larger than the total capital of the segments. In such cases, if we look in Table 1, we can use the rates of revision. The liabilities of each segment, WACC and economic capital are adjusted (Adj.) as follows:

The average as of March 31, 2008: Yen (millions)

Adj. liabilities with interest of ECM
= [(51,129 + 1,788) ∗ (1–0.4028) + (47,143 + 45,229) ∗ (1–0.5824)]/2 = 34,612

Table 1. Adjustment of the variance of the liabilities and equity: Yen (millions).

The amount on March 31	2007	2008
Liabilities with interest		
Consolidated ①	88,441	76,724
The total for the segments ②	152,698	183,742
Variance = ①−② = ③	−64,257	−107,018
Rate of revision = ④ = ③/②	−0.4208	−0.5824
Non-current liabilities without interest		
Consolidated ⑤	111,918	90,695
The total for the segments ⑥	92,679	73,694
Variance = ⑤−⑥ = ⑦	19,239	17,001
Total equity		
Consolidated ⑧	723,755	734,710
The total for the segments ⑨	517,129	538,461
Variance = ⑧−⑨ = ⑩	206,626	151,249
The total of variance = ③ + ⑦ + ⑩ = ⑪	161,608	61,237
The total capital for the segments = ② + ⑥ + ⑨ = ⑫	762,506	795,897
Rate of revision = ⑬ = ⑪/⑫	0.2119	0.0770

Adj. liabilities with interest of HA
$= [(1{,}151 + 25) * (1-0.4208) + (555 + 0) * (1-0.5824)]/2 = 456$

Adj. liabilities with interest of BP
$= [(17{,}789 + 3{,}264) * (1-0.4208) + (26{,}104 + 3{,}588) * (1-0.5824)]/2$
$= 12{,}297$

Adj. liabilities with interest of EPM
$= [(10{,}001 + 111) * (1-0.4208) + (14{,}755 + 15{,}000) * (1-0.5824)]/2$
$= 3{,}751$

Adj. liabilities with interest of AC
$= [(14{,}062 + 16{,}484) * (1-0.4208) + (14{,}755 + 15{,}000) * (1-0.5824)]/2$
$= 15{,}059$

Adj. liabilities with interest of others
$= [(6{,}321 + 30{,}573) * (1-0.4208) + (8 + 27{,}422) * (1-0.5824)]/2$
$= 16{,}412$

Therefore, the adjusted (Adj.) WACC of each segment is calculated follows:

As of March 31, 2008:

Adj. WACC of ECM
$= \{34{,}612*(1-0.422)*4.5\% + 336{,}892*7\%\}/(34{,}612 + 336{,}892) = 6.59\%$

Adj. WACC of HA
$= \{456*(1-0.307)*4.5\% + 96{,}756*7\%\}/(456 + 96{,}756) = 6.98\%$

Adj. WACC of BP
$= \{12{,}297*(1-0.390)*4.5\% + 160{,}523*7\%\}/(12{,}297 + 160{,}523) = 6.70\%$

Adj. WACC of EPM
$= \{3{,}751*(1-0.2775)*4.5\% + 82{,}732*7\%\}/(3{,}751 + 82{,}732) = 6.84\%$

Adj. WACC of AC
$= \{15{,}059*(1-0.383)*4.5\% + 133{,}068*7\%\}/(15{,}059 + 133{,}068) = 6.57\%$

Adj. WACC of others
$= \{16{,}412*(1-0.4076)*4.5\% + 70{,}236*7\%\}/(16{,}412 + 70{,}236) = 6.18\%.$

By using the rate of revision the capital in Table 1, we can calculate the adjusted economic profit (Adj. EC) of each segment, as follows:

Adj. EC of ECM
$= (51{,}129 + 1{,}788 + 50{,}670 + 192{,}145)*(1 + 0.2119) + 446*(1-0.410)*4/5$
$= 358{,}608$ Yen (millions)

Adj. EC of HA
$= (1{,}151 + 25 + 790 + 58{,}490)*(1 + 0.2119) + 0*(1-0.2756)*4/5$
$= 73{,}267$ Yen (millions)

Adj. EC of BP
$= (17{,}789 + 3{,}264 + 28{,}274 + 100{,}284)*(1 + 0.2119) + 5{,}429*(1-0.387)*4/5$
$= 183{,}976$ Yen (millions)

Adj. EC of EPM
$= (10{,}001 + 111 + 3{,}079 + 48{,}603)*(1 + 0.2119) + 1{,}074*(1-0.255)*4/5$
$= 75{,}511$ Yen (millions)

Adj. EC of AC
$= (14{,}062 + 16{,}484 + 7{,}386 + 78{,}215)*(1 + 0.2119) + 1{,}191*(1-0.423)*4/5$
$= 141{,}308$ Yen (millions)

Adj. EC of others
= (6,321 + 30,573 + 2,480 + 39,392) * (1 + 0.2119) + 1,194 * (1–0.3937) * 4/5
= 96,034 Yen (millions).

Finally, the adjusted economic profit (Adj. EP) of each segment is calculated as follows:

As of March 31, 2008:

Adj. EP of ECM = 25,782–358,608 * 6.59% = 2,150 Yen (millions)
Adj. EP of HA = 5,519–73,267 * 6.98% = 455 Yen (millions)
Adj. EP of BP = Δ405–183,976 * 6.70% = Δ12,731 Yen (millions)
Adj. EP of EPM = 5,152–75,511 * 6.84% = Δ13 Yen (millions)
Adj. EP of AC = 9,351–141,308*6.57% = 67 Yen (millions)
Adj. EP of others = 4,984–96,034*6.18% = Δ951 Yen (millions).

Thus, the calculated results using the second method are different from the results using the first method, in that three segments are in the red with the second method.

7. Conclusion

Panasonic Electric Works has been applying the management approach well in advance of the required deadline. It must be possible for us to analyze in detail the direction of decision making and performance of each business segment if we can study cases analogous to this company's case. Unfortunately, we cannot find similar cases in other companies' reports. In this paper, we were able to measure the economic profit especially based on detailed information regarding income and capital of each business segment. There is a capital information system called the "internal capital system" in Japanese management accounting practice. Therefore, in line with the original purpose of the management approach, Japanese companies would do best to disclose the capital information on each of their segments. In this regard, Japanese segment reporting is potentially more advanced.

References

Epstein, B. J. and Jermakowicz, E. K. (2007). *Willey IFPS 2007: International and Application of International Financial Reporting Standards*, John Willey & Sons.

Hiraoka, S. (2005). Valuation and goal growth rate of business segments: The case study of Matsushita Electric Works, Ltd. in *Organization Design and Management Accounting for Corporate Value*, edited by Monden, Y., Zeim-keiri-kyokai, pp. 89–99 (in Japanese).

Hiraoka, S. (2006). Valuation of business based on EVA-type metrics in Japanese companies, in *Value-Based Management of the Rising Sun*, edited by Monden, Y., Miyamoto, K., Hamada, K., Lee, G. and Asada, T, World Scientific, pp. 75–87.

Hiraoka, S. (2007). Changes in the concept of capital and their effects on economic profit in Japan, in *Japanese Management Accounting Today*, edited by Monden, Y., Kosuga, M., Nagasaka, Y., Hiraoka, S. and Hoshi, N., pp. 23–34.

Huefner, R. J., Largay, III., J. A. and Hamlen, S. S. (2007). *Advanced Financial Accounting*, 10th edn., Thompson.

Stewart, III. G. B. (1991). *The Quest for Value: The EVA™ Management Guide*, Harper Business.

Solomons, D. (1965). *Divisional Performance: Measurement and Control*, Financial Executive Research Foundation, New York.

Solomons, D. (1968). Accounting and some proposed solutions, in *Public Reporting by Conglomerates: The Issues, the Problems, and Some Possible Solutions*, edited by Rappaport, A., Peter, A. F. and Stephen, A. Z., pp. 91–104.

Young, S. D. and O'Byrne, S. F. (2001). *EVA® and Value-Based Management: A Practical Guide to Implementation*, McGraw-Hill.

Part 4

Management of Inter-firm Relations

9

How Can Management Accounting Achieve Goal Congruence among Supply Chain Partners?

Yoshiteru Minagawa
Faculty of Commerce, Nagoya Gakuin University

1. Introduction

One of the most consequential changes now rapidly occurring in many markets is the trend toward shorter product life cycles. To overcome this market challenge, it is particularly important that each company, as a partner of a supply chain to which it belongs, creates more effective and efficient information exchange and movement of goods processes within the supply chain. This increases the importance of decision making that involves the selection of a supply chain that companies may wish to join to increase their profits. Thus, competition among supply chains is becoming increasingly fierce in the current business environment.

Companies are motivated to become part of a supply chain to increase their profits by enhancing the performance of the supply chain as a whole (Schary and Skjøtt-Larsen, 2001, p. 29). However, reducing the risks of opportunistic behavior by partners is one of the most critical issues that must be dealt with in establishing an efficient supply chain management system. According to Williamson, opportunistic action is defined as self-interest seeking with guile (Williamson, 1996, p. 6). Guile includes calculated efforts to mislead, distort, disguise, obfuscate or otherwise confuse (Williamson, 1996, p. 378).

Opportunism manifests itself in the form of distortion information or agreement violation in supply chains. Self-interest seeking actions with guile allow partners to receive the benefits from without helping to pay for the cost of performing the business. However, opportunistic behavior by partners results in the failure to enhance the supply chain partnership and its integration. Partners who initially carry out their business prioritizing the increased performance of the supply chain as a whole can subsequently come to behave in an opportunistic manner and create an adverse impact (Jap and Anderson, 2003, p. 1685).

One of the most effective methods for managing opportunism is the promotion of goal congruence. This study will develop an integrated management accounting system (MAS) that can be used to achieve the goal congruence in supply chains and thereby discouraging the opportunistic behavior by partners.

2. Literature Review

2.1. *The SCOR-model*

The Supply-Chain Operations Reference-model (SCOR) was developed in 1996 and upgraded repeatedly for a decade by the Supply-Chain Council, with the aim of achieving a more efficient supply chain collaboration (Supply-Chain Council, 2008).

The SCOR-model is beneficial when standardizing the processes of supply chains (Meyr *et al.*, 2000, p. 38). The SCOR-model is based on the following five core management processes: (1) Plan. Processes for demand and supply balancing to establish the operational activities which best meet sourcing, production, and deliver requirements. (2) Source. Processes associated with procuring goods and services to meet planned or actual demand. (3) Make. Processes that transform raw materials and intermediates to finished products. (4) Deliver. Processes that provide finished goods and services. (5) Return. Processes that return or receive returned products (Supply-Chain Council, 2008). The framework of these five types of management processes has commonality with that of Porter's value chain (Porter, 1985).

The SCOR-model provides some insights into the key success factors of business performance among supply chain partners. That is, the effectiveness and efficiency of a value chain's operational execution with individual partners in a supply chain depends substantially on the level of integration of the supply chain as a whole. Furthermore, the important determinants of an individual partner's profits include increasing the effectiveness and efficiency of each operational function (i.e., sourcing, production, delivery, and return) and enhancing the integration of the value chains comprised of these functions. Moreover, the business performance of a partner within a supply chain is influenced by the degree of effectiveness and efficiency of the other partners' value chains.

2.2. *Inter-firm cost management*

Surviving the competition among supply chains depends on the ability of a supply chain to effectively and efficiently satisfy its own final customers by quickly responding to the changing market. According to Porter (1996), the achievement of sustainable growth by companies necessitates the creation of innovative and low-cost business activities. He adds that the heart of a company's success is the creation and execution of innovative activities required to generate customer value (Porter, 1996).

Activities consume resources (Kaplan and Cooper, 1998). Activity-based costing (ABC) provides managers with an economic map, based on activity-based cost, which illustrates the type and amount of resources consumed by each activity conducted in defined sections of the company. Additionally, under ABC, resource and activity drivers are helpful in establishing more effective and efficient activities and to implementing these activities successfully (Kaplan and Cooper, 1998).

As stated above, the amount of a resource consumed by the activities of an individual partner in a supply chain is determined by how efficiently the activities of the other partners in the supply chain are performed. Therefore, using ABC throughout the entire supply chain is conducive to increasing the performance level of the supply chain as a whole (Kaplan and Anderson, 2007; Cokins, 2001; Dekker and Goor, 2000).

The following section will explain the positive impacts of applying ABC across a supply chain based on Kaplan and Anderson (2007) and Dekker and Goor (2000). Consider a supply chain consisting of two partners: a producer and a retailer. The shipping and receiving activities of the producer and retailer, respectively, form boundary-spanning responsibilities assumed by each of the two companies. This leads to the interactive influence of both the shipping and receiving costs incurred by the producer and retailer. Shifting a method of procurement in a supply chain changes the amount of resources consumed by the producer in shipping as well as that for receiving and stocking by the retailer. In this case, "the method for ordering and receiving" is found to be a common cost driver of shipping and receiving activities for the producer and retailer, respectively.

Based on Kaplan and Anderson (2007, pp. 122–144) and Dekker and Goor (2000), let us suppose that the procurement method in the above-mentioned supply chain is shifted from delivering large quantities of goods at one time to shipping small quantities of goods frequently. Consider in this case how much such a change in the procurement method affects the costs incurred by the producer in shipping the goods and the retailer's receiving activities associated with them. The shifting of the procurement method from shipping large quantities collectively to delivering small quantities frequently results in the increased complexity of shipping in the producer as well as receiving in the retailer, hereby bringing about an increase in the amounts of resources consumed by both activities. Consequently, the total amount of the costs incurred by both the producer and the retailer under the frequent small quantities delivery method exceeds the total of the two companies' incurring costs under the infrequent large quantities shipping. However, when focusing on the retailer's costs of stocking goods, a shift in the procurement method to the frequent small quantities delivery method is helpful to reduce the number of days for stock-keeping, thereby decreasing the retailer's stock-keeping costs.[1]

2.3. *Time-driven activity-based costing*

What motivates companies to be part of a certain supply chain is its potential to effectively and efficiently function the customer-value-creation chains consisting of the activities performed by its partners. To achieve the sustainable growth of supply chains requires, above all, the highly enhanced relevance of their value systems to satisfy their end customers. In tackling this requirement, supply chain partners need information on the time per activity and their costs. This intelligence or information demand made by managers can be well met by time-driven activity-based costing (Kaplan and Anderson, 2007). Therefore, time-driven activity-based costing can contribute to more efficient and effective supply chain management (Kaplan and Anderson, 2007, pp. 133–148).

3. Managing Supply Chain Opportunism

3.1. *Opportunism in supply chains*

Opportunism is divided into two forms: ex ante and ex post opportunism (Williamson, 1985; Wathne and Heide, 2000). Among the former is a deliberate misrepresentation of information during the initiation phase of a new transaction. The latter involves refraining from honoring agreements in the ongoing transactions (Wathne and Heide, 2000).

According to Wathne and Heide (2000), the causes for the emergence of opportunistic behavior by partners include information asymmetry and switching costs. Information asymmetry occurs when sellers possess no information on buyers: sellers are therefore unable to detect buyers' opportunistic behavior. Switching cost-driven opportunism arises in situation in which sellers are economically locked into their relationships with buyers: sellers indulge in tolerating the buyers' opportunistic behavior as long as the losses incurred because of this behavior remain affordable to the sellers (Jap and Anderson, 2003, pp. 42, 43).

Opportunism significantly challenges partners as it can take place under any set of circumstances (e.g., Wathne and Heide, 2000). A point for consideration on the causes of opportunism in supply chains is that business exchanges in a supply chain often generate characteristics that endanger the partnership with the passage of time (Jap and Anderson, 2003, p. 1685). This means that each supply chain is always facing the risk of opportunism.

3.2. *Controlling supply chain opportunism*

This section will conduct a review of the relevant literature wherein the control of opportunism is considered.

Wathne and Heide (2000) represent four different ways to control opportunism. First, more effective monitoring of a partner's behavior and its outcomes contributes to managing opportunism. It is only if information asymmetry exists in a supply chain that partners can continue to act opportunistically without being detected. From this perspective, closer monitoring can increase the ability to detect opportunistic behavior, thereby reducing opportunism (Wathne and Heide, 2000, pp. 43–44).

Second, the incorporation of incentive systems into supply chain management is important in reducing the payoff from opportunism. At the heart of the incentive systems is the building management mechanism, wherein exerting efforts in collaboration with partners to increase the overall performance of supply chains becomes more beneficial to the sustainable growth of individual partners than acting opportunistically. The introduction of the incentive systems to reduce opportunism requires overcoming information asymmetry, and its rationale resides in the following: when information about partners remains unknown due to the existence of information asymmetry, it becomes more difficult to set up an effective reward and penalty system for partners (Wathne and Heide, 2000, pp. 44–45).

Third, according to Wathne and Heide (2000, pp. 45–46), the priori selection of partners who are inherently inclined not to act opportunistically before supply chains commence business is beneficial to managing opportunism. A key to success in the selection strategy is establishing goal congruence, which is the central theme of this study.

Fourth, opportunism in supply chains can be significantly reduced whenever the goal of supply chains as a whole can be well aligned with partners' goals (Wathne and Heide, 2000, pp. 47–48).

Jap and Anderson (2003) propose three ways to reduce opportunistic behavior by partners. First, the promotion of relationship-specific investments by supply chain partners is important to management opportunism (Jap and Anderson, 2003, p. 1687). That is, as partners of a supply chain increase their investments that are specific to other partners of the supply chain, the partnership is solidified. In addition, aligning the goals of the supply chain and the partners can keep the partners from acting opportunistically (Jap and Anderson, 2003, p. 1688). Furthermore, consolidating trust and commitment in supply chains is crucial to increasing the performance of the supply chains as a whole (Jap and Anderson, 2003, p. 1688).

4. Effects of Management Accounting on Goal Congruence in Supply Chains

According to Wathne and Heide (2000), information asymmetry is a cause of opportunistic behavior by exchange partners. As mentioned above, overcoming opportunism involves methods such as monitoring, incentives, selection, and goal congruence (Wathne and Heide, 2000). There are important factors associated with information asymmetry and its influence on opportunism: goal alignment is capable of reducing information asymmetry and information sharing among supply chain partners should, therefore, be encouraged. The theoretical rationale lies in aligning goals in supply chains to increase partner awareness of the effects of the overall supply chain performance on their own profits, which leads partners to willingly commit themselves to sharing information among themselves.

Of the measures to reduce opportunism under information asymmetry as proposed by Wathne and Heide (2000), goal congruence is the most resilient (Wathne and Heide, 2000, p. 47). That is, to the extent that partners' profits become significantly affected by the overall performance of the supply chain and the alignment of individual partners' with the overall supply chain's goals, partners can gain increased pay-offs by engaging in cooperative partnership-based behavior even when they remain unknowledgeable about partners' private information. On the other hand, monitoring and incentives as measures for managing opportunism require private information about partners. Additionally, since supply chain management is directed at encouraging partners to behave in a manner that is consistent with the overall goal of the supply chains, the essential aim of the incentive strategy is to control opportunism by effectively aligning the partners' with the supply chains' goals. Moreover, the important criterion of selecting the partners is based on the ability to collaborate with other partners to maximize the overall profits of the supply chain.

Based on an examination of the capabilities of the above-mentioned measures for managing opportunism, it can be said that goal congruence is the most effective way to overcome information asymmetry. In other words, aligning the goals of a supply chain and its partners promotes information sharing within the supply chain. Information sharing can enhance the functions of monitoring, incentives, and selection.

This study sheds light on the impacts of three management accounting systems — ABC (Kaplan and Cooper, 1998), balanced scorecard (BSC) (Kaplan and Norton, 1996, 2001) and revenue sharing — on goal congruence in supply chains. Prior to the detailed examination on the capabilities of these management accounting approaches to achieve goal congruence, a description of each follows.

First, to develop supply chain focused on customer value creation, it is especially important to effectively manage the boundary-spanning activities of partners. ABC is one of the most important managerial systems for achieving customer-value creation. The introduction of ABC across supply chain partners allows them to learn that an individual partner's activities influence the overall performances of the supply chain as well as the other partners.

Second, a key driver for attaining sustainable growth in supply chains is the use of the BSC for the inter-partner performance management. BSC is effective in the creation and implementation of customer-value focused strategies. Supply chain BSC is instrumental in the creation of a causal relationship between the strategic goals of the supply chain as a whole and the strategic planning by its partners. Consequently, supply chain BSC is substantially helpful for partners to acknowledge that their own profits are affected by the performance of the supply chain as a whole. This means that supply chain BSC encourages the promotion of goal congruence.[2]

Third, sharing the overall financial output profits of supply chains among its partners successfully promotes goal congruence within supply chains.

5. Effects of ABC on Supply Chain Integration

A key success factor in surviving the competition among supply chains is to meet consumer demands quickly and at a low cost. ABC is an effective instrument to achieve quick and efficient consumer satisfaction. To increase overall supply chain profits, it is important to manage the activities and concurrently reassign responsibilities for supply chain functions across partner boundaries. To successfully achieve these, it is critical to calculate activity-based costs. An ABC examination of both boundary-spanning activities and functional shifts within supply chains results in the enhanced combined effects of boundary-spanning activities as well as lessened overall costs.

Furthermore, introducing ABC throughout a supply chain enables its partners to become more aware of the following two requirements to establish excellent supply chain strategies. First, an individual partner's profits are affected by the activities of the other partners. Second, the overall performance of a supply chain is influenced by the activities performed by all of the partners.

Let us suppose a supply chain comprising of a part producer and a finished product producer. Moreover, assume that the part producer has completed the shift from a batch to a one-piece flow production method. This shift in the manufacturing method of the part producer results in changes in the production of the finished product for the end producer. For example, preceding the shift in the production method of the part producer, the activity-based costs of manufacturing for the two partners of the supply chain were commonly affected by batch-level cost drivers. By contrast, the manufacturing costs of both partners are determined by unit-level cost drivers subsequent to the part production method shift.[3]

With ABC data, supply chain managers can evaluate alternatives to the boundary-spanning activities of partners and the supply chain configuration. This means that inter-firm ABC within a supply chain can give rise to enhanced goal congruence.[4]

6. Using the BSC System to Promote Goal Congruence

One of the most significant benefits in participating in a supply chain is its capability to achieve quick customer satisfaction at low cost. Looking at the formulation of an individual firm's strategy, its sustainable growth is determined by the capability of satisfying the final consumer, even though it is engaged in upstream functions far removed from the final consumers. Consequently, the strategy of the entire supply chain is of great importance for the competitive advantage of all the firms, regardless of their role in the supply chain.

To effectively and efficiently achieve customer satisfaction, which is a potential capability of supply chains, it is necessary to establish collaboration and cooperation among the partners. This study focuses on the "alignment of goals between a supply chain and the partner" to encourage the partners to behave in a manner conducive to creating customer value through the supply chain.

As mentioned above, using ABC throughout a supply chain is effective in giving its partners a better understanding of the individual partner's own profits as determined by the other partners' activities and the overall supply chain's performance.

ABC data demonstrates how the partners' profits and the performance of supply chains as a whole are mutually influenced. Moreover, through the participation of supply chain BSC, the partners can better understand that the manner in which they run their own business affects the overall performance of the supply chains. This results in enhanced goal congruence.

The literature review identifies two types of or approaches to supply chain BSC. First, individual partners of a supply chain develop their own BSC, into which the perspectives relating to supply chain strategies and supply chain management are incorporated (e.g., Park *et al.*, 2005). Second, supply chain partners collaborate to establish an integrated BSC for the performance of the supply chain as a whole (e.g., Zimmermann, 2002).

Supply chain management associated with BSC is instrumental in creating a supply chain focused on customer value creation through a collaborative partnership. In supply chain BSC, all partners jointly establish the key success factors toward creating customer value, followed by setting up performance indicators as well as their targeted values for these factors. What should not be overlooked is that the establishment of strategies is identical to developing adaptive business measures that forecast a transformation in a business environment: therefore, it is likely that strategies will need to be amended to counteract unforeseen transformations in a business environment.

Supply chain BSC thrives on the creation of new strategies to successfully adapt to changes in business environments through the evaluation of performance by means of variances between actual and targeted values for strategic goals. Analyses of variances on strategic goals in BSC enable the rise of two types of signals. First, BSC generates signals indicating that the previously determined key performance in achieving the strategic goals is no longer effective in the successful execution of existing strategies. With these signals, supply chain managers can effectively amend both their tactics and key performance indicators. Second, BSC signals warn of existing strategies that have failed in continuing to enjoy competitive advantages because of drastic changes in the business environment. In this case, managers are required to create and deploy strategies that can lead to increased performance even in the face of a market shift.

Financial goals require the specific monitoring of "strategy malfunctions" to enable targeted strategic executions over a period, which are divided by the estimated overall periods for the execution of strategies. Its positive effects reside in its ability to implement phased monitoring on the deployment of strategies using analyses of variances on strategic goals over a period. A financial goal that can satisfy the requirement is a targeted cash flow of the supply chains as a whole throughout the duration of a targeted strategic execution (see Fig. 1).[5]

7. Revenue Sharing in Supply Chains

7.1. *Precedence in studies*

Sharing the overall revenue of a supply chain as a whole among its partners is conducive to the promotion of aligning individual partners' goals with the overall supply chain's goals. To actually obtain the positive effects of revenue sharing in a supply chain on goal congruence, it is essential to determine a way of accurately capturing how much effort individual partners have exerted toward enhancing value for the customers targeted by the supply chain. Thus, one of the most rational methods of deciding how to allocate the overall revenue of a supply chain to its partners is revenue sharing based on each partner's weighted overall consumed resource costs or invested capital in relation to the individual partners' investment

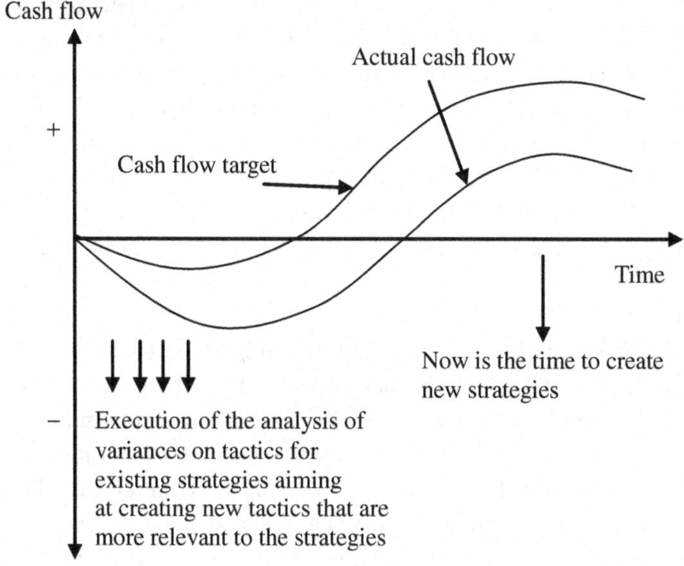

Fig. 1. Variation analysis for creating new strategies.

contributions toward the total supply chain profit (e.g., Jap, 2001; Coughlan *et al.*, 2001).

Coughlan *et al.* (2001) propose a promising method for allocating the overall profits of a marketing channel to its members. The key components of the method are outlined as follows. First, the costs of performing individual activities in the entire marketing channel as a proportion of total channel cost are calculated. Second, the customer value generated through the performance of each marketing activity is determined. Third, each marketing activity's weighted proportional cost with its value added is measured as "cost-value weight." Fourth, each channel member's weighted average cost-value as summing up the cost-value weight of activities performed by individual members is determined. Last, based on the weighted average cost-value, the allocation of the entire marketing channel profit — as calculated from the total revenue minus all costs of running the channels — to members is executed (Coughlan *et al.*, 2001).

There have been improvements on the above-mentioned allocation of total profit of a marketing channel as expounded by Coughlan *et al.* (2001). First, according to Coughlan *et al.* (2001), ABC must be used in calculating the costs of partners' activities as a component of the allocation of the entire profits of a supply chain.[6] Using ABC throughout the entire supply chain can generate the costs of all activities performed by the partners. Such ABC data within the supply chain enable the supply chain managers to correctly decide which partners to engage for certain activities as well as how to perform certain activities to increase the profits of the entire supply chain. This activity map is a good tool for estimating ABC. The estimated ABC refers to standard ABC. It is important to use the standard ABC when allocating the overall performance of the supply chain.

Second, it is not the total profit of a supply chain that is the financial output to be distributed to the partners. Rather, the entire revenue of a supply chain ought to be shared among its partners. Consider a supply chain that adopts profit sharing. Let us also assume that a partner of the supply chain succeeded in reducing the costs and increasing the profits accordingly. However, profit sharing leads the partner to receive only a fraction of the increased profit, thereby generating disincentives to invest in further cost reduction efforts. In contrast, revenue sharing does not diminish the motivation for partners to decrease their costs.[7]

7.2. *Revenue sharing based on ABC*

This section explains the means to allocate revenue using ABC data in supply chains — a method based partly on Coughlan *et al.* (2001). The issue of what part of the overall revenue or profit of a supply chain ought to be shared among the partners is not considered. First, interpartner ABC in supply chains generates standard ABC for all the activities performed by the partners as a whole. In addition, all the partners in the supply chain cooperate to decide the amount of the incremental final sales to be obtained by incurring a unit standard activity-based cost. The degree of the unit activity-based cost's contribution to the increase in final sales in supply chains needs to be measured for all activities. Second, the weighted standard ABC along with the contribution rate of the unit standard ABC to final sales in supply chains is calculated. Third, individual partners calculate their total value of the weighted standard ABC. Last, individual partners obtain their own shares of the overall supply chain revenue in proportion to their total value of the weighted standard ABC.

There is an alternative method to the above-mentioned revenue sharing of the ABC method. Activity analysis is a process of ABC systems that can identify customer value-adding and non-value-adding activities. It is conceivable to share the entire revenue of a supply chain among its partners exclusively based on the overall cost of value-adding activities in participating firms while discarding the non-value-adding activities' costs. This revenue sharing method first measures the standard activity-based cost for supply chain activities including value-adding and non-value-adding ones, and then focuses on specific value-adding activities to establish the total standard activity-based costs of value-adding activities for individual partners. Last, each partner earns its share of the entire supply chain revenue based on its total standard activity-based costs of value-adding activities.

8. Concluding Remarks

Reducing the risks associated with opportunistic behavior of partners is one of the critical issues to be solved to achieve efficient supply chain management. One of the most important means of managing opportunism is the promotion of goal congruence. This study developed an integrated Management Accounting (MA) system that can be used to achieve the goal congruence in supply chains and thereby discourage the opportunistic behavior by partners. The integrated MA system which the study explained comprises of ABC, BSC, and revenue sharing.

Endnotes

1. The discussion on the impacts of the change of order system on activity based costs of shipping, receiving, and stocking here is based on Kaplan and Anderson (2007) and Dekker and Goor (2000).
2. The discussion on BSC here is based on Kaplan and Norton (1996) and Kaplan and Norton (2001).
3. As for batch-level and unit-level cost drivers, see Kaplan and Cooper (1998).
4. The discussion on ABC here is based on Kaplan and Cooper (1998).
5. The discussion on BSC here is based on Kaplan and Norton (1996) and Kaplan and Norton (2001).
6. Coughlan *et al.* (2001) stress the importance of using ABC.
7. As for the adverse effects of profit sharing on cost reduction, see Sappington and Weisman (1996, pp. 232–233).

References

Cokins, G. (2001). Measuring costs across the supply chain, *Cost Engineering*, 43(10), 25–31.

Coughlan, A. T., Stern, L. W., Anderson, E. and El-Ansary, A. I. (2001) *Marketing Channels*, 6th edn., Prentice Hall.

Dekker, H. C. and Goor, A. R. V. (2000). Supply chain management and management accounting: A case study of activity-based costing, *International Journal of Logistics: Research and Applications*, 3(1), 41–52.

Jap, S. D. (2001). "Pie sharing" in complex collaboration contexts, *Journal of Marketing Research*, 38, 86–99.

Jap, S. D. and Anderson, E. (2003). Safeguarding interorganizational performance and continuity under ex post opportunism, *Management Science*, 49(12), 1684–1701.

Kaplan, R. S. and Anderson, S. R. (2007). *Time-Driven Activity-Based Costing: A Simple and More Powerful Path to Higher Profits*, Harvard Business School Press.

Kaplan, R. S. and Cooper, R. (1998). *Cost & Effect: Using Integrated Cost Systems to Drive Profitability and Performance*, Harvard Business School Press.

Kaplan, R. S. and Norton, D. P. (1996). *The Balanced Scorecard: Translating Strategy into Action*, Harvard Business School Press.

Kaplan, R. S. and Norton, D. P. (2001). *The Strategy-Focused Organization: How Balanced Scorecard Companies Thrive in the New Business Environment*, Harvard Business School Press.

Meyr, H., Rohde, J., Stadtler, H. and Surie, C. (2000). Supply chain analysis, in *Supply Chain Management and Advanced Planning*, edited by Stadtler, H. and Kilger, C., Springer, pp. 29–56.

Park, J. H., Lee, J. K. and Yoo, J. S. (2005). A framework for designing the balanced supply chain scorecard, *European Journal of Information Systems*, 14, 335–346.

Porter, M. E. (1985). *Competitive Advantage: Creating and Sustaining Superior Performance*, The Free Press, New York.

Porter, M. E. (1996). What is a strategy?, *Harvard Business Review*, November–December, pp. 61–78.

Sappington, D. E. M. and Weisman, D. L. (1996). Revenue sharing in incentive regulation plans, *Information Economics & Policy*, 8(3), 229–248.

Schary, P. B. and Skjøtt-Larsen, T. (2001). *Managing the Global Supply Chain*, Copenhagen Business School Press.

Supply-Chain Council (2008). *Homepage*, URL:http://www.supply-chain.org, 2008, August.

Wathne, K. H. and Heide, J. B. (2000). Opportunism in interfirm relationships: Forms, outcomes, and solutions, *Journal of Marketing*, 64, 36–51.

Williamson, O. E. (1985). *The Economic Institutions of Capitalism*, Free Press.

Williamson, O. E. (1996). *The Mechanisms of Governance*, Oxford University Press.

Zimmermann, K. (2002). Using the balanced scorecard for interorganizational performance management of supply chain — A case study, in *Cost Management in Supply Chains*, edited by Seuring, S. and Goldbach, M., pp. 363–380.

10

How to Maintain the Bargaining Position Defined in Toyota's Dealership Control?

Hiroshi Ozawa
Graduate School of Economics, Nagoya University

1. Introduction

Toyota Motor Corporation's Just-In-Time (JIT) production system with its catchphrase "producing what is needed, when it is needed, and in the quantity needed" as introduced as a production system that does not retain inventory and reduce costs. When implementing JIT, it is commonly understood that constructing a flexible production system that can respond to demand uncertainties and changes is essential.[1] Alternatively, by turning our attention to the *Keiretsu* that are unique to Japanese companies, the common explanation is that JIT is but an expression of the same thing that is implemented at the expense of affiliated parts manufacturers, and that it cannot be implemented without the existence of superior affiliated parts manufacturers.[2]

These explanations are not wrong but they only explain a part of JIT and are incomplete. This is because these explanations do not take into consideration important constraints that are inherently found in almost all production systems. Production systems require large sums of investment and are made up of many workers. So once money is invested, it is not possible to change the production volume freely. At the very least, it is impossible to completely cater to the large fluctuations in demand every season. If we wish to do so, we have to build up the production capacity in line with the estimated maximum demand volume. As a result, during periods of off-peak demand, most of the production capacity is left idle and this increases costs substantially. Affiliated parts manufacturers are in the same situation because they belong to the same industry. So if costs of parts increase, product costs will also have to increase. Assume that despite the increase in the cost of the parts, if the parts manufacturers were to sacrifice themselves and supply the parts at low costs, it would not be possible to maintain long-term affiliated business relationships within the *Keiretsu*.

Hence, because of demand uncertainties and fluctuations, we cannot have both zero inventory and reduced costs. The only exception, where we are able to have both zero inventory and cost reduction, is when the demand is certain and does not fluctuate. As a matter of fact, Toyota is able to implement JIT production because it has a system that stabilizes demand through its distributors. This is the point this thesis is advocating here. However, many theses have thus far focused only on upstream parts manufacturers, and almost none have paid attention to the presence and roles of distributors that exist between Toyota and the market. In this thesis, we shall focus on the relationship between Toyota and its distributors and explain the JIT system.

2. Framework: Production Quantity Budget and Sales Quantity Budget in Toyota

To understand the actual situation of JIT in Toyota, we have to first understand the production plan as well as the sales plan and demand forecast which it is based on. For this purpose, it is necessary to explain the method of preparing the budget, which is seldom explained in management accounting textbooks. This budget preparation method is the framework behind understanding the role of distributors and the distributor management method in Toyota.

With regard to preparing the budget, in general management accounting textbooks, the number of units that should be produced is calculated by adding the target ending finished goods inventory (units) to budget sales (units) which is the base, and then subtracting the beginning finished goods inventory (units) from it.[3] This explanation is based on the assumption that sales are exogenous variables that cannot be controlled by companies. Hence, as this budget will eventually be used to calculate the production unit, it is referred to as the production quantity budget in this thesis.

$$\begin{array}{c}\text{Budget}\\\text{sales}\\\text{(units)}\end{array} + \begin{array}{c}\text{Target ending}\\\text{finished goods}\\\text{inventory}\\\text{(units)}\end{array} - \begin{array}{c}\text{Beginning}\\\text{finished goods}\\\text{inventory}\\\text{(units)}\end{array} = \begin{array}{c}\text{Budgeted}\\\text{production}\\\text{(units)}\end{array}$$

In contrast, there is another budget that is not explained in general textbooks. This is the budget that calculates the target sales (units) by adding beginning order backlog (units) to and subtracting the target ending order backlog (units) from the expected order (units) based on demand forecast as displayed in the following equation.

$$\begin{matrix}\text{Expected} \\ \text{order} \\ \text{(units)}\end{matrix} + \begin{matrix}\text{Beginning} \\ \text{order backlog} \\ \text{(units)}\end{matrix} - \begin{matrix}\text{Target ending} \\ \text{order backlog} \\ \text{(units)}\end{matrix} = \begin{matrix}\text{Budgeted} \\ \text{sales} \\ \text{(units)}\end{matrix}$$

The budgeted sales unit is known as the "actual demand" and refers to the demands that have to be met in this period out of the total demand. In addition, as this budget will eventually be used to calculate the sales quantity, it is referred to as the sales quantity budget in this thesis. Due to the time difference that exists between occurrence of car demand and car sales, the sales quantity budget can be used in industries where companies have the room to control sales by making use of this time difference. The above equation expresses the time difference between the order (demand) and the sales as order backlogs.

Also, the sales quantity budget and production quantity budget are combined via the budgeted sales (units).

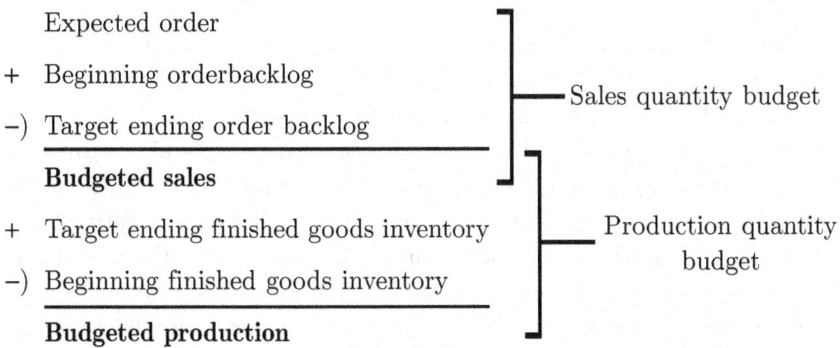

Next, to realize JIT, the management process consists of two phases. The first phase is the order backlog control phase, where the sales quantity budget is used (Fig. 1a). In this phase, the aim of the management

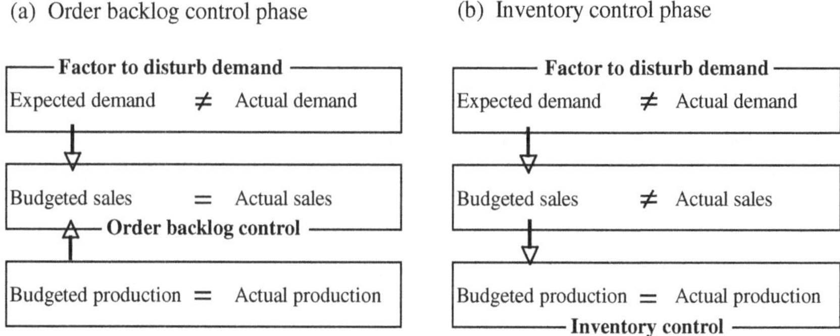

Fig. 1. Order backlog control and inventory control.

process is to make use of order backlogs to cope with demand uncertainty and achieve budgeted sales (units) = actual sales (units). If the budgeted sales units can be correctly achieved, there is no need to change the production plan midway and the production plan can be expected to progress only according to the budget. In other words, the production quantity budget and the flexible budget based on it, both of which are explained in management accounting textbooks, are unnecessary. In addition, in this phase, the budgeted sales unit will not be based on demand forecast but on production capacity, and will be decided at a level where production capacity can be most efficiently deployed.

Another thing to mention is the case whereby it is not possible to execute order backlogs control due to insufficient orders. The production quantity budget will be used in the inventory control phase. (Fig. 1b). In the case whereby the budgeted sales (units) ≠ actual sales (units), the aim is to adjust the inventory and production unit to maximize the profits. Therefore in this case, production capacity does not always have to operate efficiently.

In this way, if order (demand) is made an exogenetic variable and production capacity an endogenous variable, then it is clear that there is no room for control except to increase or decrease the order backlog and inventory. Given this, order backlog and inventory, which are important elements that stabilize production, will not be controlled by Toyota itself but by its distributors. If this is the case, then Toyota's management of distributors is an important element that supports JIT, and we will not be able to understand JIT by ignoring it.

3. Example Relating to Production Quantity Budget and Order Quantity Budget[4]

Figure 2 shows Toyota's sales quantity budget and the actual results in a given year.[5] As the actual units cannot be released, the budget values in the first month of Term 1 are relatively taken to be 100%. This will apply to all graphs henceforth. As there are times whereby the data cannot be obtained, the graph is divided into two terms (Term 1 and Term 2). Although it is a pity that the data set is incomplete, these two terms clearly show the above-mentioned two phases, which stabilize the production.

From the graph, we see that the budgeted units and actual units are almost the same in Term 1. In contrast, in Term 2, the budgeted units and actual units are wide apart. If we apply the above-mentioned two phases, order backlog control and inventory control, then Term 1 will belong to the order backlog control phase, and Term 2 will belong to the inventory control phrase.

To confirm this, let's look at the changes in order backlog and inventory. The change in order backlog is shown in Fig. 3. In Term 1, there is much order backlog but it is slowly declining. In Term 2, it is clear that the order backlog is near zero. The change in inventory is shown in Fig. 4. In Term 1, there is low inventory volume while in Term 2 the inventory is on the increase. This is because Term 1 is in the order backlog control phase while Term 2 is in the inventory control phase.

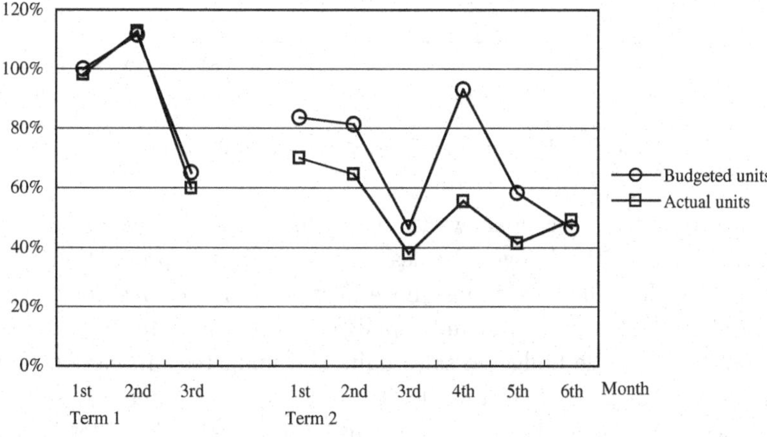

Fig. 2. Budgeted and actual units sales.

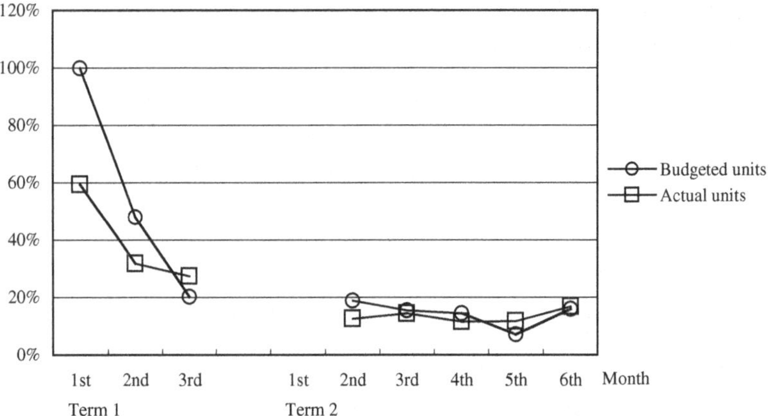

Fig. 3. Budgeted and actual units of order backlogs.

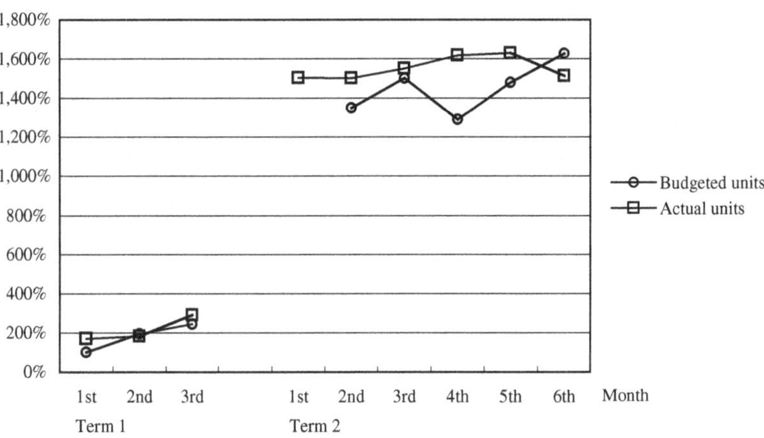

Fig. 4. Budgeted and actual units of inventories.

On top of that, Fig. 5 shows the budgeted units of sales and production. In Term 1, the budgeted sales units = budgeted production units. This shows that there is almost no adjustment of the inventory, which means that the production quantity budget was not used. In Term 2, there is a gap between the budgeted sales units and budgeted production units. Looking at Figs. 2 and 3 as a whole, it is clear that the difference is due to inventory adjustment. This is also because Term 1 is in the order backlog control phase and Term 2 is in the inventory control phase.

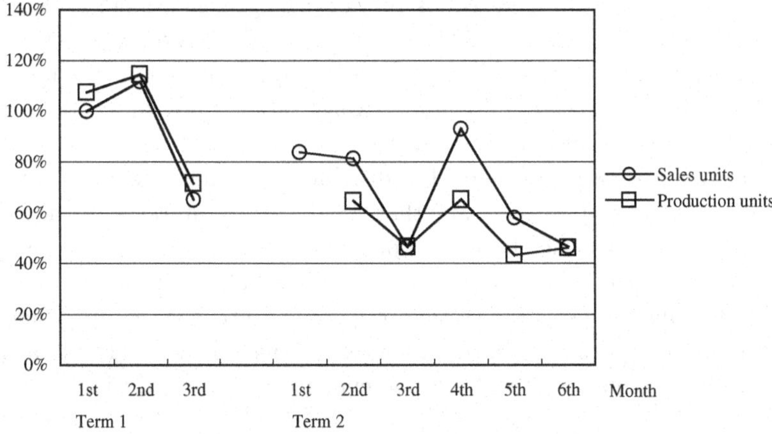

Fig. 5. Budgeted units of sales and production.[6]

4. Management of Toyota's Distributors in Japan

Toyota's production system is a mass production system. It is an order placement production that is unlike the production system of consumer electronics products. Distributors will place orders with Toyota and Toyota, upon receiving the orders, will start production. Normally, about 30–60 days are needed between order placement and completion of production. During this period, it will have to keep the customers waiting. To shorten the waiting time for customers, distributors will have to first place orders with Toyota based on forecast before receiving the orders from customers. It is the responsibility of distributors to judge whether to make the customers wait and then sell the cars or take on the risks and place orders based on the forecast.[7]

In other words, the responsibility of forecasting demand, and controlling order placement and inventory levels, does not rest on Toyota but on its affiliated distributors. The distributors have direct contact with its users, so they understand the market well and can quickly detect market changes. This makes them well suited to proactively respond to the market conditions when needed. However, what Toyota wishes of its distributors is not for them to report the evolving market trends to its production side, but to alleviate seasonal demand fluctuations and demand forecast uncertainties so that it can maintain a stable production.

Thus, Toyota established the distributor management system so that its distributors can achieve this. This system is based on two principles. The first principle is to limit, as far as possible, the range of actions distributors can take. If there are multiple options which distributors can choose from and take action, then what the distributors want will not match what Toyota wants. Hence, to ensure that distributors do not take actions that will harm Toyota, it is necessary that Toyota set limitations in the first place. The second principle of distributor management is to regulate the weakness and strengths of the actions of distributors within the limited range of available options. For this purpose, Toyota has set up different kinds of incentive systems. In the following, we shall introduce Toyota's distributor management system with reference to these two principles.

4.1. *Business structure that enables tight control*

To restrict the operations of distributors, Toyota established the monopoly system, franchise system and one region, one distributor system.

4.1.1. *Monopoly system*

Toyota's distributors only handle Toyota's products and no other companies' products. In Japan, besides Toyota, Nissan and Honda also have their own sales routes and this is considered normal. Contrast this sales method with, for example, the sales of consumer electronics products whereby products from different manufacturers are sold under the same shop.

If distributors also sell other companies' products besides that of Toyota, then they will actively sell products that bring them the greatest profits.[8] In this case, Toyota will need to approach distributors to sell its own products aggressively by acceding to their demands for an increase in sales commission, and a shorter delivery period. When this happens, distributors will no longer contribute to the stable production of Toyota. Rather they will make demands of Toyota, and disturb Toyota. This is why Toyota prohibits its distributors to sell other companies' cars and wants them to sell only its own Toyota cars.

4.1.2. *Franchise system*

Toyota builds its sales network based on the franchise system. This means that by establishing distributors in corporate entities that do not have capital ties with Toyota and separating their management from Toyota's business, it ensures that the performance of the distributors do not affect the performance of Toyota. In contrast, Nissan builds its sales network focusing on direct distributors. In the case of direct sales, the merit is that the policies of the top management are directly passed down to the sales department and executed. However, on the flip side, because the performance of the production department and the results of the sales department will ultimately make up the total sales performance of the company, the sales department has the opportunity to state their views and possesses negotiation power. As a result, it is difficult to follow the production logic alone to carry out efficient production.

In addition, in many cases, distributors of Toyota that are part of the franchise system, such as influential oil companies and transportation companies in different regions, manage the sales of the car as part of their business. Thus, they have more financial power. In contrast, in Honda's case, despite adopting a franchise system, the distributors in the franchise system are mostly former bicycle shops and car repair workshops that do not have much financial muscle. As a result, Honda's distributors do not have the ability to take on anything but their own risks, and therefore function only as "agents".

4.1.3. *One region, one distributor system*

Toyota Motor's distribution channels in Japan can be divided into five groups according to car types. In principle, in each of the groups, only one distributor is established in each region. In other words, company X is the only company that sells type A cars in a certain region. If there are several distributors (for example, companies X and Y) that sell the same type of car in the same region, companies X and Y will compete over the same customer. Competition among the distributors may make the customers happy but it only impoverishes the companies and does not bring any benefits to Toyota.

In addition, competing distributors may feel reluctant to provide accurate sales and inventory information to Toyota, being wary of the other distributors obtaining such information. It is also highly probable that such distributors negotiate with Toyota with the intention of obtaining a better contract with Toyota than those of other distributors in the same region.[9] In actual fact, by implementing the one region, one sales system, Toyota has succeeded in correctly grasping the orders and sales trends of the distributors.

In addition, because orders that are not confirmed are included in the order demand forecasts, the accuracy of the forecast is irrevocably reduced. Even though the existence of uncertainties arising from competition with other manufacturers cannot be avoided, the accuracy of the forecast is improved through the one region, one distributor system.

4.2. *Control of distributors through incentives*

Even though Toyota can avoid risks of demand uncertainties by having its distributors bear the risks, nevertheless, by doing so, it is not fully sufficient for stable production. As demand fluctuates according to seasons, it is necessary to alleviate and average out the fluctuations. Hence, despite the use of order backlog and inventory, Toyota also uses sales incentives and adopts the product allocation policy as incentives to spur distributors to get orders and retain inventory.

In addition, the source of Toyota's negotiation power with its distributors is built on a relationship whereby Toyota is in a position to provide the products that the distributors hope to sell. In other words, if distributors have the inventory and do not wish for Toyota to supply any more products, Toyota will not have any influence over them and cannot control them. The structure of the incentive is designed in full consideration of this point.

4.2.1. *Sales incentive*

The most typical incentive is the sales incentive. Toyota gives incentives to its distributors for product sales during times of weak demand or even during times booming demand when they should compete with other companies for customers, and increases order backlog.[10] The distributors can use the incentives to offer price discounts or launch advertisements.

The important point to understanding the relationship between Toyota and distributors here is that Toyota does not reduce the invoice price but rewards the distributors for actual sales. If Toyota did not provide any form of encouragement to its distributors, the unit of orders the distributors placed with Toyota would always be similar to the unit of orders users placed with distributors. However, if Toyota reduces the invoice price, it will be possible for distributors to place a higher unit of orders with Toyota as compared to the orders received from users. This is because distributors know that demand fluctuation is seasonal and they believe in placing orders in large volumes in times when products can be cheaply purchased. By keeping the goods in inventory and selling them off during times of high demand, distributors can earn higher profits.

Next, we shall talk about negotiation power which can be explained as follows. If distributors wish to have negotiation power with Toyota, it is always better that they place orders that are slightly below the supply capacity of Toyota. When sales are low, they should place orders that are less than the units supplied by Toyota and retain them as inventory. And when sales are high, distributors can liquidate inventories and channel them to sales, and also place orders that are below the units supplied by Toyota. So if distributors possess negotiation power in this manner, the order units placed by distributors will be decided without any relation to the user demand trends, and requests for a decrease in invoice price will occur. Thus, from Toyota's standpoint, having its distributors leave order backlog and supplying fewer units that distributors desire is needed to maintain its negotiation power.

Therefore, sales incentive is used as a reward for the number of units purchased by users, and this drives the demand of the users not the distributors. As a result, the number of orders placed by distributors with Toyota is similar to the orders placed by users with distributors. This will enable Toyota to maintain its negotiation power while ensuring that the distributors take up the products in a stable manner.

4.2.2. *Product allocation policy*

As mentioned, the type of products that distributors handle is decided by Toyota. Distributors have to increase the sales and profits within a limited range of products and, therefore, they wish to actively sell products with large profit margins, and products that are popular and easy to sell. Offering those products that are highly demanded by distributors is how Toyota controls the distributors.

For example, even for popular products, there are seasonal fluctuations in demand. In addition, even for unpopular products, to maintain stable production, there are situations whereby Toyota has to produce more products than distributors wish to have. In this case, Toyota will allocate popular products first, even in times of brisk demand, to distributors that ordered a lot during times of weak demand. Or Toyota will adopt the method of allocating more of the popular products to distributors that took up the unpopular products. In this way, Toyota can enjoy stable order placements from its distributors.

5. Summary

This thesis explains the essential role distributors play in alleviating demand uncertainties and fluctuations in order for Toyota to implement JIT, and the methods of control used by Toyota on its distributors.

If Toyota's management of its distributors in Japan is an important element that supports JIT, this would mean that other automobile manufacturers and manufacturing firms, which hope to learn from Toyota, have to face the difficult problem of maintaining a distribution system for the realization of JIT. For example, it may be difficult to realize JIT in the market where customers demand prompt delivery of products.

Nevertheless, we have pointed out in this thesis that the key to realizing JIT lies not in relying on the flexibility of the production system or on the parts manufacturer, but in a stable production backed by the alleviation of demand uncertainties and fluctuations. We believe that this will, at the very least, direct companies' efforts in the correct direction.

Acknowledgments

This work was supported by MEXT. Grant-in-Aid for Young Scientists (B) 21730297.

Endnotes

1. In this thesis, "uncertainty" refers to grasping the phenomenon only probabilistically due to a lack of information. "Change" is where the phenomenon which one wishes to grasp is a dynamic phenomenon. Even for a dynamic phenomenon, if we can predict the shifts in the phenomenon completely, then the phenomenon will not be uncertain.
2. Asanuma (1997) refers to this as Risk Shifting Hypothesis (RSH).
3. For example, Horngren *et al.* (2008).
4. In this section, information from Ozawa (2002a, b) is reorganized according to the framework of this thesis.
5. Created from sales data related to car model X sold and manufactured only in Japan, and production data relating to production line which manufactures only car model X.
6. Although we see that there are major fluctuations in production units every month, this is a result of the differences in monthly operational days. The monthly operational rate is approximately 80–85% in Term 1, 90–96% in Term 2. In addition, between Term 1 and Term 2, large-scale adjustment which halved the production capacity was carried out.

7. To reduce the risk of such distributors, the "season order" and "daily order" methods of ordering is adopted. This is an order method that will decide on the specification details in stages. For example, the car model is decided 30–60 days beforehand, and the engine is decided 30 days beforehand. This is followed in sequential order, starting from color, seats, and grade, which are decided 10 days beforehand. Five days beforehand, the order will be placed (Ozawa, 2002b).
8. This behavioral principle is known as equal compensation principle (Milgrom and Roberts, 1992).
9. This kind of negotiation between consumer electronics retailers and manufacturer is introduced in NIKKEI Business (2000).
10. There are various ways to design incentives including incentive per sales unit and incentive per market share within region.

References

Asanuma, B. (1997). *Mechanism of Reformative Adaptation Defined in Japanese Corporate Organization*, Toyo Keizai (in Japanese).

Horngren, C. T., Dater, S. M., Foster, G., Rajan, M., and Ittner, C. (2008). *Cost Accounting: A Managerial Emphasis*, 13th edn., Pearson Education.

Milgrom, R. and Roberts, J. (1992). *Economics, Organization & Management*, Prentice-Hall.

NIKKEI BUSINESS (ed). (2000). *Nobody Needs These Management Methods*, NIKKEI BP (in Japanese).

Ozawa, H. (2002a). Stable production and dealer management in just-in-time, *Collected Papers of AAAA in Nagoya.*

Ozawa, H. (2002b). Roles of Toyota dealerships in JIT, *The Journal of Cost Accounting Research*, 26(2) (in Japanese).

11

Royalties and Profit Sharing: Focusing on Seven-Eleven Japan Co., Ltd.

Noriko Hoshi
Faculty of Business Administration, Hakuoh University

1. Introduction

Regarding the basis of the royalty calculation used for franchise agreements in the convenience-store business, the largest number of companies uses gross profit or gross profit on sales. According to "Franchise Chains in Japan 2006" (Shogyokai, 2006), as the basis of the royalty calculation, the above gross profit or gross profit on sales is being used by 16 retailers (13.1%) out of 122 convenience-store chains, supermarket chains and other food retailers, and among those 16 retailers, most (13 retailers) are convenience-store chains. Of the 13 convenience-store chains, 10 chains use gross profit and 3 chains use gross profit on sales as the basis of royalty calculations.

In general, gross profit and gross profit on sales are taken as having the same meaning. However, when these two terms are used as the bases of royalty calculations in the convenience-store business, "gross profit on sales" means gross profit + amount of loss. At convenience stores, daily dishes, including packed lunches, are discarded after the expiration dates. In general, the prime costs for the discarded goods, called the " loss", are entirely borne by the franchise store, although at some franchise chains the franchiser bears a part thereof. What would be the reason for the inclusion of the amount of loss in the data used to calculate the royalty? This paper examines this issue and the ideal basis of royalty calculations.

2. Convenience-Store Royalties

2.1. *Mechanism of the franchise system*

The Japan Franchise Association defines a franchise as follows: "a continuing relationship between one entity (called the 'franchiser') and another entity (called the 'franchisee'), where a franchiser and a franchisee enter into an agreement, the franchiser granting the franchisee the right to use the signs representing the franchiser's business, which signs include the franchiser's logo, service mark, trade name and others as well as the franchiser's management know-how, and to conduct product sales and other businesses which bear the same image as the franchiser's, the franchisee paying a consideration therefor to the franchiser in return, providing the funds required for the business, and operating the business under the franchiser's guidance and assistance".

According to the JFA definition, a franchiser grants a franchisee the rights listed below:

(1) The right to use the franchiser's logo, service mark, and trade name;
(2) The right to use the franchiser's management know-how, including the products, services, and proprietary information developed by the franchiser; and
(3) The right to obtain continuous guidance and assistance provided by the franchiser.

These concessions are collectively called a "package"; the franchisee uses the package and pays a fee in consideration thereof. This consideration is called a "royalty".

A franchisee appears to be a branch of the franchiser, since both use the same logo and trade name, but in fact the two are independent entities. They are a "joint venture," in which each party fulfills each task imposed on it to share the profit from the venture.

2.2. *The bases of the royalty calculation*

In general, there are three bases of calculation of the royalty paid by the franchisee to the franchiser: (1) the sales amount, (2) the gross profit, and (3) the flat-rate system. A method of royalty calculation frequently used by the convenience-store business is that in which the gross profit is multiplied by a certain rate. The meaning of "gross profit" used in the convenience-store business differs slightly from that used generally. "Gross profit" in general means the sales amount after the deduction of the cost of goods sold, that is, the gross profit on sales as shown in the following expression:

$$\begin{aligned}\text{Gross profit} &= \text{gross profit on sales}\\ &= \text{sales amount} - \text{cost of goods sold.} \qquad (1)\end{aligned}$$

However, "gross profit" in the convenience-store business is understood as the gross profit on sales after the addition of both the prime cost for the food products discarded after expiry and the amount of loss from inventory, as shown in the following expression:

$$\begin{aligned}\text{Gross profit} &= \text{gross profit on sales} + \text{amount of loss}\\ &= \text{sales amount} - \text{cost of goods sold} + \text{amount of loss}\\ &= \text{sales amount} - (\text{cost of goods sold} - \text{amount of loss}). \qquad (2)\end{aligned}$$

In many convenience stores, the amount of royalty is determined by the gross profit multiplied by a certain rate.

3. Sales Cost and Amount of Loss

3.1. *Relationship between the cost of goods sold and the amount of loss*

The cost of goods sold is the cost of the goods purchased corresponding to the amount of sales, as shown in the following expression:

$$\begin{aligned}\text{Cost of goods sold} &= \text{opening inventory of goods}\\ &\quad + \text{current-term amount of goods purchased}\\ &\quad - \text{closing inventory of goods.} \qquad (3)\end{aligned}$$

Furthermore, the cost of goods sold may include the appraisal loss of goods that occurs when the market value of the goods conspicuously and irreparably falls when the cost-or-market-whichever-is-lower basis is adopted, or when the inventory shrinks in ordinary activity.

The amount of loss applied to the convenience-store business consists of the cost of goods discarded after expiry and inventory shrinkage. In accounting, this amount of loss is generally considered to be the cost of goods sold, and is included in the cost of goods sold and deducted from the amount of sales when the gross profit on sales is calculated. That is, the cost of goods sold shown in Expression (1) includes the amount of loss.

However, business accounting allows the amount of loss to be treated as a business expense, instead of its inclusion in the cost of goods sold.

3.2 *Dissatisfaction of franchisees with the accounting treatment of the amount of loss*

As mentioned above, the cost of goods sold applied to the convenience-store business excludes the amount of loss, and the gross profit is calculated as shown in Expression (2). The amount of loss excluded from the cost of goods sold is treated as a business expense. Since this method of accounting greatly differs from the generally adopted method shown in Expression (1), it is frequently raised as a point of contention in lawsuits concerning franchise agreements. In concrete terms, if the royalty is determined by the gross profit in Equation (2) multiplied by a certain rate, it means that the royalty is also imposed on the amount of loss, and franchisees consequently incur great costs. Franchisees maintain that it is unreasonable to impose a royalty on the cost of goods after expiry and inventory shrinkage.

However, in spite of the lawsuits filed by franchisees in regard to the amount of loss, the courts have never accepted the franchisees' arguments. Any franchise agreement in the convenience-store business provides that the amount of loss shall be included in the business expenses and that the franchisee shall incur any business expenses. Accordingly, the above provision can be interpreted to mean that the amount of loss is included in the gross profit; thus, the franchisees' arguments have never been accepted (Kondo, 2008).

In other words, since the above is stipulated in the agreement, even if the franchisees are dissatisfied with the fact that the amount of loss is included in the gross profit on sales instead of the cost of goods sold and consequently file lawsuits, the franchise agreement for convenience stores is interpreted as legal.

4. Gross-Profit Sharing System for Convenience Stores

The first Japanese convenience store that adopted the gross profit as the basis of royalty calculations was York Seven (currently, Seven-Eleven

Japan Co., Ltd.). When York Seven entered into a license agreement with the Southland Corp., USA, in 1973, the gross profit was used as the basis of royalty calculations in the United States.

Then, what would be the reason for using the gross profit as the basis of royalty calculations?

4.1. *Interpretation of the gross-profit sharing system*

The JFA defines royalty as referring to the consideration of the use of the package provided by a franchiser. However, regarding royalty determined based on the gross profit, i.e., royalty that is calculated by deducting the cost of goods sold, excluding the amount of loss, from the amount of sales, after multiplying by a certain rate, Seven-Eleven Japan expresses an opinion different from the usual definition and uses the term "charge" instead of royalty.

In an ordinary franchise system, the royalty is interpreted to be the price for the use by franchisee of the package provided by franchiser. The franchiser provides the franchisee with its own logo and management know-how in the form of management guidance, and in return the franchisee pays the franchiser the price therefore. However, in the philosophy of Seven-Eleven Japan, the mode of thinking centered on "price" is rejected (Kawagoe, 2001). The philosophy of Seven-Eleven Japan is as follows: while both the franchiser and the franchisee are independent entities, they are engaged in a joint venture, assuming their respective roles for the sake of prosperous coexistence. The gross profit is the outcome of the cooperation between the two independent entities. The gross profit is allotted to each party, and the rightful share of the franchiser is the "charge".

In profit sharing at an ordinary company, the management decides the method of allocation of current-term unappropriated profits to distribution, such as dividends and board members' bonuses, and to retention, such as profit reserves and voluntary reserves. Regarding the profit, the current-term profit that is the final profit is used instead of the gross profit (Table 1).

The gross-profit sharing system can be understood as a profit-oriented method in which the amount of sales and the cost of goods sold are considered important; the profit obtained as a result of active participation in the franchisee's management by the franchiser as a cooperative entity is shared, instead of the receipt of a royalty by the franchiser in consideration of the rights granted to the franchisee.

Table 1. Gross margin and net income.

Income statement	
Sale revenue	36,080
Cost of sale	30,300
Gross margin	5,780
Operating expenses	3,190
Income before taxes	2,590
Provision fro income taxes	1,200
Net income	1,390

4.2. *Role of the franchisee*

Those who play an important role in the management guidance of the Seven-Eleven franchisees are the operation field counselors (OFCs). The management advice offered by the OFC consists of the concept of order placement, proposals on selling and display techniques, in-house system architecture, analysis of business data, method of trade-area measurement, utilization of information, and so forth. These pieces of advice allow each franchisee to place orders based on his or her own judgment, with local information and weather conditions in mind.

The component ratios in terms of the amount of sales at Seven-Eleven Japan in fiscal 2007 were as follows: processed foods such as soft drinks and sweets: 29.8%; nonfood items such as cosmetics: 28.7%; fast foods such as packed lunches, rice balls and daily dishes: 28.6%; chilled groceries such as milk and desserts: 12.9% (source: Seven-Eleven Homepage). Of these items, disposal loss is the greatest in fast foods with short best-before periods. Disposal loss also occurs in processed foods and chilled groceries. The disposal loss is one of the three main business expenses that put pressure on the profit of a franchisee, the other two being inventory loss and personnel expenses (Kondo, 2008).

Since each franchisee that has received management guidance takes charge of product management (ordering and sales promotion) as one of the tasks allotted, each franchisee is responsible for finding the best way of reducing the disposal loss (Table 2).

Table 2. Tasks allotted to the franchisee and the franchiser.

Tasks of the franchisee
— Personnel management (employment, education, training, etc.)
— Product management (ordering, sales promotion, etc.)
— Business data management (sales amount, business management)
Tasks of the franchiser
— Business consultation
— Product development and product information service
— Development of the physical distribution system
— Information system service
— Advertising and promotional activities
— Lending of sales equipment
— Accounting and book-keeping service
— Development and maintenance of a system of work without anxiety

Source: http://www.sej.co.jp/corp/aboutsej/franchise.html.

To minimize the disposal loss, the order for each item should be placed based on the minimum demand therefore, to make sure that it goes out of stock. However, if the item remains out of stock, consumers gradually come to visit the store less frequently. An important task of the franchisee is to control the order quantity for each item so that the item goes out of stock less frequently and the disposal loss becomes minimal. It appears that the disposal loss is excluded from the cost of goods sold to place the responsibility for this task on the franchisee.

5. Disposal Loss and Risk Sharing

5.1. *Optimum sharing of disposal loss*

The study of Kim and Senbongi (1999) theoretically examined the optimum sharing of disposal loss using mathematical models. In their study, the cost burden on the franchiser due to the disposal loss was analyzed for three possibilities: no burden, partial burden, and total burden. In each case, the mathematical models of the amount of disposal loss, franchisee profit, cost burden on the franchiser due to disposal loss and profit for the entire franchise chain were formulated to determine the optimal solution for the profit for the entire chain. Furthermore, the analysis results were explained by classifying them into two cases.

Case 1: The disposal loss is entirely borne by the franchiser. In this case, since the franchisee does not take purchase risks, the incentive for lean and effective purchases is lost, and the purchase for each item is made based on the maximum demand therefore. This leads to greater disposal loss. Therefore, it is not desirable that the disposal loss be entirely borne by the franchiser.

Case 2: The disposal loss is partially borne by the franchiser or no disposal loss is borne by the franchiser. This case is classified into two subcases: (2.1) the franchisee considers the lack of stock undesirable and (2.2) the franchiser considers it desirable that a part of the disposal loss be borne by the franchiser, which means that the franchiser considers the lack of stock acceptable. In this case, it is preferable to minimize the disposal loss by minimizing the amount of disposal loss borne by the franchiser.

The above results would apply to those franchisees with some years' experience in convenience-store management. An inexperienced franchisee who opens a convenience store for the first time tends to purchase the minimum amount of stock for fear of risk. In such a case, the alternative is to adopt Case 1 (the disposal loss is entirely borne by the franchiser) for a limited period, to give the franchisee enough time to gain an understanding of the optimum purchase method without fear of risk. Also, there may be cases where a lack of stock may cause little inconvenience, whereas there may be cases where a lack of stock should be avoided by all means. Case 2.1 or 2.2 may be adopted depending on the product.

5.2. *Risk sharing of disposal loss*

If it is assumed that the purchase quantity of a product is based on the sales quantity expected by the franchisee, the disposal loss depends on the difference between the expected sales quantity or purchase quantity and the actual sales quantity:

$$\begin{aligned}\text{Disposal loss} &= \{\text{expected sales quantity (or purchase quantity)} \\ &\quad - \text{actual sales quantity}\} \times \text{purchase unit price} \\ &= \text{operation variance.} \qquad (4)\end{aligned}$$

The disposal risk refers to the possibility that the actual sales quantity may be less than the expected sales quantity. Also, the actual sales quantity must not be greater than the expected sales quantity (purchase quantity). If purchasing is performed only once a day, and the expected

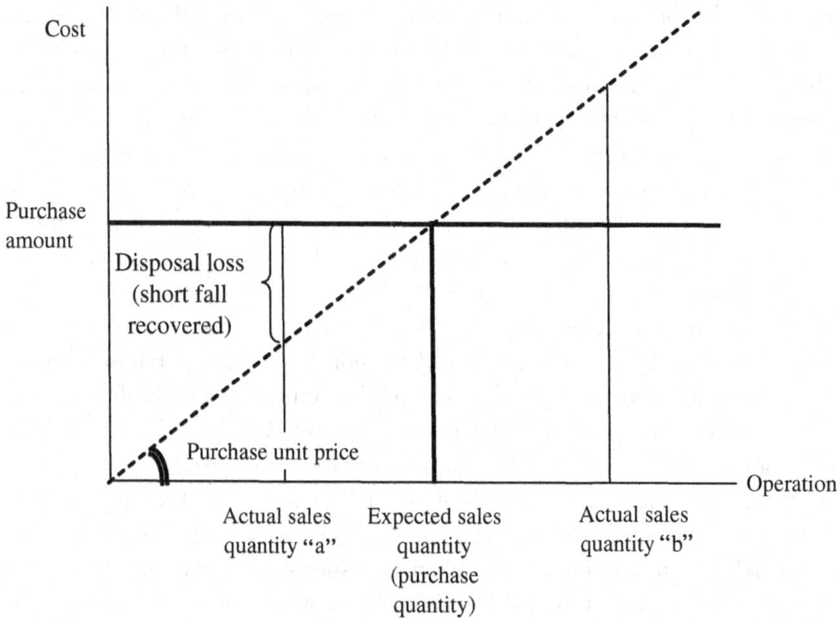

Fig. 1. Occurrence of disposal loss due to operational variance.

sales quantity (purchase quantity) is less than the actual sales quantity, and the unsold goods must be disposed of, a lack of stock occurs.

Since fast foods, and so forth, cannot be returned once they are purchased and cannot be held in stock beyond their expiry dates, the amount of purchase should be borne as a cost (Fig. 1). And since this is a cost borne regardless of whether the items are sold or unsold, this cost is similar to a fixed cost. The unrecovered portion of the fixed cost is operational variance, that is, disposal loss.

In the manufacturing industry, the operational variance is shared among the manufacturers. In the auto industry, the difference between the production volume and the actual sales quantity at a parts manufacturer is shared between the manufacturer of finished cars, such as Toyota, and the parts manufacturer. If operational variance occurs in a case where the production volume is determined using the unit price as determined by full cost accounting, the fixed cost for the parts manufacturer constitutes the risk of the cost remaining unrecoverable. As for the production volume, each parts manufacturer receives orders placed by the manufacturer of finished cars as to the delivery amount of parts based on the sales expected by the manufacturer of finished cars. Accordingly, if at a point during, for example, a two-year period of agreement the actual sales volume exceeds the initially expected sales volume, the unit part price thereafter is discounted. On the other hand, if at the time of the expiration of the two-year agreement the actual sales volume has not reached the initially expected sales volume, the manufacturer of finished cars gives a subsidy equal to the unrecovered amount of the fixed cost of the equipment investment in a specific part (for example, a metal mold). Thus, the risk is shared between the two companies.

Regarding convenience stores, is the purchase quantity ordered by the franchisee determined by the franchisee alone? Are the purchase quantities of private brand goods, and so forth, not pushed by the franchiser? Also, in convenience stores, the risk caused by the operational variance may be shared between the franchiser and the franchisee.

It appears that the method of handling the amount of loss in the franchise business is unique, in that it gives the franchisee a responsibility. Although this method of placing responsibility on the franchisee, as stipulated by the standard franchise agreement, has been deemed legal by the courts, many franchisees are unsatisfied with it. Improvements of the standard agreement would be necessary to reach a compromise between the two parties. Such improvements would optimize the profit for the entire chain and ensure prosperous coexistence, which is the original aim of the franchise business.

6. Conclusion

In the convenience-store franchise system, great importance is placed on profit, and the franchiser and franchisee assume their respective allotted roles and work together. There is a system of minimum gross profit guaranty by the franchiser. The franchiser assumes the responsibility for both the sales amount and the cost of goods sold, and supports the management of each franchise store.

It may be necessary for a franchisee to bear the entire loss amount to fulfill the obligations allocated to him/her. However, the franchisees are increasingly unsatisfied with the cost burden, in which the entire loss amount, which is said to be one of the three main business expenses, is borne by the franchisee alone, and many lawsuits have been and are being filed because of this problem. In the franchise agreement, it is stipulated that the loss amount is borne by the franchisee. However, as in profit sharing, the risk of disposal and inventory shrinkage should also be shared between the joint venture partners.

While the standard franchise agreement has been deemed legal by the courts in lawsuits filed by franchisees pertaining to disposal loss, the Japan Fair Trade Commission has conducted an on-the-spot inspection based on the consideration that the act of obliging the franchisees to dispose of close-to-expiry-date goods is an abuse of the dominant bargaining position by the franchiser (The Nikkei, 21 February 2009, p. 9). As a rule, Seven-Eleven Japan does not discount the prices of unsold goods. If the prices of close-to-expiry-date goods can be discounted, the costs of goods sold can be recovered, even if only to a small extent, thus leading to the mitigation of the royalty burden. From now on, it may become necessary to modify the relationship between the franchiser and the franchisees.

References

Kawagoe, K. (2001). *The Low of Franchising*, Shojihomu (in Japanese).

Kim, H. and Senbongi, S. (1999). The optimum distribution of abandonment loss in convenience-store business. *The Journal of Marketing and Distribution*, 364, 4–14 (in Japanese).

Kondo, K. (2008). The interpretation of case of sales cost in franchise contract, *The Journal of Administrative and Social Sciences*, 20(3), 88–119 (in Japanese).

Seven-Eleven Japan (2004). *Seven-Eleven Japan Sustainability Report* 2004.

Seven-Eleven Japan Co., Ltd web site, http://www.sej.co.jp/corp/company/pdf/yokogao/2008/711.pdf. (in Japanese).

Shogyokai (ed.). *2006 Franchise Chain in Japan*, Shogyokai (in Japanese).

The Nikkei. *Japan Fair Trade Commission Launched an Investigation of Seven-Eleven Japan Co. Ltd.*, 21 February 2009, p. 9 (in Japanese).

12

Factors Influencing Control Mechanisms in Joint Ventures: Evidence from Japanese Manufacturing Industries

Yuichi Kubota

School of Economics, Osaka Prefecture University

1. Introduction

The management of interorganizational relationships (IORs) such as joint ventures (JVs) and strategic alliances has become important in a networked age. Many companies have created values in collaboration with various partners. Interorganizational controls in hybrid organizational forms that lie between market and hierarchy are needed for collaborations (Otley, 1994; Hopwood, 1996). In Japan, the number of strategic alliances and JVs seems to be increasing, and collaborations are an important factor for the acquisition of a competitive advantage. However, prior research has found that many strategic alliances and JVs encounter problems and fail. Interorganizational control problems are the primary causes of these failures (Chua and Mahama, 2007; Groot and Merchant, 2000; Kamminga and Van der Meer-Kooistra, 2007).

The terms "alliance" and "JV" are often used ambiguously and synonymously. In fact, the structure of a JV is very similar to that of an alliance. Dekker (2004, p. 42) describes the practices common to the two IORs as follows: "joint financial investments are made, a separate organizational structure with a joint board and joint task groups is installed, specific tasks and resources are dedicated to it, and separate rules, regulations and costing and nonmarket pricing are used". Additionally, Groot and Merchant (2000) explain that JVs are of two types: equity and nonequity. Equity JVs owned by two or more partners are a prominent form of cooperative agreement. Nonequity JVs promote cooperation between partners in accordance with contractual arrangements, that is, without the creation of a new company.

The Japan Fair Trade Commission (2002) investigated the collaborations and competition among companies. The report states that nonequity JVs have become more popular than equity JVs. However, according to the results of this empirical survey, Japanese managers seem to believe that a nonequity JV partnership is easier to dissolve than an equity JV. If managers want to reduce financial investments and risks of uncertainty and share secrets and information with partners, equity JVs are preferred to nonequity ones.

Dekker (2004) classifies the control mechanisms of IORs as *ex-ante* mechanisms (goal setting, incentive systems, structural specifications, organizational structuring, partner selection, reputation, and trust) and *ex-post* mechanisms (performance and behavior monitoring, shared decision making, and goal setting). Accounting researchers have also discussed control mechanisms in JVs (Chalos and O'Connor, 2004; Groot and Merchant, 2000; Kamminga and Van der Meer-Kooistra, 2007). However, the problems related to factors influencing control mechanisms in JVs remain unsolved.

This study focused on the control problems of equity JVs in Japanese manufacturing industries. Equity JVs need to be examined as they are assumed to be managed through interdependent partnerships and to involve a longer relation than nonequity JVs. The present study aims to explore the main factors influencing ex-post JV controls and to analyze the determinants of JV control mechanisms. The next section develops the extended research model that builds on Kamminga and Van der Meer-Kooistra (2007). Section 3 explains the empirical design and variable measurement. Section 4 discusses the results of multiple regression analysis. The final section presents the conclusion and directions for future research.

2. Conceptual Framework and Literature Review

The model of Kamminga and Van der Meer-Kooistra (2007) provided four characteristics of JV control patterns: transaction, relational, control, and institutional characteristics. This study focuses on the first three characteristics and does not deal with institutional characteristics.

2.1. *Transaction characteristics*

Concepts based on transaction cost economics (TCE) have been applied in most studies of IORs. Studies on TCE have discussed organizational boundaries and the minimization of transaction costs; they also point out the risks of opportunistic behavior (ex. Gietzmann, 1996).

In particular, asset specificity has been widely drawn on in empirical research. TCE suggests that high asset specificity can lead to opportunistic behaviors, hold-up problems, and incomplete contracts (Gietzmann, 1996; Williamson, 1975, 1997). Chalos and O'Connor (2004) examined the effects of relative partner knowledge and specific asset investments on the usage of various types of control mechanisms in US-Chinese JVs. They found that partner knowledge and specific asset investments influenced a broad set of controls. Further, Kamminga and Van der Meer-Kooistra (2007) introduced and confirmed that it is not only the level of asset specificity, but also its types (physical, human, and procedural asset specificity) that matter. As they suggest, "human, procedural, and marketing asset specificity may be more difficult to settle by contract due to the tacit character of the information".

Employees of JV partners may be working for the JV firm on a contractual basis. Human asset specificity, therefore, occurs in the case of JVs. Procedural asset specificity can occur when ordering and production, techniques or tools of cost and production management, procedures of financial planning, reporting and budgeting, and internal terminology need to be standardized or unified in a JV. As a manufacturing JV operates with limited resources, in general, business processes such as cost accounting, procurement, sales, and production maintenance will be outsourced to one or some of the JV partners.

Further, TCE has certain important attributes or characteristics. Williamson (1975, 1997) shows uncertainty and frequency. However, Kamminga and Van der Meer-Kooistra (2007) assert that frequency does not play a role in the JV governance structure because the frequency of transactions is always assumed to be high. They suggest that there are two other transaction characteristics in JVs: knowledge of the transformation process and ability to measure outputs. Milgrom and Roberts (1992) point out complexity as another transaction characteristic.

2.2. *Relational characteristics*

Kamminga and Van der Meer-Kooistra (2007, p. 133) state that "in the joint venture literature, four important relational characteristics are discussed: (1) parental differences, (2) information asymmetry, (3) trust, and (4) bargaining power".

Parental differences include differences in partners' objectives, strategic interests, motivation for the JV, and cultures. For example, Groot and Merchant (2000) suggest that partners' objectives with regard to the JVs in which they become engaged differ significantly; these objectives are important to a given partner and affect choices regarding the control focus.

Second, in JVs, there is information asymmetry between parent companies and between a parent and its JV. Information asymmetry can result in problems such as hidden actions and hidden information. Sharing of information has been discussed as one of the solutions to these problems (Roberts, 2004). Tomkins (2001) analyzes the relationship between trust and information and proposes two types of information needs: the information needed to assess willingness to trust and information needed to attempt a collaborative mastery of events. He assumes that the two types of information needs are relevant to JVs as well as other IORs.

The third relational characteristic is trust. Recent investigations have demonstrated that trust is important in the governance of IORs (Dekker, 2003, 2004; Langfield-Smith and Smith, 2003; Mouritsen *et al.*, 2001; Van der Meer-Kooistra and Vosselman, 2000). For example, Dekker (2003, 2004) suggests that trust in the other's goodwill is an important informal or social control mechanism. In addition, Emsley and Kidon (2007) differentiated trust from control, and examined the relationship between the two characteristics in a JV between two international airlines.

Bargaining power is the last relational characteristic. Kamminga and Van der Meer-Kooistra (2007) argue that the extent to which parents can exercise control over a JV is regarded as the outcome of a bargaining process. They, however, note that the mere possession of power by a parent does not imply that this power will actually be exercised.

2.3. *Control characteristics*

Geringer and Hebert (1989) believe that control is a critical concept for the successful management and performance of JVs, and present a conceptualization of JV control. The dimensions of JV control are as follows: (1) mechanisms by which parents exercise control; (2) extent of control exercised over a JV, namely, dependence on centralization or the locus of the decision-making process; and (3) scope of the JV activities (relatively wide or narrow) that parents focus on when they choose to exercise control. In addition, Geringer and Herbert suggest three components of control mechanisms: context-oriented mechanisms (encompassing a wide variety of informal and culture-based mechanisms), content-oriented mechanisms (formal and bureaucratic), and process-oriented mechanisms (exercising control through reporting relationships or influence on JV planning and decisions). Some previous studies used this conceptualization of JV controls (Groot and Merchant, 2000; Kamminga and Van der Meer-Kooistra, 2007).

Groot and Merchant (2000) identify three distinct types of control mechanisms: action controls, results controls, and personnel/cultural controls. Action controls involve steps taken by parents to ensure that certain desirable actions are implemented. Results controls are used to determine performance, to monitor performance reports, and to provide rewards. Third, personnel/cultural controls are those that make personnel willing and able to perform well; alternatively, they could refer to the JV culture and its role in motivating the employees to perform well. Further, Groot and Merchant (2000) explain the concepts related to the extent of control (control tightness) in Merchant (1998) — namely, tighter and looser control. For example, they suggest that action controls are tight from the partner perspective in cases where approval reviews are frequent, detailed, and performed by a knowledgeable person.

Kamminga and Van der Meer-Kooistra (2007) also distinguish three control patterns on the basis of control characteristics: content-based control pattern, consultation-based control pattern, and context-based control pattern. The control characteristics they discuss include focus, tightness, JV types (shared/dominant/split/independent), control mechanisms, and contract type. Borrowing Geringer and Hebert's terminology, they break the control mechanism down into two components: content-based and context-based. Moreover, they suggest that the consultation-based control pattern serves as the medium between the content-based and context-based components, depending on the relative control complexity.

2.4. *Research model and expectations*

The literature on control in IORs has demonstrated the choice of governance structures (Dekker, 2004; Langfield-Smith and Smith, 2003; Van der Meer-Kooistra and Vosselman, 2000). Governance structures are related to

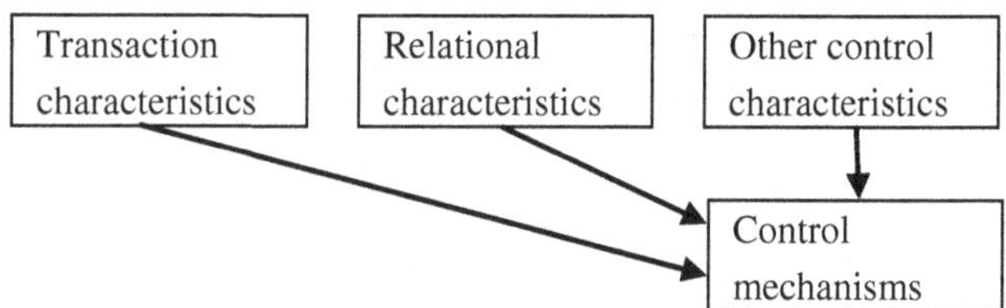

Fig. 1. Research model.

the control mechanisms of IORs. Further, measures and causal factors explaining differences in JV control systems, such as transaction, relational, and control characteristics, have been explored and founded. However, little is known about the factors influencing (ex-post) control mechanisms in Japanese JV practices and their determinants. Therefore, a research model is provided and examined (see Fig. 1). The research expectation is that the control mechanisms are affected to some extent by the transaction, relational, and other control characteristics.

3. Research Method

3.1. *Sample*

Survey data were collected through questionnaires administered to Japanese JV managers. A total of 275 JVs were selected from *The Group Companies in Japan* (2006) database. Since 1990, JVs have begun to be formed in Japan for development and production; typically, the parents in these JVs are one or more of the listed Japanese manufacturing companies. Moreover, some of the JVs seem to be strategically important to one or some of the parents. The questionnaire for the study was sent in March 2007 and responses were received from 58 JVs (valid responses: 55, valid response rate: 20.0%). The respondents were asked to answer some of the questions from the viewpoint of the largest shareholder (one parent) of the JV.

3.2. *Variable measurement*

This study conducted exploratory factor analysis to examine a priori types of measures. The questionnaire contained questions for measuring transaction, relational, and control characteristics, followed by the research expectation. Each item was rated on a seven-point Likert-type scale (7 = high, 4 = medium, 1 = low). Table 1 provides an overview of the survey items in the factor analysis.

First, the transaction characteristics were measured to examine the constructs about environmental uncertainty (4 items) and complexity (3 items), measurability of performance and efficiency (3 items), parent's knowledge (4 items), and asset specificity (10 items). With regard to the relation between transaction uncertainty and environmental uncertainty, Kamminga and Van der Meer-Kooistra (2007) explained that both increased and decreased environmental uncertainty may lead to uncertainty regarding the activities of transacting parties. Langfield-Smith (2008, p. 346) state that "environmental uncertainty arises from conditions that are outside of the control of an alliance, but which may affect the execution of agreements and the outcomes of cooperation". This study applied environmental uncertainty (instead of transaction uncertainty) and environmental complexity for a similar reason. As a result of the principal factor analysis of uncertainty, complexity, measurability, and knowledge, one factor was retained for each construct. For asset specificity, three factors whose eigenvalues were greater than 1 were identified: (1) asset specificity of planning and reporting processes (planning), that is, the extent to which the JV's planning and reporting processes are consistent in the parent's workflows, (2) asset specificity of the processes of specified tasks (operation), and (3) physical and human asset specificity. The first and second factors can be interpreted as process and procedural asset specificity.

Second, the relational characteristics comprised parental similarity (2 items), information sharing between partners (16 items), trust (4 items), and bargaining power (1 item). The items under similarity are concerned with the parental "objectives" and "cultures". As information sharing is closely linked to information asymmetry and the management of Japanese companies is, in general, characterized by tendencies toward a high level of sharing, several items were set in this construct. The items of similarity and bargaining power were directly utilized. The analysis of information sharing revealed two factors: (1) maintaining current relationships and (2) building long-term relationships. Although these factors have been interpreted as types of information needs (Tomkins, 2001), they do not coincide with each other. Moreover, through the factor analysis, one component was identified for the items measuring trust between JV partners.

Third, the control characteristics were divided into control mechanisms and other control characteristics. The 18 items of control mechanisms

Table 1. Results of factor analysis for JV management control ($n = 55$).

Factors and Cronbach alphas	Factor loadings I	II	III	IV
A. Uncertainty (α = 0.719) (Eigenvalue = 2.18, % of variance = 40.53)				
Frequency of new product development	0.81			
Competitiveness of product market	0.62			
Difficulty of demand forecasting	0.54			
Pace of technology obsolescence	0.54			
B. Complexity (α = 0.570) (Eigenvalue = 1.65, % of variance = 36.31)				
Diversity of product market	0.43			
Similarity/commonality in technology (reverse)	0.49			
Diversity of sales promotion	0.82			
C. Measurability (α = 0.750) (Eigenvalue = 2.00, % of variance = 51.36)				
Measurability of JV performance	0.82			
Identification of performance drivers and measurement	0.72			
Visibility of JV operation (stipulating operation task)	0.59			
D. Knowledge (α = 0.814) (Eigenvalue = 2.60, % of variance = 54.98)				
Knowledge and information about development/production for JV	0.90			
Knowledge and information about technology for JV	0.76			
Knowledge and information about management techniques for JV	0.73			
Knowledge and information about sales and marketing for JV	0.53			
E. Asset specificity (α = 0.842)				
I. Planning (Eigenvalue = 4.24, % of variance = 24.41)				
Business planning process	0.96	0.08	0.22	

(*Continued*)

Table 1. (*Continued*)

Factors and Cronbach alphas	Factor loadings I	II	III	IV
Budgeting process	0.83	0.17	0.15	
Financial reporting process	0.66	0.27	0.32	
II. Operation (Eigenvalue = 1.41, % of variance = 17.56)				
Ordering process	0.17	0.87	0.04	
Engineering design and production process	0.32	0.79	0.26	
Procuring/purchasing parts or materials	0.01	0.44	0.33	
III. Physical/human (Eigenvalue = 1.25, % of variance = 16.66)				
Sending JV employees to parents for training	0.30	0.03	0.79	
Sending parent's employees (engineers) to JV	0.19	0.14	0.56	
Renting equipment, machines, facilities, and land from JV partners	0.08	0.17	0.51	
Technical support to JV	0.34	0.17	0.36	
F. Information sharing between partners (α = 0.961)				
I. Maintaining (Eigenvalue = 10.17, % of variance = 34.47)				
Assessment of JV's competitive position	0.79	0.31		
Strategic analysis for JV	0.78	0.33		
Potential risks for JV	0.73	0.48		
Information on plans (goals for profits, costs, and quality, etc.)	0.73	0.42		
Progress of goals/targets	0.72	0.47		
Values and ethics for JV	0.64	0.48		
Detailed financial positioning and structure of JV	0.63	0.33		
Satisfactory JV financial results	0.57	0.55		
Detailed investment appraisal	0.57	0.49		

(*Continued*)

Table 1. (*Continued*)

Factors and Cronbach alphas	Factor loadings I	II	III	IV
II. Building (Eigenvalue = 1.02, % of variance = 31.36)				
New business development possibilities	0.35	0.83		
Partners' contribution to JV operations	0.35	0.77		
Openness in reporting of information on all operations of JV to parent organization	0.41	0.69		
Concrete suggestions from partner to JV and reaction to the same	0.49	0.67		
Detailed cost data of JV	0.31	0.64		
Detailed information of partners' request to JV	0.50	0.64		
Providing more reliable open data	0.51	0.54		
G. Trust (α = 0.930) (Eigenvalue = 3.31, % of variance = 77.28)				
Competence trust	0.96			
Goodwill trust	0.89			
Reciprocal trust and willingness to contribute	0.85			
Contractual trust	0.81			
H. Autonomy of JV (α = 0.862)				
I. Profit center level (Eigenvalue = 4.30, % of variance = 44.63)				
Authority to develop and enter a new market	0.91	0.08		
Authority to select buyers	0.90	0.13		
Authority to change product design or technical specification	0.84	0.02		
Authority to decide the plan with regard to production and sales volume	0.79	0.26		
Authority to select suppliers	0.67	0.36		

(*Continued*)

Table 1. (*Continued*)

Factors and Cronbach alphas	Factor loadings I	II	III	IV
II. Investment center level (Eigenvalue = 1.66, % of variance = 21.70)				
Authority to employ and dismiss the members of JV	0.13	0.85		
Authority to promote and demote managers within JV	0.36	0.71		
Authority to purchase an asset and to transfer or dispose one	0.00	0.53		
I. Tightness of NFT (α = 0.804) (Eigenvalue = 2.15, % of variance = 57.92)				
Tightness of cost reduction targets	0.79			
Tightness of quality targets	0.78			
Tightness of nonfinancial and operational targets	0.70			
J. Control mechanisms (α = 0.929)				
I. Participation (Eigenvalue = 9.20, % of variance = 23.76)				
Participation in setting quality targets	0.87	0.28	0.08	−0.07
Participation in setting cost reduction targets	0.78	0.18	0.24	0.06
Involvement in cost management activities	0.77	0.27	0.19	−0.21
Involvement in Kaizen activities	0.76	0.22	0.08	−0.13
Participation in setting nonfinancial targets	0.75	0.17	0.14	−0.06
Involvement in quality management activities	0.72	0.38	0.02	−0.15
Participation in setting financial targets	0.61	0.12	0.47	−0.05
II. Monitoring of nonfinancial measures (Eigenvalue = 2.88, % of variance = 22.06)				
Frequency in monitoring lead-time variability	0.22	0.91	0.12	0.07

(*Continued*)

Table 1. (*Continued*)

Factors and Cronbach alphas	Factor loadings I	II	III	IV
Frequency in monitoring product design and specification compliance	0.22	0.89	0.20	–0.04
Frequency in monitoring customer satisfaction	0.22	0.81	0.14	0.13
Frequency in monitoring product quality	0.29	0.81	0.21	–0.03
Frequency in monitoring operational activities	0.40	0.70	0.20	0.05
Frequency in monitoring manufacturing costs	0.29	0.66	0.49	–0.04
III. Monitoring of financial measures (Eigenvalue = 1.94, % of variance = 14.40)				
Frequency in monitoring financial performance	0.18	0.06	0.93	0.00
Frequency in monitoring sales volume	0.02	0.37	0.76	0.15
Involvement in JV administrative support activities and tasks	0.52	0.11	0.58	–0.16
Frequency in monitoring investment and its result	0.15	0.31	0.57	–0.10
Frequency in monitoring market share	0.38	0.30	0.40	0.12
IV. Cooperative coordination (Eigenvalue = 1.80, % of variance = 9.71)				
Collaboration and cooperative coordination among JV employees	–0.19	–0.02	–0.09	0.85
Mutual reliance between employees	–0.02	0.03	–0.03	0.76
Communication among JV employees	–0.08	0.08	0.10	0.73

Loadings are based on principal factor analysis with varimax rotation. One or more factors are retained for each construct. The constructs all have eigenvalues greater than 1.

were developed in relation to participation in setting targets, involvement in JV activities, monitoring of financial and nonfinancial measures, and cooperative coordination. Four factors emerged from the items of control mechanisms: participation, monitoring of nonfinancial measures, monitoring of financial measures, and cooperative coordination in JV operation. The first factor seems to be an ex-post mechanism wherein a parent participates in setting the JV's targets and directly supports the JV for operational management activities (ex. cost management, quality management, and Kaizen activities). In particular, this mechanism may involve the exercise of control over processes "for mastery of events by the relationship as an entity itself" (as pointed out by Tomkins (2001)) and contain both outcome and behavior controls. The second factor can be related to behavior monitoring based on nonfinancial measures, and the third factor can be interpreted as an ex-post outcome control mechanism related to financial performance monitoring. The fourth factor seems to be an ex-post social control mechanism.

Other control characteristics included the constructs of autonomy (8 items), tightness (4 items), comprehensive contracts (1 item), and detailed agreements (1 item) and prior consultation (1 item) between parents to avoid conflicts. The items of contract, agreement, and prior consultation were directly used. The construct of autonomy was set because it seemed be relevant for controlling focus and empowerment (Simons, 2005). As a result of the analysis, two factors were retained because both had eigenvalues above 1; these factors were characterized by the authority of (1) profit center level and (2) investment center level. In addition, from the factor analysis of tightness, the item of "tightness of financial targets" was removed owing to its low communality. As a result, one factor was identified within three items: "tightness of nonfinancial targets (NFT)".

4. Results and Discussion

Using each factor score of the above analysis, multiple stepwise regression analysis was performed to examine the relationships between control mechanisms as the dependent variables and the independent variables measuring transaction, relational, and other control characteristics. The results of the regression analysis are presented in Table 2.

First, "monitoring of financial measures" would be positively associated with "planning", "maintaining", "comprehensive contracts", "profit center level", and "detailed agreements"; on the other hand, it would be negatively associated with "complexity". The most important variable explaining the extent of the monitoring of financial measures was

Table 2. Multiple regression analysis of control mechanisms ($n = 55$).

	Monitoring of financial measures		Monitoring of nonfinancial measures		Participation		Cooperative coordination	
	β	t	β	t	β	t	β	t
Transaction characteristics								
Complexity	−0.217*	−2.382	0.322*	2.670				
Knowledge					0.206^{+}	1.742		
Asset specificity								
Planning	0.562***	6.283						
Operation			0.233^{+}	1.974	0.339**	2.876		
Physical/Human					0.317*	2.659		
Relational characteristics								
Bargaining power							−0.315*	−2.390
Trust							0.278*	2.110

(*Continued*)

Table 2. (*Continued*)

	Monitoring of financial measures		Monitoring of nonfinancial measures		Participation		Cooperative coordination	
	β	t	β	t	β	t	β	t
Information sharing								
Maintaining	0.155+	1.712			−0.208+	−1.721		
Other control characteristics								
Comprehensive contract	0.186+	1.951						
Autonomy								
Profit center level	0.275**	3.112	−0.419**	−3.455				
Tightness of NFT			0.187	1.623				
Detailed agreements	0.215*	2.259						
F	16.562***		6.788***		5.796***		4.204*	
Adjusted R^2	0.634		0.300		0.262		0.106	

Significance levels: ***$p < 0.001$, **$p < 0.01$, *$p < 0.05$, $^+p < 0.1$ (two-tailed). The beta values are standardized coefficients from the final regression equation. The stepwise method was applied to select the best set of predictor variables for the regression equation (F-value to enter = 2, F-value to remove = 1.96). Each model with the highest adjusted R-square was chosen. Tests of multicollinearity: no variance inflation factor (VIF) scores were greater than 2.00, indicating that multicollinearity is not a problem.

"planning" ($\beta = 0.562$), which means that the asset specificity of planning and reporting processes increases the frequency of the monitoring of the JV's financial measures by a parent. Moreover, if a parent at least gives the JV managers authority of the profit center level, it can control the JV by monitoring the financial measures. The lower the level of a JV's environmental complexity and the more detailed agreements between partners, the greater is the monitoring of financial measures that the parent will undertake.

Second, "complexity" and "operation" have significantly positive effects on "monitoring of nonfinancial measures" while "profit center level" has a negative effect. It seems that a parent could exercise control through the monitoring of nonfinancial measures, which is the exact opposite of monitoring financial measures, in cases involving a low level of authority as a profit center and a high level of environmental complexity. Although the effect of "operation" is statistically insignificant at 10%, it seems that the monitoring of nonfinancial measures entails the matching of the JV's processes for specified tasks to the parent's workflows.

Third, "knowledge", "operation", and "physical/human" have positive effects on "participation" while "maintaining" has a negative effect. If a parent participates in the setting of the JV's targets and directly supports the JV, it is accordingly required to have a higher level of knowledge. In addition, in this case, it is necessary to match the JV's processes for specified tasks to the parent's workflows and to contain a greater level of physical and human asset specificity. This result implies that the type of JV (shared/dominant/split/independent) could affect the extent of participation.

Finally, "trust" has a positive effect and "bargaining power" has a negative effect on "cooperative coordination". When one of the JV partners has more power than the others and the power linearly translates into the parent's control, cooperative coordination may not be achievable or desirable. In a case where cooperative coordination is necessary, the bargaining power must be exercised very carefully. In addition, the greater the level of trust between JV partners, the more cooperative coordination can be improved.

5. Concluding Remarks

This study has explored transaction, relational, and control characteristics and analyzed the determinants of ex-post control mechanisms.

The results may be summarized as follows. In the exploratory factor analysis, four factors in the construct of control mechanisms were clarified: participation consisting of outcome and behavior controls, monitoring of financial measures mainly as outcome control, monitoring of nonfinancial measures as behavior control, and cooperative coordination related to social control. In particular, it seems to be necessary to examine the parents' participation in setting targets and directly supporting the JV's operational activities under various conditions. Moreover, some determinants of each mechanism were found. This research revealed that the two types of monitoring were positively or negatively associated with the levels of environmental complexity and autonomy as a profit center. Specifically, for the monitoring of financial measures, it may be necessary to match the JV's planning and reporting processes to the parent's workflows. Furthermore, it was estimated that participation can differ according to the type of JV. As a matter of course, trust and bargaining power have an effect on cooperative coordination. These results seem to be relevant to the detail-oriented management style of Japanese JVs. However, the style has yet to be adequately examined — a task that can be undertaken by future multilateral studies.

Another suggestion for future research is an integrated study of these controls. These control mechanisms are never exercised in isolation (Malmi and Brown, 2008). Moreover, their operation may differ across the stages/phases of the JV's growth. Although this research dealt with JVs in the start-up phase, there may be individual variations in the way JVs develop. The pace of growth of JVs is one of the control issues that remain to be examined.

Acknowledgement

This research was partially supported by a Grant-in-Aid for Young Scientists (B) No. 20730306 from the Ministry of Education, Culture, Sports, Science & Technology, Japan.

References

Chalos, P. and O'Connor, N. G. (2004). Determinants of the use of various control mechanisms in US-Chinese joint ventures, *Accounting, Organizations and Society*, 29(7), 591–608.

Chua, W. F. and Mahama, H. (2007). The effect of network ties on accounting controls in a supply alliance: Field study evidence, *Contemporary Accounting Research*, 24(1), 47–86.

Dekker, H. C. (2003). Value chain analysis in interfirm relationships: A field study, *Management Accounting Research*, 14(1), 1–23.

Dekker, H. C. (2004). Control of inter-organizational relationships: Evidence on appropriation concerns and coordination requirements, *Accounting, Organizations and Society*, 29(1), 27–49.

Emsley, D. and Kidon, F. (2007). The relationship between trust and control in international joint ventures: Evidence from the airline industry, *Contemporary Accounting Research*, 24(3), 829–858.

Geringer, J. M. and Hebert, L. (1989). Control and performance of international joint ventures, *Journal of International Business Studies*, 20(2), 235–254.

Gietzmann, M. B. (1996). Incomplete contracts and the make or buy decision: Governance design and attainable flexibility, *Accounting, Organizations and Society*, 21(6), 611–626.

Groot, T. L. C. M. and Merchant, K. A. (2000). Control of international joint ventures, *Accounting, Organizations and Society*, 25(6), 579–607.

Kamminga, P. E. and Van der Meer-Kooistra, J. (2007). Management control patterns in joint venture relationships: A model and an exploratory study, *Accounting, Organizations and Society*, 32(1–2), 131–154.

Langfield-Smith, K. (2008). The relations between transactional characteristics, trust and risk in the start-up phase of a collaborative alliance, *Management Accounting Research*, 19(4), 344–364.

Langfield-Smith, K. and Smith, D. (2003). Management control systems and trust in outsourcing relationships, *Management Accounting Research*, 14(3), 281–307.

Malmi, T. and Brown, D. A. (2008). Management control systems as a package: Opportunities, challenges and research directions, *Management Accounting Research*, 19(4), 287–300.

Milgrom, P. and Roberts, J. (1992). *Economics, Organization and Management.* Englewood Cliffs, NJ: Prentice Hall.

Mouritsen, J., Hansen, A. and Hansen, C. Ø. (2001). Inter-organizational controls and organizational competencies: Episodes around target cost management/ functional analysis and open book accounting, *Management Accounting Research*, 12(2), 221–244.

Roberts, J. (2004). *The Modern Firm: Organizational Design for Performance and Growth*, Oxford University Press.

Simons, R. (2005). *Levers of Organization Design: How Managers Use Accountability Systems for Greater Performance and Commitment.* Boston, MA: Harvard Business School Press.

The Japan Fair Trade Commission. (2002) *The Report on the Survey of Collaborations and Competition Among Companies* (in Japanese).

Tomkins, C. (2001). Interdependencies, trust and information in relationships, alliances and networks, *Accounting, Organizations and Society*, 26(2), 161–191.

Van der Meer-Kooistra, J. and Vosselman, E. G. J. (2000). Management control of interfirm transactional relationships: The case of industrial renovation and maintenance, *Accounting, Organizations and Society*, 25(1), 51–77.

Williamson, O. E. (1975). *Markets and Hierarchies: Analysis and Antitrust Implications*. New York: Free Press.

Williamson, O. E. (1997). Hierarchies, markets and power in the economy: An economic perspective, *Transaction Cost Economics: Recent Developments*, ed. C. Menard, Chapter 1, Edward Elgar.

13

Does Inter-Firm Cooperation Contribute to the Performance of Japanese Firms?

Junya Sakaguchi
Graduate School of Accountancy, Kansai University

1. Introduction

From the 1980s to the beginning of the 1990s, Japanese manufacturing companies demonstrated overwhelming competitiveness in the world markets by producing multifunctional and high-quality products at low costs and providing such products at low prices. With this as a background, studies on the management of Japanese manufacturing companies have been actively pursued around the world, and a number of unique activities and programs undertaken by Japanese manufacturing companies have been introduced (Clark and Fujimoto, 1991). Similarly, in the field of management accounting, target cost management (cost management activities in the product development phase), the Just-in-Time (JIT) production system (which aims to reduce inventories on the basis of production instruction sheets called "kanban") and the inter-organizational cost management system (cost reduction activities involving parts suppliers) have been widely introduced as techniques incorporated into "Japanese Management Accounting" (Hiromoto, 1988; Monden and Sakurai, 1989; Cooper, 1995, 1996).

In particular, regarding inter-firm cooperation in cost reduction between manufacturers and parts suppliers, some previous studies have pointed out, based on an analysis of some cases of Japanese manufacturers, (1) that manufacturers set the target prices for parts they purchase from suppliers and continuously evaluate individual suppliers' target achievement levels, (2) that manufacturers and suppliers share various information about products and parts, and cooperatively generate new ideas for cost reduction, and (3) that these inter-company efforts have yielded dramatic improvements in cost reduction (Cooper, 1995, 1996; Cooper and Slagmulder, 1999, 2004; Cooper and Yoshikawa, 1994). These studies commonly describe inter-firm cooperation, i.e., cost reduction activities involving parts suppliers, as an important system that contributes to strengthening the competitiveness of Japanese manufacturers.

As stated above, inter-firm cooperation among Japanese manufacturers has been widely introduced as an excellent system that enables them to produce multifunctional and high-quality yet low-priced products at low costs. However, looking at the present condition of Japanese manufacturers, it appears that some have lost their competitiveness. This study considers the question of "whether inter-firm cooperation contributes, even today, to the performance of Japanese companies", on the basis of the results of a questionnaire survey targeting Japanese manufacturers. The purpose of this study is to clarify, through consideration of the above question, the present status of inter-firm cooperation among Japanese manufacturers. Section 2 discusses the actual state of inter-firm cooperation among Japanese manufacturers; Section 3 examines the relationship between inter-firm cooperation and performance. Based on these, this paper concludes with a description of the limitations of this study and directions for future research.

2. Actual State of Inter-Firm Cooperation

A questionnaire survey used in this study was conducted between January 29, 2008 and February 23, 2008, targeting 376 companies in the processing and assembly industry (general machinery, electrical machinery, transportation machinery, and precision machinery), all listed on the first section of the Tokyo Stock Exchange. The number of survey respondents by the type of industry is as follows: 30 companies in the general machinery industry (out of a total of 122 companies), 49 companies in the electrical machinery industry (out of a total of 165 companies), 15 companies in the transportation machinery industry (out of a total of 63 companies) and 6 companies in the precision machinery industry (out of a total of 26 companies). The overall response rate was 26.6% (100/376), which is relatively high compared with other questionnaire surveys. The results of the survey used in this study are therefore considered to accurately represent the actual condition of Japanese manufacturing companies today. This study analyzed the responses of 97 companies (25.8%) that answered all the questions relevant to this study.

Before discussing the actual state of inter-firm cooperation today among Japanese manufacturers, let us look at the trends in Japanese manufacturers' attitude toward parts suppliers. First, let us consider manufacturers' attitude toward a continuous long-term business relationship with their parts suppliers. In the questionnaire, the respondents were asked to select one of the three choices (1 = positive, 2 = neutral, and 3 = negative) in response to the statement: "Our company and suppliers have maintained a long-term business relationship. Therefore, we wish to maintain a long-term business relationship with the suppliers in the future". Secondly, let us consider manufacturers' attitude toward cost reduction benefit sharing with their parts suppliers. In the questionnaire, the respondents were asked to select one of the three choices (1 = positive, 2 = neutral, and 3 = negative) in response to the statement: "Our company successfully achieved cost reduction targets by cooperatively working with our suppliers before and after mass production. Therefore, we believe that we should share the profits derived from cost reduction efforts, according to the degree of efforts". Table 1 shows the Japanese manufacturers' attitude toward long-term business relationship and cost reduction benefit sharing with their parts suppliers.

As shown in Table 1, it can be concluded that many Japanese manufacturers are trying to sustain a cooperative relationship with their parts suppliers. These results also suggest that inter-firm cooperation, beyond the boundaries of individual companies, has been still important.

Based on these results, the following part in this section examines the actual state of inter-firm cooperation today among Japanese manufacturers. As mentioned in the previous section, some previous studies regarding inter-firm cooperation have pointed out: (1) the control aspects of inter-firm cooperation, i.e., the facts that manufacturers set targets for price/cost, delivery and quality of purchased parts and

Table 1. Manufacturers' attitude toward parts suppliers (created by author).

	Positive	Neutral	Negative
Long-term business relationship	45/97 (46.4%)	40/97 (41.2%)	12/97 (12.4%)
Cost reduction benefit sharing	56/97 (57.7%)	40/97 (41.2%)	1/97 (1.0%)

continuously evaluate individual suppliers' target achievement levels; (2) the interactive aspects of inter-firm cooperation, i.e., the fact that manufacturers and suppliers share various information about products and parts, and cooperatively generate new ideas for cost reduction; and (3) effects of inter-firm cooperation, i.e., the fact that inter-organizational efforts bring great benefits in terms of reduced costs and improved quality to manufacturers who purchase parts from suppliers. To examine these three points, survey questions were developed for this study, using previous studies as a reference (Kato, 1993; Nishiguchi, 1994; Asanuma, 1997). In the survey, respondents were asked to rate each question using a five-point Likert scale (1 = strongly disagree and 5 = strongly agree). Taking into account characteristics of parts and materials that manufacturers procure from suppliers, questions were asked separately for "custom parts and materials" (which are tailored to a particular manufacturer (purchaser)'s specifications and products) and for "standard parts and materials" (which are not tailored to a particular manufacturer (purchaser)'s specifications and products) (Nobeoka, 1999).

First, (1) the survey results regarding the control aspects of inter-firm cooperation are presented. In this study, to investigate manufacturers' practice of evaluating suppliers' performance, four questions were asked about "target price/cost setting," "evaluation of target price/cost achievement", "evaluation of on-time delivery," and "quality level evaluation". Table 2 shows the responses to each of the questions regarding control aspects.

Regarding control aspects, as can be seen in Table 2, "evaluation of on-time delivery" and "quality level evaluation" were widely performed. These

Table 2. Control aspects of inter-firm cooperation (created by author).

	Custom parts/ materials			Standard parts/ materials		
	n	Mean	S.D.	n	Mean	S.D.
Target price/cost setting	97	3.70	1.072	97	3.35	1.137
Evaluation of target price/ cost achievement	97	4.14	0.854	97	3.95	0.940
Evaluation of on-time delivery	97	4.61	0.531	97	4.56	0.629
Quality level evaluation	97	4.67	0.515	97	4.45	0.842

results indicate that in inter-firm cooperation, the level of achievement of the delivery and quality targets is evaluated on a continuous basis. Looking at the results by the type of parts/materials, "target price/cost setting (t-value = 4.040, $p < 0.01$)" and "quality level evaluation (t-value = 3.065, $p < 0.01$)" are more widely practiced in the case of custom parts/materials. These results suggest that control based on accounting and quality data is prevalent particularly in the case of custom parts/materials.

Next, (2) the survey results regarding the interactive aspects of inter-firm cooperation are presented. In this study, four questions were asked about "sharing of various types of information", "sharing of various events", "sharing of various problems", and "joint problem solving". Table 3 shows the responses to each of the questions regarding interactive aspects.

Regarding interactive aspects, as can be seen in Table 3, "sharing of various types of information (t-value = 6.217, $p < 0.01$)", "sharing of various events (t-value = 5.872, $p < 0.01$)", "sharing of various problems (t-value = 6.462, $p < 0.01$)", and "joint problem solving (t-value = 6.319, $p < 0.01$)" are more actively conducted in the case of custom parts/materials. From these results, it can be said that information sharing and joint problem solving, which are the interactive aspects of inter-firm cooperation, are common practices, particularly in the case of custom parts/materials. It can also be assumed that information sharing and joint problem-solving activities provide manufacturers and their parts suppliers with plenty of opportunities to cooperatively generate new cost reduction ideas and to share those ideas.

Lastly, (3) the survey results regarding the effects of inter-firm cooperation on manufacturers' performance are presented. In this study, to

Table 3. Interactive aspects of inter-firm cooperation (created by author).

	Custom parts/ materials			Standard parts/ materials		
	n	Mean	S.D.	n	Mean	S.D.
Sharing of various types of information	97	4.09	0.693	97	3.62	0.883
Sharing of various events	97	4.26	0.650	97	3.79	0.877
Sharing of various problems	97	4.39	0.605	97	3.96	0.853
Joint problem solving	97	4.41	0.625	97	3.99	0.823

Table 4. Effects on performance (created by author).

	Custom parts/ materials			Standard parts/ materials		
	n	Mean	S.D.	n	Mean	S.D.
Quality improvement	97	4.06	0.788	97	3.86	0.854
Cost reduction	97	4.18	0.707	97	4.04	0.763
Lead-time reduction	97	4.04	0.828	97	3.87	0.874

determine the effects of inter-firm cooperation on manufacturers' performance, three questions were asked about "quality improvement", "cost reduction", and "lead-time reduction". Table 4 shows the responses to each of the questions regarding performance.

As can be seen in Table 4, most manufacturers reported positive effects in terms of "cost reduction". This supports the findings of previous researchers who argued that inter-firm cooperation contributed to improve cost reduction performance of Japanese manufacturers. Looking at the results by the type of parts/materials, improvement in "quality improvement (t-value = 3.911, $p < 0.01$)" and "lead-time reduction (t-value = 3.087, $p < 0.01$)" is more pronounced in the case of custom parts/materials. This suggests that particularly in the case of custom parts/materials, inter-firm cooperation with parts suppliers is widely recognized as an important activity that contributes not only to reducing cost, but also to improving the quality level and lead-time performance.

This section discussed the present state of inter-firm cooperation among Japanese manufacturers, based on the results of a questionnaire survey. The discussion of this section is summarized as follows.

1. Control aspects of inter-firm cooperation: Continuous evaluations of parts suppliers' performance in terms of delivery and product quality are widely performed by manufacturers. Accounting control (target price/cost setting) and quality control are actively exercised particularly in the case of custom parts/materials.
2. Interactive aspects of inter-firm cooperation: Particularly in the case of custom parts/materials, manufacturers and parts suppliers actively share various types of information and solve problems cooperatively, leading to increased opportunities to generate and share new ideas for cost reduction.

3. Effects of inter-firm cooperation on performance: Positive effects in cost reduction are widely recognized by manufacturers. It is also widely recognized that inter-firm cooperation greatly contributes to improving product quality and shortening lead-time, particularly in the case of custom parts/materials.

As stated above, inter-firm cooperation actively takes place among Japanese manufacturers today, and it is widely recognized that inter-firm cooperation contributes to improved performance of manufacturers. This tendency seems particularly strong in the case of custom parts/materials. Then, how do the control and interactive aspects of inter-firm cooperation relate to manufacturers' performance? The next section discusses this point further.

3. Relationship between Inter-Firm Cooperation and Performance

The fundamental question of this study is "whether inter-firm cooperation contributes, even today, to the performance of Japanese companies". This section examines how (1) control aspects and (2) interactive aspects of inter-firm cooperation relate to (3) the performance of manufacturers.

In this study, with respect to the control aspects of inter-firm cooperation, the following one composite variable was used as an independent variable: "control aspects" (an average of "target price/cost setting", "evaluation of target price/cost achievement", "evaluation of on-time delivery", and "quality level evaluation"). With respect to the interactive aspects of inter-firm cooperation, one composite variable was used as an independent variable: "interactive aspects" (an average of "sharing of various types of information", "sharing of various events", "sharing of various problems", and "joint problem solving"). With respect to the performance of manufacturers, "performance", one composite variable obtained as an average of the following three: "quality improvement", "cost reduction", and "lead-time reduction", was used as a dependent variable. Table 5 shows the descriptive statistics regarding "control aspects", "interactive aspects", and "performance". Table 6 shows the results of multiple regression analysis of the impact of the control and interactive aspects of inter-firm cooperation on manufacturers' performance.

Table 5. Control aspects, interactive aspects, and performance (created by author).

	Custom parts/ materials			Standard parts/ materials		
	n	Mean	S.D.	n	Mean	S.D.
Control aspects	97	4.2809	0.56511	97	4.0773	0.66081
Interactive aspects	97	4.2887	0.51329	97	3.8402	0.72814
Performance	97	4.0928	0.66795	97	3.9210	0.70181

Table 6. Relationship between control/interaction and performance (created by author).

	Custom parts/materials	Standard parts/materials
	Performance	Performance
Control aspects	0.366 (2.799)**	0.321 (2.839)**
Interactive aspects	0.219 (1.524)	0.224 (2.182)*
Constant	1.588 (2.771)**	1.750 (4.078)**
F-value	10.300**	13.155**
Adjusted R-square	0.162	0.202

* Indicates statistically significant at 5% level.
** Indicates statistically significant at 1% level.

As shown in Table 6, the "control aspects" of inter-firm cooperation has a noticeable positive impact on "performance". This indicates that the accounting-based control, such as target price/cost setting and achievement evaluation, and the continuous evaluations of quality and delivery time have a strong impact on the improvement of performance by manufacturers (purchasers) in terms of cost reduction, quality improvement, and lead-time reduction. However, the "interactive aspects" of inter-firm cooperation does not have a significant impact on the improvement of manufacturers' performance in the case of custom parts/materials. This result can be interpreted as indicating that inter-organizational information sharing and joint problem-solving activities, as well as the generation and sharing of new ideas for cost reduction, do not contribute noticeably to the improvement in manufacturers' performance, regarding inter-firm cooperation between manufacturers and custom parts/materials suppliers.

This section discussed the relationship between inter-firm cooperation among Japanese manufacturers and their performance, on the basis of the results of a questionnaire survey. Below is a brief summary of the discussion of this section.

1. Relationship between the control and interactive aspects of inter-firm cooperation and performance: The "control aspects" have a significant positive impact on the improvement of overall manufacturers' performance.
2. However, from the fact that the "interactive aspects" do not have a significant impact on manufacturers' performance in the case of custom parts/materials, it is thought that the generation and sharing of cost reduction ideas do not contribute significantly to the improvement in manufacturers' performance, regarding inter-firm cooperation between manufacturers and custom parts/materials suppliers.

4. Conclusion

This study addressed the question of "whether inter-firm cooperation contributes, even today, to the performance of Japanese companies". On the basis of the results of a questionnaire survey of 97 Japanese manufacturing companies, this paper discussed the actual state of inter-firm cooperation among Japanese manufacturers and the relationship between inter-firm cooperation and performance.

As a result, it was found that continuous evaluations of parts suppliers' performance on delivery and quality are widely conducted by manufacturers; and that information sharing and joint problem-solving activities actively take place, particularly in the case of custom parts/materials. Furthermore, it was also found that the control aspects of inter-firm cooperation had a noticeable positive impact on the performance of manufacturers. These results support the findings of previous studies. However, it was found that the interactive aspects did not have a noticeable impact on manufacturers' performance in the case of custom parts/materials.

However, since the analysis results of this study were largely descriptive, it is necessary to conduct further analysis. To understand the actual status of Japanese manufacturing companies in more detail, interview surveys should be conducted in future.

Additionally, with respect to activities related to inter-firm cooperation and their usefulness, there are only a limited number of studies from the parts supplier's perspective; studies are largely from the perspective of manufacturers (purchasers). Therefore, in future, it is necessary to consider what kind of activities exist, when seen from the parts supplier's perspective, and what impact these activities have on the usefulness of inter-firm cooperation. By considering these, the actual situation of inter-firm cooperation among Japanese companies, which is stereotypically considered "excellent" in the field of management accounting, will become clearer.

References

Asanuma, B. (1997). *The Organizations in Japanese Companies*, Toyo-keizai (in Japanese).

Clark, K. and Fujimoto, T. (1991). *Product Development Performance: Strategy, Organization and Management in the World Auto Industry*, Boston, Harvard Business School Press.

Cooper, R. (1995). *When Lean Enterprises Collide: Competing through Confrontation, Boston*, Harvard Business School Press.

Cooper, R. (1996). Costing techniques to support corporate strategy: Evidence from Japan, *Management Accounting Research*, 7(2), 219–246.

Cooper, R. and Slagmulder, R. (1999). *Supply Chain Development for the Lean Enterprise: Interorganizational Cost Management*, Portland, Productivity Press.

Cooper, R. and Slagmulder, R. (2004). Interorganizational cost management and relational context, *Accounting, Organizations and Society*, 29(1), 1–26.

Cooper, R. and Yoshikawa, T. (1994). Inter-organizational cost management systems: The case of the Tokyo-Yokohama-Kamakura supplier chain, *International Journal of Production Economics*, 37, 51–62.

Hiromoto, T. (1988). Another hidden edge: Japanese management accounting, *Harvard Business Review*, July/August, 22–26.

Kato, Y. (1993). *Target Costing: Strategic Cost Management*, Nihon-keizai-sinbunshya (in Japanese).

Monden, Y. and Sakurai, M. (1989). *Japanese Management Accounting*, Cambridge, Productivity Press.

Nishiguchi, T. (1994). *Strategic Industrial Sourcing: The Japanese Advantage*, New York, Oxford University Press.

Nobeoka, K. (1999). Changes in component procurement network in the Japanese automobile industry, *Kokumin-keizai Zassi*, 180(2), 57–69 (in Japanese).

14

Concept of Incentive Price for Motivating Inter-Firm Cooperation

Yasuhiro Monden
Professor-Emeritus, Tsukuba University

1. The Purpose of This Paper

The function of price mechanism in the traditional economics is supposed to be only the one for balancing the supply and demand in the market. Since such price as a "supply–demand equilibrium price" has a goal of socially optimal allocation of resources, it could be called as a "global optimal price". The papers applied to the corporate divisional transfer pricing are all based on such a "supply-demand equilibrium price." (See Hirshleifer (1956); (1957), Cook (1955); (1957) and Gould (1964).)

On the contrary to such price, the author will propose a new concept of the price called an "incentive price". This is the price that will be attached to the good or service transferred between the seller and buyer, to allocate the joint profit earned through their cooperation. (The earlier papers of such concept of incentive price are Shubik (1962), Schneider (1966) and Ronen & McKinney (1970), but they are not explicitly coined it as an incentive price and show the accounting way of its measurement from the viewpoint of intangible assests.)

The incentive price has a purpose for the seller or buyer of the resource to decide if they should participate in the network organization as its member or not, considering the amount of such allocated profit. The "participation" in this context implies that (1) an independent company will get into the network organization as its member company, and/or (2) an existing participated member company will enhance their self-efforts in the network.

Therefore, the incentive price has no goal of determining the quantity of supply and demand or the global optimal allocation of resources, unlike the supply–demand equilibrium price. The determination of quantity is made by the central authority of the core company in the network organization.

Moreover, the monetary equivalence between the supply–demand equilibrium price and the incentive price could not be necessarily assured. The amount of price will be usually different between two of them.

This paper will clarify the difference between these two prices and contend the raison d'être for the new concept of incentive price. For this purpose, we will use some numerical examples.

2. Comparison of the Incentive Price and the Price for Supply and Demand Equilibrium: Numerical Examples

2.1. *Problem setting*

A certain consolidated business group has two subsidiary companies. The first one is the zinc buyer company X purchasing from a zinc mining and refining company, and the second one is the zinc-vessel manufacturing and selling company Y. The group central company calls each of these two companies as two divisions.

This zinc-vessel manufacturing and selling company Y makes three kinds of zinc vessels. But, there is a limit to the zinc quantity that the zinc buyer company X can purchase, and since this quantity limit is a bottleneck for the manufacturing company, it makes a product-mix decision based on the *contribution margin (i.e., gross profit) of each product per 1 kg of zinc.* The author quoted this example from famous German Schmalenbach (1947) (pp. 66–) and arranged it to clarify the points.

The accounting information for each of the zinc products A, B, and C are as follows and shown in Table 1.

$$\text{Unit contribution margin} = \text{sales price} - \text{variable outlay-cost}$$

where the variable outlay cost = zinc purchasing cost per unit of product + variable processing cost.

Also since both the zinc market and the zinc vessels market are imperfect competition markets, there exists the acquisition constraint for zinc and the sales constraints for each products.

Table 1. Data for the product-mix decision.

Product variety	Contribution margin per unit product	Necessary quantity of zinc per unit	Contribution margin per 1 kg of zinc	Purchase cost per 1 kg of zinc (MC)	Net marginal revenue per 1 kg of zinc (NMR)	Maximum sales capacity
	(1)	(2)	(3) = (1)/(2)	(4)	(5) = (3) + (4)	(6)
Product *A* (all-zinc vessel)	400 Yen	2.0 kg	200 Yen	200 Yen	400 Yen	1,000 units
Product *B* (tin galvanized vessel)	300 Yen	0.4 kg	750 Yen	200 Yen	950 Yen	2,500 units
Product *C* (electric zinc vessel)	200 Yen	0.2 kg	1,000 Yen	200 Yen	1,200 Yen	10,000 units

Table 2. Optimal allocation of resource under the constraints of resource and sales capacities.

Selction rank of products	Maximum sales capacity	Necessary quantity of zinc per unit product	Maximum demand for zinc	Optimal allocation of zinc
	(6)′	(2)′	(7) = (6)′ × (2)′	(8)
C (1st rank)	10,000 units	0.2 kg	2,000 kg	2,000 kg
B (2nd rank)	2,500 units	0.4 kg	1,000 kg	800 kg (accumulated quantity 2,800 kg)
C (3rd rank)	1,000 units	2 kg	2,000 kg	0 kg

Seeing from the column (1) the rank of the contribution margin per unit of product is $A \rightarrow B \rightarrow C$, whereas seeing from the column (3) the contribution margin of each product per 1 kg of zinc has the order of $C \rightarrow B \rightarrow A$ because the zinc supply constraint is 2,800 kg. Therefore, the zinc should be allocated according to the order of $C \rightarrow B \rightarrow A$, but the sales constraints for each product in column (6) should also be considered to determine the amount of allocation quantity itself.

Now take a look at column (7) of Table 2. Because the allocation order of zinc is $C \rightarrow B \rightarrow A$, the product *C* will be given 2,000 kg at first and the remaining 800 kg will be given to the product *B* of the second order. Product *B* will have a shortage of 200 kg, while the product *A* will not be given any amount of zinc. Then, the quantities produced will be 10,000 units of *C*, 2,000 units of *B* and 0 unit of *A*.

2.2. *"Supply and demand equilibrium price" when the resource demand exceeds its supply*

In the following Fig. 1, the horizontal axis shows the quantity; the supply quantity of the supplying company *X* of zinc and the demand quantity of the demanding company *Y* of zinc, who makes and sells final products. Although the former is the quantity of zinc supply and the latter is the sales quantity of zinc-made vessels, the sales quantity of final products are also measured by the contained zinc quantity (i.e., weight of kg).

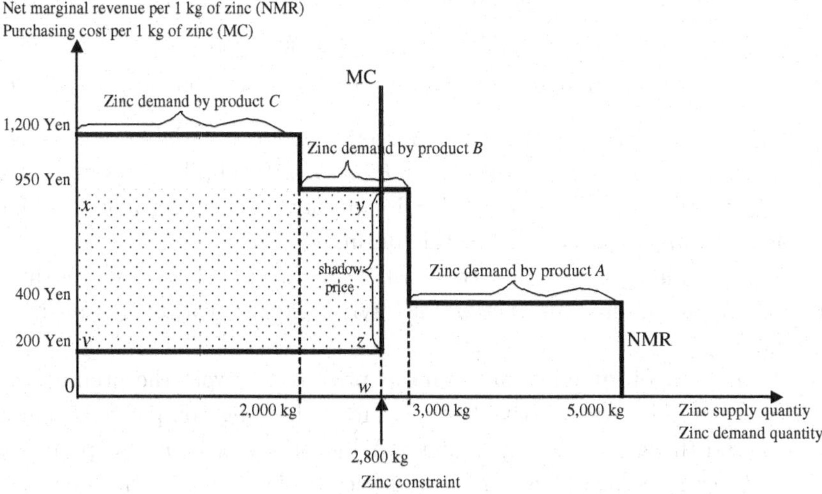

Fig. 1. Case of the resource demand that exceeds the resource supply.

In Figure 1, it will be defined that

MC = marginal cost
= acquisition cost of 200 yen per 1 kg of zinc
= variable outlay-cost 200 yen per 1 kg of zinc

$$\text{NMR} = \text{net marginal revenue}$$

$$= \left(\frac{\text{contribution margin per unit of product}}{\text{required quantity of zinc per unit of product}}\right) + \text{acquisition cost of zinc per 1 kg.}$$

$$\text{NMR of product } C = (200 \text{ yen}/0.2 \text{ kg}) + 200 \text{ yen} = 1{,}000 \text{ yen} + 200 \text{ yen} = 1{,}200 \text{ yen}/1 \text{ kg}$$

In Fig. 1, the point where MC is equivalent to NMR is the quantity of the point where MC curve will merge NMR curve that is 2,800 kg of zinc constraint.

At this point the transfer price of zinc is the line yw, which is 950 yen. This price is the supply and, demand equilibrium price. (The readers should note that Fig. 1 does not deal with a final consumer good, but it deals with the supply and demand equilibrium price of *raw-material good* of zinc.)

This transfer price is composed of

Transfer price = (variable outlay-cost of 1 kg zinc; 200 yen)
+ (contribution margin per 1 kg zinc; 750 yen) = 950 yen.

In other words, the transfer price has exceeded the variable outlay-cost (i.e., acquisition cost) and got the *premium* of 750 yen. This is due to the fact that demand for zinc exceeded its supply of 2,800 kg and the zinc became a *scarce* resource within this business group.

This premium is the one that will be attached to zinc when three product segments had an *auction* for buying the zinc within this business group.

As a result of applying this transfer price of 950 yen, the premium of 750 yen per 1 kg was attached to the zinc supplying company X in this group, and the zinc receiving company Y lost their profit by this premium amount per 1 kg zinc. This will be numerically shown in the income statements of both companies X and Y by Table 3.

2.3. *"Incentive price" when the resource demand exceeds the resource supply*

Now, according to the supply–demand balancing price as a transfer price, the profit of the supplying company became 2,100,000 yen that is equivalent to the shadowed rectangular $xyzv$, whereas the profit of the zinc receiving company is only 500,000 yen. The manager of product company Y, however, will not approve such an allocation of profits.

Certainly under the supply and demand relations of Fig. 1, the bottleneck of this business group lies in the zinc supply company X. Thus, it may be reasonable to allocate much profit to this company X, to motivate the supplying company X expand its capacity.

However, such allocation scheme will attribute all of the shadowed profit in Fig. 1 to the supplying company and the efforts of the product manufacturing and sales company Y who contributed to achievement of the joint profit 2,600,000 yen (= 2,100,000 + 500,000) was neglected at all. (Note that there exists also another joint profit in Fig. 1 that belonged to Product C, which is the white colored space above the shaded one.)

Zinc-vessels manufacturing company also has been developing the profitable products, expanding the sales-network under the market sales constraints and making efforts to increase the sales. In other words, they have generated the *intangible assets* such as the product development technology and sales-network. Such contribution made by the final product

Table 3. Income statements of both companies X and Y, based on the supply–demand balancing price.

Income statement of zinc supply company		Income statement of zinc demand company	
Expense 560,000 yen (= variable outlay cost of zinc × zinc supply quantity = 200 × 2,800)	Sales 2,660,000 yen ⟹ (= transfer price × zinc supply quantity = 950 × 2,800)	Expense 2,660,000 yen (= transfer price × zinc supply quantity = 950 × 2,800)	Net sales 3,160,000 yen (= Σ (marginal revenue per 1 kg zinc × zinc used quantity) = 1,200 yen × 2,000 kg + 950 yen × (2,800 – 2,000 kg)
Profit 2,100,000 yen		Profit 500,000 yen	
2,660,000 yen	2,660,000 yen	3,160,000 yen	3,160,000 yen

company Y for a long time must be awarded. Without such remuneration or reward, the managers of the product company Y will lose their morale and as a result, their self-help efforts for the company will be badly affected.

Here is the reason why the incentive price has to appear on stage.

An incentive price stands for the transfer price of goods that has the purpose of allocating the joint profit to each division appropriately corresponding to their respective contribution and thus motivates the managers of all divisions to make their participation and self-help.

Therefore, the profit attributed to the zinc supplying company should be allocated to the product sales company, too.

The profit attributed to the zinc supplying company X

= (zinc transfer price − variable outlay cost per 1 kg of zinc)
× total quantity of zinc supplied
= (950 yen − 200 yen) × 2,800 kg = 2,100,000 yen.

Now let us measure the contribution level of each company to realization of the joint profit by use of the *investment amount* of each company. This investment amount can be measured by the *book value* applying the "cost approach" of business valuation. Also, it can be measured by the *stand-alone market value of the firm* (= book value amount of investment + estimated value-created; or *the market value of tangible assets & identifiable intangible assets* + good will), which is a stand-alone business value by the "market approach".

Suppose that

Investment amount to the zinc supply company
= 1,080,000 yen
investment amount to the zinc-vessel manufacturing company
= 1,620,000 yen.

Then, the following formula will be applied

Allocated profit to the zinc supply company
= Joint profit

$$\times \frac{\text{Investment amount to the zinc supply company}}{\text{Investment amounts to the zinc supply and the zinc demand companies}}$$

+ stand-alone profit of zinc supply company
= {2,600,000 yen × [1,080,000 yen/1,080,000 + 1,620,000) yen]} + 0 yen
= 1,040,000 yen.

Table 4. Income statements of zinc company X and product company Y, based on *incentive price.*

Income statement of zinc supply company		Income statement of zinc demand company	
Expense 560,000 yen (= variable outlay cost of zinc × zinc supply quantity = 200 × 2,800) Profit 1,041,600 yen	Sales 1,601,600 yen ⟹ (= transfer price × zinc supply quantity = 572 × 2,800)	Expense 1,601,600 yen (= transfer price × zinc supply quantity = 572 × 2,800) Profit 1,558,400 yen	Net sales 3,160,000 yen (= Σ(marginal revenue per 1 kg zinc × zinc used quantity) = 1,200 yen × 2,000kg + 950 yen × (2,800–2,000 kg)
1,601,600 yen	1,601,600 yen	3,160,000 yen	3,160,000 yen

Therefore the transfer price per 1 kg of zinc
= (allocated profit to the zinc supply company
÷ total quantity of zinc supplied)
+ acquisition cost per 1 kg of zinc
= 1,040,000 yen ÷ 2,800kg + 200yen = 372 + 200 = 572 yen.

Thus while the profits of each company were 2,100,000 yen vs. 500,000 yen respectively under the supply–demand equilibrium price, the allocated profits changed to 1,041,600 yen vs. 1,558,400 yen under the incentive price. The figures of the transfer prices themselves were different between two prices; the supply-demand equilibrium price = 950 yen, while the incentive price = 572 yen (see Table 4).

2.4. *"Supply and demand equilibrium price" when the resource supply exceeds its demand*

Regarding the case of the supply–demand equilibrium price when the zinc supply exceeds its demand, Schmalenbach (1947) did not treat it all.

In this case because the zinc supply has enough amount so that some remaining amount will appear in the *auction* for zinc in the inner-business group, the premium will not be attached to the zinc, unlike the case of over-demand.

Therefore the transfer price will be

Transfer price = variable outlay cost per 1 kg of zinc = 200 yen.

Under this situation, the zinc supply company X has to supply the zinc to the product company Y with the price of 200 yen that is equivalent to the acquisition price of zinc from the zinc mining company, the company X will not be given any amount of profit at all and all amount of joint profit will be attributed to the zinc vessels producing company.

2.5. *"Incentive price" when the resource supply exceeds the resource demand*

Now according to the supply–demand equilibrium price, total amount of joint profit was allocated to the zinc receiving company Y and none of profit was attributed to the zinc supply company X. Is such allocation approved by the zinc supply company? No!

Suppose, for instance, that the zinc supply company has expanded their capacity of buying the zinc through their enormous efforts during this period because their acquisition capacity was small in the preceding period. Then, the top management of this business group should compensate for their contribution. Again here comes the reason why the incentive price has to appear on stage.

Thus, the profit exclusively allocated to the product sales company should be partially allocated to the zinc supply company, too. Therefore, again as like as the previous case in Section 2.3 the level of the contribution of each company to realization of the joint profit will be measured by the *investment amount* of each company.

3. Problem of the Supply–Demand Equilibrium Price: *Redundant* Decentralized Decisions

3.1. *Opportunity cost of the constrained resource and the transfer price*

In the above case of zinc transfer price in the Section 2.2, the premium amount of 750 yen per 1 kg of zinc that will be gained by the final use of zinc under the zinc constraint of 2,800 kg has the meaning of *opportunity cost*. The reason is as follows:

When we see this zinc-vessels manufacturing company as an independent firm, the premium amount of profit 750 yen will be lost if the final unit of zinc was lost or wastefully used or kept unused. Therefore each product manager who wishes to utilize 1 kg of zinc must earn *at least* 750 yen when they use it for product A or B or C.

Thus the premium amount of 750 yen is the opportunity cost in the meaning of the "*minimum necessary profit*" to be attained per 1 kg zinc use.

Then the product manager of product A cannot bear the opportunity cost of 750 yen per 1 kg of zinc. The product B is a barely permissible product because its profit will be zero under this opportunity cost, while only the product manager of C can earn the positive profit of 250 yen per 1 kg of zinc.

If such opportunity cost of 750 yen plus the acquisition cost of 200 yen are used as a transfer price, then managers of each product can make a decentralized decision about whether or not their use of zinc resource is profitable.

In other words, the decentralized decision making will be possible by the transfer price based on opportunity cost. (In the situation where the sales revenue is a function of the sales price under a certain "elasticity of price", any products will not break-even unlike the product B in the above Fig. 1 example. Thus the decentralized decision can be made clearly.)[1]

However, the transfer price based on the opportunity cost itself must be calculated centrally by the central headquarters that collected the date of all divisions, which are Tables 1 and 2 or Fig. 1. Also at the same time when the transfer price is calculated the globally optimal production plan (i.e., zinc allocation plan and the production plan of each product) will be centrally determined. Therefore, the decentralized decision by use of a supply–demand equilibrium price will be *redundant.*[2]

Therefore, it follows that the supply–demand equilibrium price will be unnecessary to the network organization, where the core company can make a centralized "quantity decisions".[3]

3.2. *"Shadow price" as the opportunity cost*

The numerical example in Section 3 had only one capacity constraint of zinc supply that commonly had dealt with multiple products. That was why the problem of determining the optimal product-mix was easily solved by the accounting method. On the other hand, in the general situations there are more than two constraints such as various machines that will be used to manufacture the multiple products. In such general case, the mathematical programming method must be applied.

The zinc allocation problem of Schmalenbach also can be formulated as a linear programming (LP) model (see Opfermann und Reinerman, 1965). The opportunity cost or premium 750 yen per 1 kg of zinc will be calculated as the "shadow price" of zinc constraint equation by the LP model.

For the case of Section 2.4 when the resource supply exceeds the resource demand, the LP model will solve the problem. And the zinc resource will be found as "excessive" and its shadow price will be zero, which is corresponding to the zero amount of zinc opportunity cost.

In general the shadow price will take zero value when the resource in question is *excessive* (i.e., the profit will not be attached to such resource supply in our example). On the other hand, the shadow price will be nonnegative (i.e., positive or zero) when the resource in question is *scarce* (i.e., the profit will be attached to such resource supply in our example).[4]

4. Conclusion: Long-Term Contribution to Realize the Synergy Effect

Kaplan (1982) posed a negative opinion for the use of shadow prices as supply–demand equilibrium price, from the viewpoint of incentives to the divisional managers. Under the shadow price method if each manager of individual division has known that only the bottleneck division can be given profit allocation, they would not tell the candid information about their sales or production capacity to the central headquarters. In other words, the shadow price method may induce a dysfunctional behavior of each divisional manager or strategic manipulation of their information. That is the so-called "incentive comparability" that induces truthful information will not be assured.

4.1. *Merits of incentive pricing*

Instead of the incentive comparability problem as Kaplan noted, the author will contend from the motivation theory such as "expectancy theory" that the shadow price method or the supply–demand equilibrium pricing cannot motivate the manager of *affluent* resource capacity to make their self-help efforts after the *next period*, because he will not be given any profit allocation in *this period* and thus his reward based on the measured profit performance will be smaller.

According to the mathematical programming algorism (complementary slackness theorem), only the relationship of resource supply and demand in the business group will affect the joint profit allocation as stated above. However, since the relationship of resource supply and demand in the business group will be determined by the short-run conditions such as seasonal fluctuation during a year, the shadow price also varies depending on the monthly conditions. Then do people trust such a *variable* evaluation criteria?

On the other hand, according to the incentive pricing method, the joint profit will be allocated by the long-term accumulated efforts of divisional manager and employees, which will make the intelligent assets or intangible assets. Such a long term allocation measure will earn more acceptance by the divisional managers and employees as much fair, than the short run measure.

As such long-term contribution factors, there are tangible and intangible assets, and the division that has much amount of such resources can contribute more to achieving the joint profits than others. The examples of such intangible assets are the sales network in the sales division and the know-how of production management such as JIT or TQM in the manufacturing division, and also the engineering know-how of R&D in the development or production divisions. Tangible assets are also another contributor to the joint profit. Thus, the amount of investments to the tangible and intangible assets or the cost outlay to the human resources (i.e., amount of labor costs) is contributing to the realization of joint profits.

Thus, the participants of network organization will better satisfy to the allocation of joint profit based on such long-term contribution measure.[5]

The shadow price method reflects the short-run scale of holding resources, while the incentive price method reflects the long-run scale of holding resources.

Finally, let us confirm the purpose of the incentive price again. The incentive price is the transfer price of resource that has the purpose of motivating all divisional managers to do their participating or self-help efforts by allocating the joint profit according to the long-term profit contribution. Since the decisions of participation or self-help efforts are the long-term commitment of each member to the network organization, the long-term contribution measure should be utilized for the allocation of synergy effect.

4.2. *Forming the socially optimal organizational structure through the incentive price*

Although the incentive price differs from the supply–demand equilibrium price that was supposed by Adam Smith as an "invisible hand", it has some automatic adjusting function for the allocation of business resources in a society as a whole.

The network organization is an open system where any firm can depart from or enter in the network in question. Thus any member-candidate firm will naturally get into the network that they select as the best for them based on the amount of incentive price.

If a certain member candidate did not participate in the network as its central headquarters expected, it means that the member candidate could not be satisfied with the amount of profit allocated by the center. Then the separated candidate in question will go independently or may participate in another network that can satisfy this member candidate through their suggested profit allocation.

Endnotes

1. In this case, the problem formulated as a mathematical programming model has a nonlinear objective function. And if each division solved its own *local* optimization problem by using the shadow price of *global* model, then each manager can get a *globally* optimum solution.
2. Similar criticism was made long before by Hax (1965a,b) S.208f in German literature.
3. When a manager faced the decision problems such as the "*make or buy*" and the "*sell outside or transfer to inside*", and so forth, the problems can be solved by applying the "incremental cost" analysis or by the "differential cost" analysis as so-called "special cost studies". Because, if the resource has a constraint, then the opportunity cost will be included in the incremental cost or differential cost. The function of the transfer price should be confined to the profit allocation goal to motivate managers under inter-firm relations or inter-divisional relations.
4. This theorem is called the "complementary slackness theorem" in the mathematical programming. There are many kinds of decomposition solution methods in mathematical programming models that resemble decentralized managerial decisions (see Dantzig and Wolf (1960), Kornai and Liptak (1965), Adam and Röhrs (1967), Adam (1970), Ruefli (1971), Kornbluth (1974), etc.).
5. In the well-known "prisoner's dilemma" of game theory all players will not betray any others in the long-term repetitive games. This result suggests that long-term contribution measure will be the incentive system that induces the "truthful information" transmission.

References

Adam, D. and Röhrs, W. (1967). Ein Algorithmus zur Dekomposition linearer planungsprobleme, *Zeitschrift für Betriebswirtschaft*, June, 395–417.

Adam, D. (1970). *Entscheidungsorientierte Kostenbewertung*, Betriebswirtschftlicher Verlag.

Cook Jr., P. W. (1955). Decentralization and transfer pricing, *Journal of Business*, 1153 (April) 87–94.

Cook Jr., P. W. (1957). New technique for intracompany pricing, *Harvard Business Review*, 35(4), July–August. 74–80. (reprinted in: *Decentralized Management Series*. HBR Supplement).

Dantzig, G. B. and Wolf, P. (1960). Decomposition principle for linear programs, *Operations Research*, 8(January–February), 101–111.

Gould, J. R. (1964). Internal pricing in firms when there are costs of using an outside market, *Journal of Business*, XXXVII(January), 61–67.

Hax, H. (1965a). Kostenbewertung mit Hilfe der mathematischen Programmierung, *Zeitschrift fur Betriebswirtshaft*, April SS, 197–210.

Hax, H. (1965b). *Die Koordination von Entscheidungenn: Ein beitrag zur Betriebswirtschaftlichen Organizationslehre*, Carl Heymanns Verlag.

Hirshleifer, J. (1956). On the economics of transfer pricing, *Journal of Business*, XXIX(July), 172–184.

Hirshleifer, J. (1957). Economics of the divisionalized firm, *Journal of Business*, XXX(April), 96–100.

Kaplan, A. (1982). *Advances in Management Accounting*, Prentice-Hall.

Kornai, J. and Liptak, T. (1965). Two level planning, *Econometrica*, 33(1), 141–169.

Kornbluth, J. S. H. (1974). Accounting in multiple objective linear programming, *The Accounting Review*, April 284–295.

Milgrom, P. and Roberts, J. (1992). *Economics, Organization & Management*, Prentice Hall.

Opfermann, K. and Reinerman, H. (1965). Opportunitatskosten, Shattenpreis und Optimale Geltungszahl, ZFB, (4, SS). 233–234.

Ronen, J. and McKinney, G. III. (1970). Transfer pricing for divisional autonomy, *Journal of Accounting Research*, 8(1), (Spring), 99–112.

Ruefli, T. W. (1971). A Generalized goal decomposition model, *Management Science*, 9–6 (June), B649–B518.

Schmalenbach, E. (1947). *Pretiale Wirtschaftslenkung*, Band 1, *Die optimale Geltungszahl*, Industrie-u. Handelsverlag Walter Dorn Gmbh.

Schneider, D. (1966). Zielvorstellung und innerbetriebliche Leistungspreise in privaten und öffentlichen Unternehmen, *ZfbF*, 3.

Shubik, M. (1962). Incentives, Decentralized control, the assignment of joint costs and internal pricing, *Management Science*, (April), 325–342.

Part 5

Inter-Organizational Learning and Autonomous Organizations

15

Management of Population-Level Learning and Inter-Organizational Relations in Japan

Hiroki Kondo
Faculty of Business Administration, Mejiro University

1. Introduction

The role of long-term transaction practices that characterize Japanese corporate groups and *keiretsu* relationships is not only a coordination mechanism of strategic behavior among group organizations, but also a channel of learning that transfers new practices and allows for the sharing of knowledge among group organizations. Moreover, through these inter-organizational learning processes, trust among *keiretsu* group companies is encouraged, again accelerating the sharing of more knowledge about each other (Manabe and Nobeoka, 2002). In addition, in some local industrial accumulations or clusters, knowledge sharing and imitating each other among geographically approximate firms provide regions with the potential to develop as learning regions.

However, according to behavioral organizational learning theorists (Levitt and March, 1988; Levinthal and March, 1993), learning does not necessarily improve corporate efficiency, and thus dysfunction often occurs. In fact, a level of performance is widely dispersed among each company group and each *keiretsu* group in Japan. A long-term relationship is not a sufficient condition for learning. Furthermore, some industrial accumulations fall into disuse with their core technology or products that is obsolete, such as the traditional local industry.

Therefore, the problem is how to control the inter-organizational learning that easily deteriorates into dysfunction. There should be good management practices to promote effective learning. Therefore, this paper aims to propose a framework for controlling inter-organizational learning using collective strategy as a channel of learning. For this purpose, routine-based (Levitt and March, 1988) and population-level learning (Miner and Haunschild, 1995) are examined as an analytical framework for the dysfunction of inter-organizational learning. In addition, a collective strategy framework (Astley and Fombrun, 1983) is introduced to classify the channel of population-level learning.

2. Brief Overview of Population-Level Learning

2.1. *Routine-based learning theory*

From the standpoint that considers organizational learning not only as the development of knowledge but also a change in the knowledge system and the action pattern, organizational learning is not necessarily useful for the survival of an organization. Levitt and March (1988), the representative advocates of behavioral organizational learning theory, proposed some constraints on organizational learning and its dysfunctional outcomes. Considering learning as a "process" rather than "outcome" and illustrating the dysfunctional aspects of learning, they ask how organizational learning can be effective.

Within their framework, "organizations are seen as learning by encoding inferences from history into routines that guide behavior" (p. 320). Their framework is based on the characteristics of behavioral organization theory — "routine-based", "history-dependent", and "target orientation" — characteristic of organizational action. Given these characteristics, the legitimacy and plausibility of selected routines are more important than the calculated choices or logical sequence with regard to the circumstances or intention. Moreover, the frame of interpretation of historical experiences makes a large difference on the selection of routines and, consequently, the entire organizational action.

The term "routines" include "the forms, rules procedures, conventions, strategies, and technologies around which organizations are constructed and through which they operate. It also includes the structure of beliefs, frameworks, paradigms, codes, cultures, and knowledge that buttress, elaborate, and contradict the formal routines" (p. 320). Beliefs, frames, and paradigms are the foundation for interpreting the past experiences. Therefore, learning new frames for interpretation and unlearning the old actualize radical learning such as double-loop learning (p. 324).

2.2. Competency traps and the exploration–exploitation problem

Such transformation in behavioral patterns through organizational learning does not necessarily contribute to the effectiveness of organizations. March's theory indicates the possibility of organizational dysfunction. *Competency trap* involves the inability of organizations to shift to new routines of potentially higher performance when old routines based on sufficient experiences guarantee organizations the satisfaction with their present performance. March (1991) classified two modes of learning: *exploitation* and *exploration*. Exploration leads to competency traps, so an organization must adopt exploration to an extent in which it will not fall into *failure traps*.

However, Levinthal and March (1993) argue that organizations that learn from their own experiences are likely to fall into competency traps due to their myopic tendency. To promote effective learning, organizations gravitate to making the environment simple and comprehensive, and specialized organizational divisions deal with each aspect of the environment separately. This tendency makes learning myopic. The authors also classify three types of myopia. *Temporal myopia* refers to the tendency to put greater emphasis on short-term rather than long-term performance. *Spatial myopia* refers to the tendency in failing to see the entire system in terms of local experiences. *Failure myopia* refers to the tendency to stick to successful experiences and forget failures. Thus, it becomes easy to fall into competency traps, as organizations try to learn effectively from their own experiences.

Competency traps are the outcomes that result from incremental learning on the basis of one's own experience. As a solution to avoid falling into competency traps, organizations can draw on other companies' experiences. But in such a *vicarious learning* process, an interpretation of the relationship between routine and performance is more ambiguous than that in the case of own experience. Thus, vicarious learning tends to lead organizations to *superstitious learning* by mistaking the relationships between routine and performance and adopting irrelevant routines. In this way, a clue to resolve the antinomy between exploitation and exploration would exist in inter-organizational learning or vicarious learning about another organization's experience. However, to avoid superstitious learning, the evaluation or interpretation of routines must be discussed among peer organizations.

2.3. *Framework of population-level learning*

Miner and Haunschild (1995) applied routine-based learning theory to population-level analysis. Population-level learning is defined as a "Systematic change in the nature and mix of organizational action routines in a population of organizations, arising from experience" (p. 115). A population is defined as "a set of organizations that share at least one major semistable trait, activity or resource utilization pattern" (Miner and Anderson, 1999, p. 6). Researchers can consider various collectives of organizations as a unit of analysis in light of the broad definition of population. They consider an industry as a type of population, and "a regional collection of organizations might also represent a local organizational population" (p. 6). Once an organization introduces a new routine, it is imitated and diffused to other organizations by vicarious learning. It can be said that population-level learning seems to be generated when a routine is diffused to an entire population, and thus the mix of organizational routines is changed.

As with March's theory, learning does not necessarily bring adaptation at the population level. The outcome of population-level learning appears as a change in the distribution of routines in a population. Competency or failure traps occur in an entire population causing a decline of industry or local industrial districts. The subject of inter-organizational learning research is the practices that an organization attempts to obtain new routines through interaction with other organizations and its research interest is in the survival of individual organizations. On the other hand, the primary focus of population-level learning is the survival and growth of the entire population and an individual organization is merely a vehicle of organizational routines.

Populations in which the same routines have been diffused through population-level learning come to competitive relationships with other populations that have substitutive routines. In such cases, the timing of learning affects the survival of populations (Miner and Haunschild, 1995). In the event that the timing of learning is too early, the diffusion of an underdeveloped routine begins before alternatives are fully explored. The second-best routine, which would be inferior to the optimum state, is selected and introduced to the population. On the other hand, in the event that the timing of learning is too late, it is possible that a competing population would invent a routine superior to that of the focal population. The timing of diffusion is important to the survival of an individual organization in each population in terms of making a forking point of competitive advantage for the entire population.

2.4. Research implication of population-level learning

The survival of populations is a central concern in population-level learning, but it is also quite important to individual organizations. In particular, it has already seen that individual organizations will try to avoid competency traps through vicarious learning that seeks a source of exploration in other organizations. Individual organizations in that population would fall into competency or failure traps unless the mix of exploration and exploitation could be balanced.

Miner and Haunschild (1995, p. 116) illustrate such balancing of exploitation and exploration in two examples. A major pharmaceutical manufacturer in the United States has been carefully studying the behavior of newly founded biotech firms. Once it becomes clear which venture firm would be successful, major firms cautiously imitate that routine through head hunting, licensing, or investing in patents that are peripheral to seemingly valuable technology. Early period in which biotech venture firms were established worked as a period of exploration learning for major firms. On the other hand, the semiconductor industry in the United States established corporative R&D institutions called the Microelectronics and Computer Consortium (MCC) and Semiconductor Manufacturing Technology (SEMATECH) on the basis of the successful experience of Japanese companies (Aldrich and Fiol, 1994).

In this paper, following Miner and Haunschild (1995), the diffusion of routines among a population is classified in three patterns. First, *contact transmission* refers to a direct transfer of routines from one organization to another. It includes technology transfer from other firms, inferential imitation by observing seemingly successful competitors, acquisition of routines through formal and informal personal networks, interlock of directors, mergers and acquisitions, and so on. Second, *broadcast transmission* refers to the diffusion from an authoritative source to other organizations in the entire populations. It is carried out through promulgation by professionals such as certified accountants and lawyers, regulation by nation states, establishment of educational systems, transfer of technology transfer from research institutions such as universities, and so on. Third, *a population-level routine* includes a foundation of trading associations and R&D consortiums, standard lobbying or implicit price-fixing cartels, and so on.

These are routines for collective strategy and cannot be adopted by any one or a few organizations.

3. Collective Strategy and Population-Level Learning

Population-level learning is based on the diffusion of routines through interaction among inter-organizational networks and coordinated activity among organizations. Individual organizations within a population are embedded in multiple relationships that include networks or hierarchical coordination among independent organizations. Astley and Fombrun (1983) classified these relationships into four types and conceived strategies to control each relationship. We can see these collective strategies as a channel for the diffusion of routines. Moreover, individual organizations may use collective strategy to control the dynamics of population-level learning and avoid the dysfunctional effects of learning.

3.1. *Brief overview of collective strategy*

Collective strategies were originally conceived as strategies to deal with a turbulent environment (Astley and Fombrun, 1983). Because turbulence of environment arises from complex interactions on the part of organizations acting independently, a collective strategy aims to reduce environmental uncertainty by making the behaviors of each other predictable. Organizational theories that emphasize environmental selection, such as population ecology, depreciate the strategic choices made by individual organizations, considering that the environment rigorously restricts the autonomy of organizations. Astley and Fombrun (1983) argued that strategic choices can be possible at the collective level if the competitive relationships among organizations can be overcome using collective strategies. Collective strategy has been presented as a theoretical and practical solution to the selection–adaptation debate in organization theory.

Astley and Fombrun (1983) classified the relationship between organizations and the four types using two axes. One axis denotes whether the relationship is competitive or corporative (commensalism or symbiosis) and another axis denotes whether the resource transfer among organizations is direct or indirect. Commensalism refers to the relationship in which organizations compete over the same resources and share the same selection pressure from the environment. Symbiosis refers to the relationship in which organizations do not compete over any resources and exchange resources reciprocally. A collective strategy can be conceived for each relationship, as seen in Table 1.

Agglomerative collectives consist of organizations of the same species that compete over the same limited resources. In such associations, inter-organizational relationships would be coordinated by information flow, especially price information. A competitive relationship is restricted by a centralized coordinative mechanism such as lobbying by industry organizations and price agreements by cartels.

Confederate collectives occur in an oligopolistic industry. In such relationships, price information would not be important; rather, personnel transfer is more important in inter-organizational coordination. Collusion enhanced by informal contacts is a coordinative mechanism.

Conjugate collectives occur in interdependent relationships among relative industries. In such a relationship, stabilization of workflow by the prolongation of transactions is important in reducing the turbulence. A collective strategy is the improvement of a relationship by the cooptation of partner organizations through joint ventures and interlocking directors.

Organic collectives consist of independent organizations that belong to unrelated industries having no direct transaction with each other. An increase in the interrelations among organizations in such associations accelerates environmental turbulence and gives organizations an unintended outcome. Therefore, control of the network is attempted through restrictions by political influence.

3.2. *Control of population-level learning*

In each type of collective, collective strategies work as a channel through which organizational routines are diffused by the vicarious learning of organizations. We can classify the modes of population-level learning proposed in Miner and Haunschild (1995) into four organizational collectives. Population-level learning can be controlled to enhance organizational learning or to avoid dysfunctional learning by influencing the flow of the diffusion of routines through collective strategies. However, if a collective strategy operates incorrectly, population-level learning would result in dysfunctional effects.

In agglomerative collectives, population-level learning is promoted by diffusion of routines through imitation between organizations in

Table 1. Framework of collective strategy (Astley and Fombrun, 1983, Table 2).

	Agglomerative collectives	Confederate collectives	Conjugate collectives	Organic collectives
Sub-structural relationships				
Forms of internal interdependence	Indirect commensalisms	Direct commensalism	Direct symbiosis	Indirect symbiosis
Resource flow through network	Information flows	Personnel flows	Work flows	Influence flows
Super-structural relationships				
Form of control	Economic sanction	Social sanction	Regal sanction	Political sanction
Emergent structures of coordination	Cartel, trade, and professional associations	Collusion Informal leadership	Agreement/ contract Interlocking directorates Joint ventures	Network organizations' institutionalized rule structures

competitive relationships. Because imitation by vicarious learning is performed by inference about the experiences of other organizations, processes of inferences or results from mis-inferences invent rich blind variations. This process can affect the growth of the entire population by enhancing the knowledge base of the population and the entry of new firms (Aldrich and Fiol, 1994). At the same time, trade associations acquire population-level routines.

In confederate collectives, imitation among large organizations in oligopolistic competition would promote population-level learning, similar to agglomerative collectives. In addition, personnel transfer among competitors may also facilitate the diffusion of routines, though this has not occurred to a great extent in Japan thus far. An R&D consortium would be founded to coordinate the development of technology and set industrial standards among competitors.

In conjugate collectives, routines are diffused through the interaction between organizations that make transactions with each other. Similar to contact transmissions, broadband transmissions that take the shape of guidance of the coordinative organizations promote population-level learning. For example, large distributors or assemblers who control their districts or groups instruct their subcontractors to adopt certain routines.

In organic collectives, there is less coercive force to restrict the strategic behavior of organizations than in other collectives; therefore, organizations can establish inter-organizational relationships more autonomously. Cross-industrial association between various industries becomes the route for the transmission of knowledge between organizations. The failure of the interpretation that arises from vicarious learning is reduced by the sharing of knowledge in the association.

4. A Case of Population-Level Learning in Japan

Individual organizations are usually involved simultaneously in four types of collectives. They use different strategies in each collective to try to restrict the turbulence caused by a complex interaction of organizations. Moreover, collective strategies work as a coordinative channel that affects the outcome of population-level learning. In particular, in Japan, these collective strategies have been used not only to restrict turbulence, but also to share knowledge.

4.1. *Flexibility of fixed transaction relationships*

Numagami (1995) argues about the cause of the differences between Japan and the United States in the choice of technology for the display of an electronic watch in the 1970s. At that time, the following two technological alternatives were available for an electric watch display: Light Emitting Diode (LED) and Liquid Crystal Diode (LCD). The LED consumed considerable power, so the user would have to light the display every time to confirm time. On the other hand, the LCD consumed less power and could produce a continuous display, but its production cost was expensive. However, the second generation (TN-LCD) had the potential to clear up the problem of the production cost as compared to the first generation (DSM-LCD). Nevertheless, watchmakers in the United States did not decrease their supply of LED watches until 1977, though it was clear that the second generation had been launched, and that the LCD had exceeded the LED in 1975. In the United States, the volume of consumption of the LCD and the LED was reversed in 1978. On the other hand, no Japanese firms selected the LED from the outset.

Numagami (1995) contends that the differences in the transaction system between the Japanese and US industry affected the choice of technology. The industrial system of the United States is a flexible one that consists of market transactions, and it is possible to procure both the LED and the LCD relatively freely from an outside company. On the other hand, the industrial system of Japan is a fixed one, and Japanese firms customarily procure parts from suppliers in a long-term relationship. If Japanese companies want to use the LCD in future, they must select a fixed transaction with a certain parts supplier or an in-house production from the outset. Thus, due to the lack of flexibility with parts suppliers, a large number of companies had to choose the LCD from the outset. Therefore, investment and technological progress occurred in the LCD and the peripheral technology.

Numagami (1995) concludes that if endogenous technological progress is great, consensus among industrial systems about technology in the next generation is more important than flexible transactional relationships. If the possibility of technological change in the future is relatively clear and endogenous technology development is important, a technological conversion will be delayed in a flexible rather than in a fixed industrial system. Due to the lack of flexibility, technological choice has to be undertaken carefully in a fixed industrial system. The fixed relationship between the organizations automatically forms the selection criterion of right technology. Even when the future technology is uncertain, this selection mechanism can be supplemented by sharing knowledge about technology at the industry level and prompting an appropriate interpretation of the situation that influences the industry.

4.2. Collective strategies related to growth of local industry

In the *Okawa* region of Fukuoka Prefecture in the northern part of Kyushu, Japan, 838 companies related to woodwork gathered in a small town comprising 40,000 people in 2007. In addition, in the same year, in the *Fuchu* region of *Hiroshima* Prefecture in the western part of mainland Japan, 262 companies related to woodwork gathered in a small town comprising 45,000 people. These two towns came to compete with each other intensely after high-consuming regions, including *Osaka* and *Tokyo*, became important markets with the development of transportation routes such as railways and tracks beginning with the period of rapid economic growth in Japan. In both regions, under the instruction of industrial associations and traditional craft institutes, almost all companies learned and adopted production techniques from Germany (flash structure, Dübel construction method, and so forth) in 1950s and shifted from the craftsman's process to the assembly line operation. Both regions acquired a large market share through low-cost strategy using cheap local manpower.

At that time, the painting process was the greatest bottleneck in whole manufacturing process. However, companies in the *Hiroshima* region introduced the curtain flow coater from Germany, which was the most up-to-date process at that time, in 1959, and was able to apply uniform, beautiful painting at a high speed. By introducing this expensive machine, companies in the *Hiroshima* region shifted from a system of specialization involving manufacturing processes coordinated by large producers or distributors to an integrated system of production from raw material to the finished product. Therefore, the *Hiroshima* region achieved four times more productivity than in the *Okawa* region and was able to overwhelm in both the price and quality of its product during the 1960s. Thus, during the 1950 and the 1960s, population-level learning was promoted and routines in entire regions were changed through broadband transmission by trade associations in agglomerative collectives.

In the *Okawa* region, which had been left behind by the *Hiroshima* region, the first company that adopted the Numerical Control machine appeared in 1967. With this event, many operators of the NC router became independent, which resulted in an increase in the trade of decoration of furniture parts. In addition, as the coating technology advanced and the painting processes became more important, this aspect of the operations often came to be subcontracted out to independent specialists. The lease contracts of the NC router made the entry barrier very low for the subcontractor. Moreover, because the *Okawa* region consisted of innumerable small firms that did not have sufficient facilities and manpower to implement these processes, large numbers of orders piled up from these firms. Thus, the specialization of manufacturing processes was restructured. This specialization led to the coexistence of economy of scale and rapid technological change in the NC decorating process and the coating process. In the *Okawa* region during the 1970s and the 1980s, adaptation was achieved by decoupling exploitation in the assembling routine that was developed in the 1950s and exploration of rapid technological changes in the coating and decorating processes.

Japan has been in a long economic depression since the 1990s. Moreover, due to the high valuation of the yen, extraordinarily low-priced wooden furniture has been imported from China into the Japanese market. In such poor economic conditions, the *Karimoku group* in *Aichi* Prefecture is the only Japanese manufacturer that has been expanding its market share in Japan. *Karimoku* adopts a management style that exerts consistent control from manufacturing to retailing. A *brand management system* develops brand product lines targeted to every lifestyle and age group, and the *marketing center* makes a request for implementation of details of planned products to manufacturing division. In the factory, managers of manufacturing divisions set up *engineering activity* to respond to the demands of the *marketing center*. Through this *engineering activity*, they offer *kaizen* in the procurement, draft, manufacturing operation, inventory control, and so forth, to the *marketing center*. In 2008, *Karimoku* surpassed the entire *Okawa* region that consisted of over 800 companies by sales of wooden furniture.

Karimoku introduced a market-directed management style by using a top–down approach, while the small manufacturers in the *Okawa* region have tried various projects by forming inter-firm groups cooperatively. The three groups presented below tried to introduce themselves by building their own brands of products at the outset. They assumed that the only recourse the Japanese manufacturers could take against Chinese products was to produce a complete set of interior furnishings for Japanese consumers, which consisted of a set of special furniture produced by each company in the group. They assumed that a Chinese manufacturer that is geographically distant from the Japanese market could not produce a set of furniture for a complete interior style. However, based on consumers' responses directly to large retailers in *Tokyo*, it appeared that their own brand products made with a product-oriented approach did not appeal to customers.

Two of these groups therefore abandoned their own brand products and the product-oriented approach that they had at first. The first group, *Order Seven*, assumed that small retailers exist everywhere in Japan as customers, and started to create a merchandising plan with such retailers cooperatively, proposing planning and designing of store space that is customized for each location and customer traffic. The second group, *Collabostyle*, started OEM manufacturing for various retailers and house builders, introducing the JIT manufacturing system and making the best use of the flexibility of SMCs. In contrast, the third group, *MOST*, did not follow any transformation of style from product-oriented to market-in.

Organizations outside the groups, such as large retailers or trade associations, are influenced by the strategic changes of each group. For the first and second groups, the large retailers in *Tokyo*, *Tokyo-Marui*, and *Otsuka Furniture* are joining temporarily as *referent organizations* that redefine the *problematique* faced by the population (Trist, 1983). However, for the third group, which was formed under the mentorship of a trade association, the authoritative consensus about the goal setting and the understanding of business environment worked as regulative pressure. Therefore, the failure experienced in transactions with outside retailers was also interpreted in light of that consensus and a product-oriented concept was repeated in the changing membership of the group.

5. Discussion

In the first case of the watch industry, we see population-level learning restricted by inter-organizational relationships in conjugate collectives. Correcting the relationships between contracting firms would have worked as a motive to communicate with each other to invest in new technology, and thereby avoid the second-best choice of technology. Moreover, as Numagami (1995) argued, a collective understanding about future technology can complement the flexibility of the fixed industry system when the future technology is uncertain. This could be understood as a case in which the appropriate usage of the collective strategy can restrict the dysfunctional aspect of population-level learning.

In the second case of the traditional local industry of wooden furniture, we see that the effect of population-level learning changes along with the local industry's stage of development. In the first stage of development, broadband transmission by a trade association in the agglomerative collective worked to establish the modernization of the furniture assembly process. In the second stage, contract transmission between woodwork manufacturers and independent subcontractors of the NC router and the coating processes enhanced the flexibility of the entire region by decoupling exploitation in the assembly process and exploring the complex NC router and coating technology. During this period, contact transmission in conjugate collectives worked to balance the exploitation and exploration processes in the entire region. In the third stage, broadband transmission in conjugate collectives worked as a redefinition of *problematique*, or double-loop learning, by learning a routine in the shape of the frame of the interpretation of past experiences.

In this paper, I have offered some tentative assumptions that collective strategy should be considered as a vehicle to control population-level learning. In population-level learning, the balance between exploitation and exploration would be a core issue to be discussed in terms of an evolutionary perspective. Partly, it was seen in these cases that learning through collective strategies may be attempted to study about exploration by other organization to imitate from geographically approximate organizations to another segment or industry. How the balance between exploitation and exploration is resolved collectively at the population level of analysis would be a future research topic.

References

Aldrich, H. E. and Fiol, M. C. (1994). Fools rush in? The institutional context of industry creation, *Academy of Management Review*, 19, 645–670.

Astley, W. G. and Fombrun, C. J. (1983). Collective strategy: Social ecology of organizational environments, *Academy of Management Review*, 8(4).

Levitt, B. and March, J. G. (1988). Organizational learning, *Annual Review of Sociology*, 14, 319–340.

Levinthal, D. A. and March, J. G. (1993). The myopia of learning, *Strategic Management Journal.* 14, 95–112.

Manabe, S. and Nobeoka, K. (2002). Constructing trust in network: Inter-organizational learning system of Toyota, *Hitotsubashi Business Review*, 50(3) (in Japanese).

March, J. G. (1991). Exploration and exploitation in organizational learning, *Organization Science*, 2, 71–87.

Miner, A. S. and Anderson, P. (1999) Industry and population level learning: Organizational, interorganizational, and collective learning processes, *Advances in Strategic Management*, 16, 1–30.

Miner, A. S. and Haunschild, P. R. (1995). Population-level learning, *Research in Organizational Behavior*, 17, 115–166.

Numagami, T. (1995). Adaptive capacity of fixed industrial system to the technological change. Research group of corporate behavior (eds.), *Adaptive Capacity of Japanese Company*, Ch. 8, Nihon keizai shinbun sha (in Japanese).

Trist, E. (1983). Referent organizations and the development of interorganizational domains, *Human Relations*, 36, 269–284.

16

Management Control System in an Empowered Organization

Katsuhiro Ito

Department of Economics, Seikei University

1. Characteristics of Empowered Organizations Observed in Japanese Companies

Among Japanese companies, there are some that have been designed and managed based on a logic different from that of traditional centralized organizations on which management accounting theory was originally premised. The JAA Special Committee (2006) has conceptualized those organizations represented by such Japanese companies with organizational principles different from those of centralized organizations as empowered organizations. Today, even in Europe and the United States, an organizational design (empowered organization, individualized corporation) different from that of organizations (centralized organizations) assumed by management accounting theory at its birth is attracting attention as an alternative. The change in organizational context (movement to empowered organization) is discussed in some documents (Hamel and Breen, 2007; Ghoshal and Bartlett, 1997). The empowered organization therein is contradistinguished from the centralized organization, which is under "command and control" through official positions and hierarchy. As characteristics of empowered organizations, the following three can be listed: (1) emergence of strategy, (2) distributed execution of field operational decision making (autonomous judgment by each organizational unit), and (3) renewal of organizational routines by front-line personnel. This paper discusses mainly (3).

2. Importance of Organizational Learning in Empowered Organizations

Organizational learning is one of the means by which an empowered organization accommodates itself to its surroundings. In the midst of ever-increasing environmental changes, the promotion of organizational learning has become an important management task. Then, what role can the management control system play in this task?

2.1. *Significance of organizational learning*

Learning, unlike problem solving, means that changes in potential implementing abilities continue and establish themselves. For example, there is a clear difference between the success of a company in the development of a product and the improvement in the company's product development capability itself. The former is a problem-solving task within the framework of the existing product development capability, whereas the latter is a learning process for the acquisition of greater product development capability. Organizational learning results in organizational routine. Therefore, organizational learning can be defined as a change in organizational routine (Cyert and March, 1963; Hedberg, 1981). Organizational routine refers to a program that gives continuity or consistency to organizational behaviors. Organizational routines are present as formulated/documented regulations, standard business procedures, manuals and job description forms, and take the form of customs, beliefs, knowledge, technologies, strategies, cultures, and so forth, shared among organizational members (Levitt and March, 1988).

Individual learning is the fundamental element of organizational learning. However, the sum total of individual learning does not amount to organizational learning. Organizational learning is the sharing of the results of individual learning among the organizational members, and the acceptance of a common interpretation thereto; thus, a new organizational routine is formed or an existing organizational routine is modified (Huber, 1991; March, 1991). The accumulated organizational routines remain in the organizational memory irrespective of the time lapse or the changes in the member roster, and serve as guides for future organizational behaviors. That is, organizational routines are the "memory" which allows the preservation of the continuity or consistency of organizational behaviors (Levitt and March, 1988), and are "genes" that are inherited over generations (Nelson and Winter, 1982).

2.2. Change in the process of organizational routine formation

In the preceding Section, organizational learning was defined as a change in organizational routine. An important fact to note here is that, nowadays, certain changes are observed in the process of organizational routine formation. That is, in the past, organizational routines used to be formed by specific organizational members such as top executives, their staff or engineers, and were not modified in the absence of substantial changes in the conditions. However, today, more diversified organizational members (from top executives to frontline workers) have come to participate in the formation of organizational routines, and frequent updates thereof are being widely observed especially in Japanese leading companies such as Toyota, Seven Eleven Japan and Kao. The continuous improvement activities in the manufacturing operations of Japanese companies are a typical example of organizational learning by all employees. The design of the operation process was once the task of engineers. However, nowadays, those actually engaged in the production process have come to suggest or propose a wide range of ideas as well, and such suggestions or propositions have contributed to the day-to-day evolution of the production methods (Fujimoto, 1997; Satake, 1998).

The change in the process of strategy formation as well as the frequent modification of organizational routines is an important point in characterizing the empowered organizations. Although emergent strategy has recently come to attract attention, it was once considered that management strategy should be formulated by top executives and their staff members, and that field personnel should only carry out the strategy given by their superiors (Mintzberg, 1987, 1994). Nowadays, it has come to be understood that the actual strategies are realized through slow changes in the initially intended strategies brought about by the removal of inappropriate parts and the addition of new ideas, as they are being implemented on-site (Simons, 1987, 1995, 2000).

2.3. Two-step model for organizational learning

If the formation of frontline-entry-type organizational routines in empowered organizations is assumed, it is natural for organizational learning to consist of the two steps shown in Fig. 1. The two stages refer to the memories of individual organizational members and the organizational memory as a whole, that is, organizational routines.

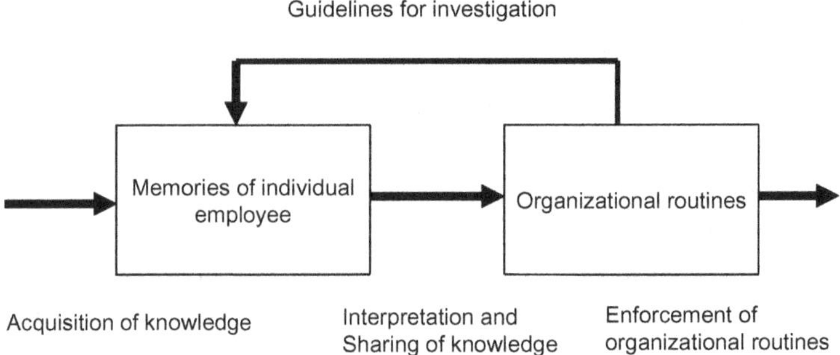

Fig. 1. Two-step model for organizational learning.

New information or knowledge is initially acquired by individual organizational members. Of various types of information or knowledge, knowledge useful for the attainment of organizational goals is shared among the members and is given a common interpretation for the whole organization; thus, such knowledge is committed to corporate memory in the form of organizational routines. The memorized organizational routines are imposed on the members by some method, and the members are required to follow them. This two-step model for organizational learning can be well applicable to Japanese business practice such as TQC/TQM, TPM, and Kaizen Costing.

If the formation of organizational routines in an empowered organization is assumed, those organizational members who take part in the first step of organizational learning are not limited to certain organizational members such as top executives and their staff. Instead, employees and managers who are engaged in various sectors, including manufacturing and sales, of value chains are expected to take part therein. If this is the case, to achieve more efficient and effective organizational learning, some sort of management would be required to direct this process. That is, the formation of organizational routines in an empowered organization also affects the role of the management control system. However, before discussing this issue, let us briefly examine a few cases in the next section.

3. Cases of Empowered Organization

The Toyota production system of Toyota and the on-premise ordering system of Seven-Eleven Japan Co., Ltd. are discussed below as examples of the formation of organizational routines in empowered organizations. The mechanisms of both systems are familiar, but the most important point to be noted here is that both systems have been gradually formed over many years through the participation of many organizational members.

3.1. *The Toyota production system of Toyota*

The Toyota production system is a production system with the ultimate aim of cost reduction by productivity improvement. It is a complex system consisting of various elements, but the two main pillars of the system are just-in-time (JIT) and JIDOKA (autonomation). Autonomation can be described as "intelligent automation" or "automation with a human knowledge".

Initial studies of the Toyota production system elucidated its structure and mechanism, and analyzed and proved why it is more effective than other systems (for instance, Clark and Fujimoto, 1991; Monden, 1991; Ohno, 1978). The results of those studies are summarized as follows: the Toyota production system has established and maintained its superiority over other production systems by overcoming trade-offs in terms of quality, costs and delivery time, realizing flexibility in manufacturing activities and incorporating the mechanism of incessant improvements into the system (Fujimoto, 1997).

Meanwhile, recent studies have focused on the development/formation process, such as how the Toyota production system was formed or why only Toyota has been able to create such a system (Fujimoto, 1997; Satake, 1998). These questions are far more difficult to answer than those addressed in the initial studies, and, to date, no clear explanations have been given. However, one certain thing is that the Toyota production system is the result of historical evolution. That is, "the Toyota system was not established at a certain point in time by a certain person or persons, but was gradually formed as a result of the merging of various elements at different times before and after World War II (Fujimoto, 1997)." In fact, an examination of the formation process of the Toyota production system shows this clearly. For example, multiprocess handling (TAK-OUTEI-MOCHI), which is the main element of Toyota Production System, was already adopted in 1947. Also, regarding the JIT inventory management, which is the main element of JIT, the pull system had already been worked out in 1948. Thus, it was as late as 1970 that, as a result of the accumulation of various ideas, the Toyota production method was organized into a system, albeit imperfect; that is, some 20 years passed after the initial spark. Thereafter, experiments and examinations have been accumulating over a period of nearly 40 years (Toyota Motor Corp., 1987; Ogawa, 1994).

Regarding those who worked out the Toyota production system, some engineers, including Taiichi Ohno, are named from time to time as the inventors of the system. However, considering the length of time it took for the creation of the system and its utter complexity, it is quite natural to assume that numerous engineers and front line workers took part therein. Also, it has been pointed out that, besides these individuals, numerous on-site employees and managers contributed thereto as well.

As described above, the Toyota production system focuses on the formation of organizational routines in an empowered organization. The contents of the organizational routines have been and will be improved through organizational learning.

3.2. *The on-premise ordering system of Seven-Eleven Japan*

Let us now discuss the on-premise ordering system of Seven-Eleven Japan. The "ordering" refers to the decision of each store on the daily purchase of specific products, including the number of units to be bought. Seven-Eleven places the ordering affairs into the hands of each affiliated store, considering that the owner (store manager) and store personnel who attend to their customers in their daily business grasp the customer needs best (Yahagi, 1994). Yet, it is not easy for the owner and a few part-timers to determine the daily orders for as many as 3,000 items. They may be susceptible to the temptation to place the same orders as those on the previous day, even though they know very well that the ordering is an important matter.

Therefore, Seven-Eleven has systemized the policy and procedure of the ordering operation, and called the ordering system "hypothesis verification-type ordering". The basic concept of this system is that each order should be placed based on a clear hypothesis regarding the expected sales quantity of each specific product the next day and the reason therefore, and that the sales results based on such hypothesis should be verified utilizing the point-of-sale (POS) system data, so that such results may be reflected in the next order. In the practice of "hypothesis verification-type ordering", the on-premise ordering system is very helpful.

The on-premise ordering system provides a wide range of detailed information, and information of special importance is displayed in such a manner that the person in charge of ordering can notice it very easily. So, the person in charge of ordering figures out the order quantity for each item based on the hypothesis, while verifying the information on the terminal dangling from his or her neck with the stock status on the shelf.

It is said that, at Seven-Eleven, the above-mentioned on-premise ordering system has enhanced the ordering accuracy, thus contributing to the increase of the average daily sales and stock reduction for each store, and consequently to the consistently good business results of Seven-Eleven Japan. However, the on-premise ordering system of Seven-Eleven was not created all at once, just as in the case of the Toyota production system. In fact, the concept of "hypothesis verification-type ordering" did not exist at the time of its foundation.

It was in 1978, immediately after the foundation of Seven-Eleven, that the company started the development of the on-premise ordering system. The initial purpose of the first system of 1978 was merely to save labor for ordering by printing bar codes on products, and the order quantity was decided based on the principle of replenishment; that is, sold items were reordered.

Since then, Seven-Eleven Japan has sustained its efforts to improve the on-premise ordering operation and the information system supporting it. The main arena for such improvements was the management conferences held every week, in which supervisors and managers gathered from all over the country discussed various issues with the top management. At these management conferences, the problem of inaccuracy in the orders placed by stores was repeatedly raised, and possible solutions were discussed. As a result, in 1982, the POS system was adopted to have a firm grasp on the sales for each product. And in 1985, the function of graphing and analyzing the sales data was added to the system. Through this process, the mechanism of hypothesis verification-type ordering, in which orders are placed based on hypotheses and the results are verified by the sales data, was created (Kawabe, 1994; Ogawa, 2000).

The hypothesis verification-type ordering operation of Seven-Eleven is unimaginable without the on-premise ordering system that supports the ordering operation. In fact, the personnel in charge of system planning and development have examined the details of the improvements to be made by frequently visiting the stores, and so forth, to support the improvements in the ordering operation in terms of the ordering system. Also, they were always present at the above-said management conferences held every week, to gain a proper understanding of and share on-site operational problems, as well as cope with and solve each problem if it was relevant to the information system. Thus, the cycle of problem occurrence and troubleshooting was completed (Ogawa, 2000).

As just described, it is clear that both the hypothesis verification-type ordering operation of Seven-Eleven and the on-premise ordering system supporting this operation are also an example of the formation of organizational routines in an empowered organization.

4. Change in the Role of the Management Control System

In the preceding sections, the significance and process of organizational learning were elucidated, and the concept and cases of the organizational routine formation process in an empowered organization were discussed. In this section, the change in the role of the management control system due to the change in the formation process of organizational routines is examined.

4.1. *Traditional role of MCS*

In view of the aforesaid two-step model of organizational learning, the traditional management accounting technique was helpful for forcing organizational members to comply with the routines. Also, in the formation of organizational routines, the participation of those who carry out the routines, such as on-site employees and managers, was not expected. Instead, top executives and engineers prepared the routines before the implementation of the operation.

For example, in standard cost accounting, cost standards are given as targets to the manufacturing premise upon the decision on the product specifications. Since the cost standards are determined based on the standard operation procedure for the production of the relevant product, it is possible to monitor whether or not the standard operation procedure is followed through an analysis of the differences from the actual costs. Budget management is basically the same. That is, since a budget assumes the standard operation procedure and detailed work planning, we can learn whether or not these are accomplished through an analysis of the differences from the results.

4.2. Roles of MCS in an empowered organization

In an empowered organization, MCS should enforce the efficient implementation of organizational routines and contribute to the modifications (improvements) thereof. MCS was forced to play a new role, that is, to facilitate organizational learning.

As a result, the traditional view of MCS has changed. The concept of management control assumed by Anthony (1965) focused on formal financial information. With the 1980s as a momentum, the concept of management control expanded, covering organizational culture, management creed, and so forth.

According to Machin and Lowe (1983), one of the most potent myths in the field of the study of the management control system is that management control is the synonym of management accounting, and they pointed out, management control can no longer be said to be near equal to management accounting. In Collier (2005), the management control system includes the management accounting system and other control means, that is, he clearly expressed the idea that management accounting is a subset of the management control system. Similarly, Chenhall (2007) indicated, the management control system is a wide concept covering other controls such as clan control, in addition to the management accounting system.

As just described, the concept of management control gradually changed from that defined by Anthony to a wider concept covering control means other than management accounting. Merchant (1985) and Merchant and Van Der Stede (2007) defined management control more widely. In that context, management control refers to *all* the means or systems used by managers for the purpose of mating the behaviors and decision making of employees with the objectives and strategy of an organization. An important fact to be noted here is that a wide variety of the means of control, such as direct supervision, employee recruitment criteria and norms of conduct, as well as measured financial results that are utilized for control by output, came to be covered. Otley (1999) also defined it relatively widely.

The idea of control mix came to be adopted because the concept of management control spread and various means of control were brought into view at the same time. Control mix (or control package) refers to a selection of the means of control (control mechanisms) from among a wide range of possible means of control, integrated into one system for the purpose of attaining one goal (Abernethy and Chua, 1996). As examples of control means that are included in the control mix, Abernethy and Chua (1996) listed the standard operation procedure, office regulations, supervision and guidance by superiors, budget management system, achievement measurement, remuneration system, internal control, allocation of official authority, personnel affairs/selection, education and training, and so forth.

Because an empowered organization was assumed, the frequent and effective updating as well as efficient implementation of organizational routines became the roles of MCS. This mechanism is inherent in those Japanese companies that consistently achieve the solid results.

References

Abernethy, M. A. and Chua, W. F. (1996). A field study of control system "Redesign": The impact of institutional processes on strategic choice, *Contemporary Accounting Research*, 13(2), 569–606.

Anthony, R. N. (1965). *Planning and Control Systems: A Framework for Analysis*, Division of Research, Graduate School of Business Administration, Harvard University.

Birkett, W. P. (1995). Management accounting and knowledge management, *Management Accounting,* November, 44–48.

Chenhall, R. H. (2007). Theorizing contingencies in management control systems research, in *Handbook of Management Accounting Research,* Chapman, C. S., Hopwood, A. H. and Shields, M. D. (eds.), Vol. 1, pp. 163–205. Elsevier.

Collier, P. M. (2005). Entrepreneurial control and the construction of a relevant accounting, *Management Accounting Research,* 16, 321–339.

Clark K. B. and Fujimoto, T. (1991). *Product Development Performance*, Harvard Business School Press.

Cyert, R. M. and March, J. G. (1963). *A Behavioral Theory of the Firm,* Prentice-Hall.

Davenport, T. H., DeLong, D. W. and Beers, M. C. (1998). Successful knowledge management projects, *Sloan Management Review,* 39 (Winter) 43–57.

Dent, J. F. (1987). Tension in the design of formal control systems: A field study in a computer company, in *Accounting and Management: Field Study Perspectives,* Bruns, Jr. W. J. and Kaplan, R. S. (eds.), Harvard Business School Press.

Drury, D. H. and Mc Watters, C. S. (1998). Management accounting paradigms in transition, *Journal of Cost Management,* May/June, 32–40.

Fujimoto, T. (1997). *Evolutionary Theory of the Production System*, Yuhi-kaku (in Japanese).

Ghoshal, S. and Bartlett, C. A. (1997). *The Individualized Corporation: A Fundamentally New Approach to Management.* Harper.

Hamel, G. and Breen, B. (2007). *The Future of Management.* Harvard Business School Press.

Hansen, D. R. and Mowen, M. M. (1997). *Cost Management: Accounting and Control*, 2nd edn. South-Western College Publishing.

Hedberg, B. L. T. (1981). How organizations learn and unlearn, in *Handbook of Organizational Design,* Nystrom P. C. and Starbuck W. H. (eds.), Oxford University Press.

Huber, G. P. (1991). Organizational learning: The contributing processes and the literature, *Organization Science*, 21, 88–115.

Kawabe, N. (1994). *The History of Seven Eleven Japan*, Yuhi-kaku (in Japanese).

Levitt, B. and March, J. G. (1988). Organizational Learning, *Annual Review of Sociology*, 14, 319–340.

Machin, J. L. and Lowe, T. (1983). Introduction, in *New Perspectives in Management Control,* Lowe, T. and Machin, J. L. (eds.), pp. 3–21. St. Martin's Press.

March, J. (1991). Exploration and exploitation in organization learning, *Organization Science,* 21, 1–13.

Merchant, K. A. (1982). The control function of management, *Sloan Management Review,* 23(4), 43–55.

Merchant, K. A. (1985). *Control in Business Organizations,* Ballinger.

Merchant, K. A. and Van Der Stede, W. A. (2007). *Management Control Systems: Performance Measurement, Evaluation and Incentives*, Prentice Hall.

Mintzberg, H. (1987). Crafting strategy, *Harvard Business Review*, 654, 66–75.

Mintzberg, H. (1994). *The Rise and Fall of Strategic Planning,* Prentice-Hall.

Monden, Y. (1991). *Toyota System*, Kodan-sya (in Japanese).

Nelson, R. R. and Winter, S. G. (1982). *An Evolutionary Theory of Economic Change,* Harvard University Press.

Ohno, T. (1978). *Toyota Production System*, Diamond (in Japanese).

Ogawa, E. (ed.) (1994). *Research on Toyota Production System*, Nihon-Keizai Shinbun (in Japanese).

Ogawa, S. (2000). *Source of Innovation*, Chikura (in Japanese).

Otley, D. (1999). Performance management: A framework for management control systems research, *Management Accounting Research*, 10, 363–382.

Otley, D. (2003). Management control and performance management: Whence and whither? *The British Accounting Review*, 35, 309–326.

Satake, H. (1998). *Toyota Production System: Formation, Development and Transformation*, Toyo-Keizai (in Japanese).

Simons, R. (1987). Planning, control, and uncertainty: A process view, in *Accounting and Management: Field Study Perspectives,* Bruns, Jr., W. J. and Kaplan, R. S. (eds.), Harvard Business School Press.

Simons, R. (1995). *Levers of Control: How Managers Use Innovative Control Systems to Drive Strategic Renewal*, Harvard Business School Press.

Simons, R. (2000). *Performance Measurement and Control Systems for Implementing Strategy: Text and Case,* Prentice-Hall.

Thompson, J. D. (1967). *Organizations in Action.* McGraw-Hill.

Toyota Motor Corporation (1987). *The History of Toyota* (in Japanese).

Yahagi, T. (1994). *Innovation of Convenience Store System*, Nihon-Keizai-Shinbun (in Japanese).

Index